QUANTIFYING BEHAVIOR THE *JWatcher* WAY

# QUANTIFYING BEHAVIOR
## the *JWatcher* WAY

## Daniel T. Blumstein and Janice C. Daniel

*Department of Ecology and Evolutionary Biology,
University of California, Los Angeles*

**Sinauer Associates, Inc.** *Publishers*
*Sunderland, Massachusetts U.S.A.*

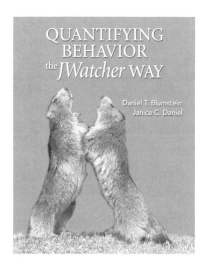

### The Cover

Two Alpine marmots (*Marmota marmota*) playboxing in France. Photo © Cyril Ruoso/JH Editorial/Minden Pictures.

### QUANTIFYING BEHAVIOR THE *JWatcher* WAY

Address inquiries and orders to:
  Sinauer Associates, Inc.
  23 Plumtree Road
  Sunderland, MA 01375 U.S.A.

  www.sinauer.com
  FAX: 413-549-1118
  orders@sinauer.com
  publish@sinauer.com

### Notice of Trademarks

Throughout this book trademark names have been used and depicted, including but not necessarily limited to Microsoft Windows, Macintosh, Microsoft Excel, Java, and QuickTime. In lieu of appending the trademark symbol to each occurrence, the authors and publisher state that these trademarked names are used in an editorial fashion, to the benefit of the trademark owners, and with no intent to infringe upon the trademarks.

### Library of Congress Cataloging-in-Publication Data

Blumstein, Daniel T.
  Quantifying behavior the JWatcher way / Daniel T. Blumstein and Janice C. Daniel.
    p. ; cm.
  Includes bibliographical references and index.
  ISBN 978-0-87893-047-0 (alk. paper)
  1. Animal behavior—Computer simulation. 2. JWatcher. I. Daniel, Janice C., 1965- II. Title.
  [DNLM: 1. JWatcher (Computer program) 2. Behavior, Animal. 3. Software. 4. Automatic Data Processing—methods.
  QL751.65.D37 B658q 2007]

QL751.65.D37B58 2007
591.50113—dc22

                                    2007011510

Printed in U.S.A.

5 4 3 2 1

# Contents

# Preface and Acknowledgments

*Quantifying Behavior the JWatcher Way* was initially conceived and developed in collaboration with Chris Evans at Macquarie University, in Sydney, Australia. We all shared the frustrations of using some commercially available event recorders and we wanted a powerful tool that we could use with our Macintosh computers. We decided to develop the program we wanted to use in Java, the operating system created by Sun Microsystems that theoretically could run within most other existing operating systems. Chris previously wrote a simple event recorder (Evans et al. 1984) that was based on the concept of parallel streams of behavior that are represented in traces. This heuristic fundamentally underpins the algorithms used in *JWatcher*. We shared many enjoyable hours with Chris "white boarding" out ideas and honing the algorithms that form the basis of *JWatcher*.

After completing our 0.9 version of *JWatcher* (which works perfectly well and has been downloaded by thousands of researchers and used as an educational tool by thousands of undergraduates), we wanted to create new features that would make *JWatcher* even more useful. Additionally Java, like all new technologies, has evolved, and some people had difficulties installing *JWatcher* on newer computers. *JWatcher* Version 1.0 and *JWatcher Video* reflect the changes and modifications we made to the software while working here at UCLA.

We intend to continue to distribute *JWatcher* without charge as a service to the research community. We wrote this book to help others get the most out of *JWatcher*. Our intended audience is anyone who has a behavioral question that can be addressed by making focal observations and combining that with continuous recording. *JWatcher's* audience includes neuroscientists, psychologists, human factors experts, veterinarians, and behavioral ecologists. We hope that our step-by-step discussion of using *JWatcher* combined with strategies that we've found helpful over the years in our studies of marmots, birds, fish, and macropodid marsupials will help you, the reader, focus your research questions and use *JWatcher* to help answer any behavioral questions.

Initial *JWatcher* development was supported by a Macquarie University Research Infrastructure Block Grant. During initial development, Dan Blumstein was supported by an Australian Research Council Postdoctoral Fellowship, and Chris Evans by an Australian Research Council Large Grant. We thank Fiona Walkerden, Xuhong Li, and Derek Renouf of Adaptive Arts Pty. Ltd. (www.adaptive-arts.com); Linda Evans for creating the *JWatcher* icon, and members of the Macquarie University Animal Behavior Lab for help with detailed testing of Version 0.9. Development of Version 1.0 and *JWatcher Video* was generously supported by the U.S. National Institute of Health grant 5R21MH065226. We thank the UCLA Life Science Computing staff for help distributing *JWatcher* and a number of 0.9 users for suggesting additional features. We particularly thank Terry Ord and Barbara Clucas for ongoing comments and Barbara for help developing educational exercises. For programming, we are extremely grateful to Nada and Jose da Viega of Convolution L.L.C. (www.convolution.ws). Finally, it's been a genuine pleasure to transform our manuscript into a book with the direction of Graig Donini, Andy Sinauer, Sydney Carroll, Chris Small, and Janice Holabird at Sinauer Associates and Michele Ruschhaupt at The Format Group.

Dan Blumstein and Janice Daniel,
Gothic, Colorado and Los Angeles, California 2007

# CHAPTER 1

# An Introduction to Quantifying Behavior

## 1.1 Why Quantify Behavior?

Quantifying behavior is a fundamental problem in many academic disciplines, and for a variety of theoretical problems (e.g., Altmann 1974; Lehner 1999; Irwin and Bushnell 1980; Whiten and Barton 1988; Martin and Bateson 1993; Sanderson et al. 1994; Alberto and Troutman 1995). For instance, developmental psychobiologists seek to understand how behavior changes over time (e.g., Brown and Dixson 1999; Dawson et al. 1999); pharmacologists must determine whether and how drugs affect the behavior of humans or model systems (e.g., Redolat et al. 2000); veterinary researchers seek to understand how disease affects behavior (e.g., Corke and Broom 1999); neurophysiologists study the effect of lesions on behavior (e.g., Oxley and Fleming 2000); primatologists, comparative psychologists, and behavioral ecologists quantify natural animal behavior (e.g., Goodall 1986; Eckstein and Hart 2000; Hill 2000); and human-factors researchers focus on human behavior to better understand efficiency, causes of pathology, and accidents (e.g., Ketola et al. 2001; Wright and McGowan 2001).

We are behavioral ecologists, and we quantify behavior to understand behavioral diversity and its function. Human and nonhuman animals produce a rich variety of sounds and engage in a remarkable variety of activities. This includes human behavior (why do boys fall down more than girls? e.g., Coss and Goldthwaite 1995), and nonhuman behavior (why do broad-bandwidth repeated sounds elicit mobbing behavior in birds whereby individuals are attracted to the sound and may attack the nearest predator-related stimulus or speaker broadcasting the sound? (Catchpole and Slater 1995). Like the biodiversity that is the subject of considerable ecological and evolutionary study, behavioral diversity can begin to make sense when it is cataloged, described, and quantified.

There are different ways to quantify behavior. We could look at a group of schoolchildren and note each time a child falls and the sex of the child. For this all occurrence sampling (Martin and Bateson 1993), the entire schoolyard may provide many observations of falling behavior. However, this sort of sampling protocol will not allow us to identify the context of falling. For instance, is falling preceded by a child looking toward another child? Or does falling occur only after the child has been climbing on the jungle gym for a certain amount of time? To understand the context of certain behavioral events, we must have a more detailed and comprehensive sampling protocol.

Thus there are good reasons why we might want to go out and focus our observations on a single individual at a time. Focusing on one individual at a time is called focal observation (Martin and Bateson 1993). So, to study children's falling behavior, we might go out and watch children, one at a time, for a set amount of time, in a schoolyard, during recess. To study the response of birds to broad-bandwidth sounds, we might want to conduct a simple playback experiment, in which we would broadcast a variety of sounds to a set of individual birds, record each individual's behavior before the start of the playback, and then continue recording its behavior during and following the playback of different sounds. Observing focal subjects is the basis of many observational and experimental studies of behavior.

Once we have decided to conduct focal observations, we then must make a decision about how we are going to record behavior. Are we going to time sample, whereby we record what our focal subject is doing, say, once every 10 seconds, or are we going to continuously record behavior? We obtain much more information about behavior when we continuously record behavior.

*JWatcher* is a program that allows you to quantify focal observations by focusing on one individual at a time and continuously recording all of that individual's behavior. But what do we mean when we say that we record all of the behavior? Specifically, we mean that we record behavioral transitions.

In our example of children falling, a behavioral transition occurs when a boy in the schoolyard stops talking with another child and begins walking to the jungle gym. Another transition occurs when he stops walking and begins climbing. A transition occurs when the boy stops climbing upon reaching the top of the jungle gym. Another one occurs when he begins to climb back down, or when he falls.

In our avian playback experiment, a behavioral transition occurs when a focal bird stops pecking at the ground and begins looking toward a hidden speaker broadcasting a particular sound. Depending upon the detail with which we record behavior, we might be interested in quantifying each peck at food on the ground, or each time the head moves and the eyes fixate. A transition would occur when the bird begins walking or flying toward the speaker, and another transition occurs when the bird lands on the speaker and begins pecking at it.

*JWatcher* is a computer program that can help you answer these and countless other questions. It is based on continuous recording of focal observations in which you, the user, focus on one subject at a time and score behavioral transitions.

## 1.2 Preliminaries to Quantifying Behavior with *JWatcher*

### Develop a Focused Question

You *must* have a focused question before conducting an observational or experimental study using *JWatcher*. Framing a focused question is often the most difficult part of quantifying behavior. We are going to work through a series of real-life examples in which we used *JWatcher* to help answer the questions. Let's begin with a question about kangaroos and wallabies. If you are interested in rats, monkeys, or humans, fear not; the principles we discuss should be easily adaptable to other focused questions. All questions have some context, and it is important to understand the context of our questions.

Virtually all species at some point in their lives face some risk of predation, and there is a truly remarkable variety of antipredator behaviors that share the common goal of reducing the risk or likelihood of predation (Caro 2005). One common antipredator behavior is aggregating with others. When animals are in groups, the risk faced by any given individual is much smaller than the risk faced by the individual on its own. Imagine that you want to go surfing but you realize that there is some risk of being killed by a great white shark. (Note: while striking, this is really a *very* hypothetical example; many more people are killed by bee stings each year than those few unfortunate ones killed by sharks—Ropeik and Gray 2002.) You have a few options. You could paddle out and stand on your surfboard looking around to try to detect a shark. By doing so, you are not going to catch many waves. This does not sound like too much fun. Or, you could surf with others. By surfing with others, you might not be able to catch every wave yourself, but you are effectively reducing the likelihood of a shark's attacking any single person. Importantly, the larger the group you are surfing with, the less the likelihood that a shark will attack you. Specifically, if you make the convenient assumption that a shark will attack only one surfer, and that larger groups do not attract more sharks, then you have some small probability of being killed when you surf alone, and half that probability when you surf with one other person. The probability decreases in a nonlinear way. If you surf with two other people, each of you has 33% of the original risk of predation when surfing alone. Here is a hypothetical graph illustrating the probability of predation as group size increases:

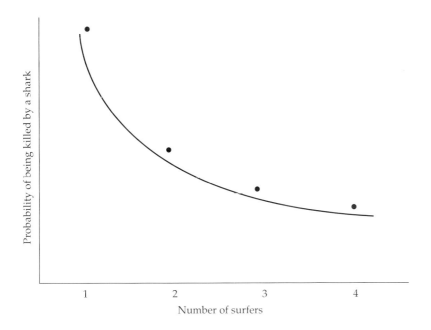

Behavioral ecologists (biologists who study the evolutionary basis of animal behavior; see Alcock 2005) have developed several models to explain how predation risk decreases with increasing group size (discussed in Krause and Ruxton 2002). One model focuses solely on risk dilution, whereby per capita attack rate declines with increasing group size. Another model focuses on the amount of time that you would have to allocate to looking for sharks. If you are surfing with others, each surfer could still spend time looking around for sharks, but the fact that you are surfing in a group means that each individual can catch relatively more waves and look relatively less. Such group size effects, whereby individuals look less as group size increases, have been reported in numerous species (Bednekoff and Lima 1998). We have studied their evolution in kangaroos and wallabies (Blumstein and Daniel 2005) by comparing group size effects in many different species.

Now let's apply this idea to a nonhuman example. Imagine an individual that is constrained in the amount of time that it can forage. Such constraints may be induced by daylight (there are only so many hours in a day), climatic conditions (it may be too hot to be out in the middle of the day), or other factors such as gut capacity (after eating for a while, it may be necessary to digest a meal before eating anything else). The bottom line is that while it is important to forage, foraging individuals expose themselves to some risk of predation. Assume there are two ways to die: you can be killed by a predator, or you can starve to death (Brown 1999). If you stay in a safe refuge, such as a burrow or in dense cover, you can protect yourself from predation, but you are likely to starve to death. Thus you must leave your burrow or other refuge to forage.

Assume that you have left your refuge and have reached a location where you can forage. Should you forage alone or forage with others? If you forage with others and your food is depletable, you will have to compete with others for this food. However, in many cases the antipredator benefits of foraging with others outweigh the costs of increased competition.

We conducted a number of studies in which we focused on foraging kangaroos and wallabies and asked the precise question, "how does time allocated to vigilance change with group size?" Our goal in asking these questions was to study the evolution of "group size effects"—the observation that some species allocate more time to foraging and less time to antipredatory vigilance when aggregated.

If you are following this example so far, you will see that we have two focused null hypotheses:

> Hypothesis 1: there is no relationship between time allocated to vigilance as a function of group size.
> Hypothesis 2: there is no relationship between time allocated to foraging as a function of group size.

How do we now evaluate these hypotheses? We chose to conduct focal observations on individual kangaroos and wallabies. In theory, we could work with captive animals and systematically manipulate group size (Blumstein et al. 1999), or with wild animals focusing opportunistically on individuals found in different sized groups (Blumstein and Daniel 2002). In both cases, we would need to estimate time allocated to vigilance and foraging, and in both cases we would want to use regression analysis to regress group size against these measures of time allocation.

How do we go about quantifying time allocated to vigilance and foraging? We must create an ethogram, which is a catalog of behaviors of interest.

### *Develop an Ethogram of Sufficient Detail*

An ethogram is a catalog of behaviors. The specific ethogram used in a study will depend upon the question asked and how accurately, and with what specificity, a particular behavior can be scored. Clearly the entire behavioral repertoire of a species is complex. However, if your question is focused (which we strongly advocate), the set of behaviors that you might need to keep track of is much reduced. How do you develop an ethogram? You must go out and conduct preliminary observations in the context of your experiment. For instance, recall our example of falling rates in children. If we were focused only on schoolyard activity during recess, we would have to go out and watch children during recess. At this point of a behavioral study, it is probably best to conduct unstructured "ad-lib" observations (Martin and Bateson 1993) in which you try to identify different behaviors and write them down. Video recordings are particularly useful at this early stage of ethogram creation because they allow you to compare different examples of climbing, walking, running, and falling. Depending upon the specificity of your question, you might want to distinguish among many different types of these activities.

In our foraging kangaroo and wallaby example, we elected to have a rather simple ethogram. This was largely because we had to observe the animals at night, often in the field, and with image intensifiers. Our ethogram for kangaroos and wallabies consisted of the following behaviors:

### LOCOMOTION

Pentipedal walk (abbreviated "w"): Focal subject uses forefeet, hindfeet, and tail to move forward.

Hop (abbreviated "h"): Focal subject hops on hind feet slowly.

Run (abbreviated "n"): Focal subject hops on hind feet quickly, tail vigorously pumps up and down like a water pump with a long arm.

### VIGILANCE

Lie down and look (abbreviated "d"): Focal subject lies down on its side with legs and tail extended, head held upright and immobile. For this and other types of vigilance, each time the head moves and fixates, an additional look is scored.

Stand and look (abbreviated "s"): Focal subject stands pentapedally with all four legs and tail on the ground, head held upright and immobile. For this and other types of vigilance, each time the head moves and fixates, an additional look is scored.

Rear and look (abbreviated "r"): Focal subject stands tripedally on hind legs and with the tail on the ground, head held upright and immobile. For this and other types of vigilance, each time the head moves and fixates, an additional look is scored.

### FORAGING

Stand and forage (abbreviated "f"): Focal subject stands pentapedally with all four legs and tail on the ground and is ingesting food.

Rear and forage (abbreviated "g"): Focal subject stands tripedally on hind legs with the tail on the ground and is ingesting food.

### OTHER ACTIVITIES

Self-grooming (abbreviated "l"): Focal subject runs fur through forepaws or mouth.

Groom pouch (abbreviated "p"): Focal subject holds open her pouch with her forepaws and inserts her head into the pouch. This is often associated with vigorous head movement.

Social activities (abbreviated "a"): One of a number of social activities that the focal subject could be involved in: includes aggressive and affiliative behaviors.

Out-of-sight (abbreviated "o"): Focal subject has moved out of sight and it is not possible to see what the individual is doing.

You will notice immediately that this is a rather depauperate ethogram. Kangaroos and wallabies have more than 45 different unique behavior patterns (Coulson 1989) and more than 50 unique agonistic activities (Ganslosser 1989). We left most of those out. Why? Because we have a focused question and our ethogram focuses on the activities that we are most interested in: vigilance and foraging. We have conceived all of these behavioral categories to be mutually exclusive; that is, the onset of each behavior turns off the preceding behavior, such that no behavioral categories can exist simultaneously. Nevertheless, you will notice that the ethogram is arranged hierarchically. Thus, in the future it will be possible to combine various behaviors into a larger category (e.g., total locomotion, total foraging, total vigilance).

You will also notice that we included a type of behavior we called "out-of-sight." Whether you are studying animals in the wild or in captivity, it is common to lose sight of your focal subject for some period of time. It could walk behind a feeding dish or move behind vegetation. Another subject could walk in between you and the focal subject, temporarily blocking its view. Thus, it is generally important to have a behavioral category of "out-of-sight" which can be used whenever you are unsure about the behavior in which a subject is engaged.

There are several important things to realize at this stage of your investigation.

First, make sure you conduct sufficient preliminary observations so that you can develop an ethogram with sufficient detail to evaluate your hypotheses. The worst thing is to conduct too few preliminary observations only to realize a few months into a study that there really is an important behavior type that you neglected to quantify (note: *JWatcher* will accommodate this situation, but since you essentially will have changed your methods midway through a study, your results will be somewhat suspect).

Second, do not go overboard with your ethogram. Keep it simple. It is difficult to score behavior precisely if you are working with a large and complex ethogram. This is not to say that it is impossible to do so, but a considerable amount of training is required. Third, try to have intuitive abbreviations. In theory, it does not matter if standing and foraging is abbreviated as "f" or "y" or "z." However, if possible make these intuitive; by doing so, you will find it is easier to learn to score behavior and your scoring is likely to be more precise.

Fourth, write out your ethogram, and if possible include photographs and/or videos to illustrate prototypical examples of each activity. This is particularly important if you want to train others to score behavior, and especially if your study will take several years to complete. Something we call "method creep" is the bane of behavioral (and other) studies. You want to ensure that what you are scoring as "standing-and-foraging" when you first start recording behavior is the same behavior that you are calling "standing-and-foraging" after two years of study.

Here are some photographs (taken from a video) of tammar wallabies (*Macropus eugenii*) engaged in various behaviors. Note that these are wallabies we studied in captivity (e.g., Blumstein et al. 1999) and they each have a key chain with reflective tape hanging from a leather collar to aid in identification both during the day and at night.

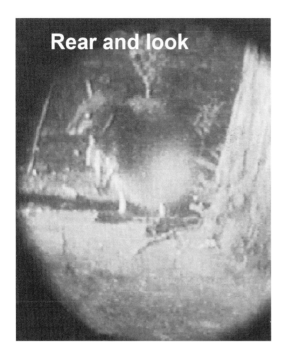

## Practice Scoring Behavior

We live at a really great time in history for behavioral research: very high quality audio and video recording equipment is widely available at affordable prices. Take advantage of this when planning your observations. Video record your subjects. Watch them repeatedly. Slow down playback to look for nuances that you might not see at full speed. For instance, maybe boys fall more because they are glancing around more than girls, and maybe a quick glance precedes each fall. Without video records, it might take a long time to detect this. However, once you are trained to detect this, it might be unmistakeable.

Use your video recordings to practice scoring behavior. You will want to practice until your intra-observer reliability is very high. This means that if you score the same video twice, you should have the same result. *JWatcher* has tools to help you quantify your reliability.

Use video recordings to help train other observers. In addition to paying attention to intra-observer reliability, you must be concerned with inter-observer reliability if more than one person scores behavior. Using *JWatcher*, you can calculate inter-observer reliability, too, and there is no better way to train others than by repeatedly scoring a variety of videos.

## Design Your Data Collection Protocols

You should be very concerned about how you collect your data. Your final conclusions are only as robust as your experimental design. Thinking through the design of your observational sampling protocol, or the design of any experimental manipulation, is essential before going out and collecting any data for analysis.

It is vital that observations of individuals are randomly collected and are independent. "Random" means that you have selected subjects in an unbiased manner. For example, if you are interested in the difference between adult males and adult females, you would not want to collect all observations on adult males before collecting observations on adult females. If you did this, any differences between adult males and adult females might result from some change that took place between the times you collected the male observations and the female observations (e.g., seasonal differences). Thus you should randomize or systematically vary your observations so that you alternate between collecting data on males and females.

Statistical independence means that your final data set will contain (typically) one observation per subject. In some cases, however, you might explicitly design your sampling protocol such that you have repeated measurements on individuals. Statistics that account for these repeated measures must then be used for analysis. Siegel and Castillian (1988) describe nonparametric tests for repeated measures analyses when normality and/or homogeneity of variance in your resulting data cannot be assumed. When normality and homogeneity of variance in your data can be assumed, within-subjects ANOVA and repeated measures General Linear Models are powerful statistical tools for analyzing fully balanced data sets (i.e., each subject received every treatment). If your data are not balanced—meaning that each subject was not exposed to every treatment or condition—linear mixed-effects models (e.g., Verbeke and Molenberghs 2000) can be used. Details of these analyses are beyond the scope of this book, but it is always a good idea to consult with a statistician at the beginning of a study to make sure that you are collecting data that can be analysed to answer the questions you wish to address.

If you have two conditions or treatments, systematically balancing your data collection is particularly useful. Although you could flip a coin and use heads to conduct a focal on a randomly selected male and tails to focus on a randomly selected female, it is not impossible to *randomly* get eight heads in a row. Thus, to ensure a balanced data set, you might want to systematically vary your observations between males and females such that you watch M F M F M F M F M F M F M F M F. . . .

If you have three or more conditions or treatments, and if you are collecting only one observation per subject, you could collect them either randomly (A A C B A A B C C C A B C . . .) or in a predetermined order (e.g., A B C A B C A B C A B C . . .). To randomize treatments you will need to have a random number table or you will have to generate a set of random numbers. If you use Microsoft Excel, the equation to calculate a random number between 0 and 1 is "=rand()." Multiply this by 10, and create a column of random numbers that can be used to help select the order that you will use to expose animals to a particular treatment. Thus, if you have three treatments, you might look down this list and focus only on the numbers 1, 2, and 3. A random presentation order would be the order in which these occurred. Predetermined random orders are particularly useful when your sample size is small and when true random selection might lead to very unbalanced results.

Repeated measures designs, in which individuals are subjected to multiple treatments or conditions, are very powerful ways to collect data. They have the important benefit of being able to "factor" out individual variation. We all know that individual humans have unique personalities. A growing literature on nonhuman "personality" (Gosling 2001; Sih et al. 2004) demonstrates that this is true for other species as well. Given these systematic differences among subjects, allowing each subject to serve essentially as its own control increases our ability to detect the effects of different treatments or conditions.

In the case of an experiment with three treatments (e.g., we might conduct a playback experiment in which we broadcast a territorial song, the "mobbing" call, and an alarm call from the same species of bird), you might consider collecting data using the following guide, where A = alarm call, B = territorial song, and C = mobbing call:

| Subject | 1st treatment | 2nd treatment | 3rd treatment |
|---------|---------------|---------------|---------------|
| 1 | A | B | C |
| 2 | B | C | A |
| 3 | C | A | B |
| 4 | A | B | C |
| 5 | B | C | A |
| ... | | | |

Balancing out treatments like this can eliminate carryover or "order" effects by which the subject's response to a future stimulus is changed after some initial experience. For instance, if subjects always heard the alarm-call playback first, it is likely that they would increase their vigilance and might respond more to subsequent bird song.

Latin Square Designs (e.g., Winer 1962; Campbell and Stanley 1963) are an extension of this to four conditions/treatments, whereby the first individual gets the treatments A B C D, the second B A D C, the third C D A B, the fourth D C B A, and so on.

If you do not have such experimental control (e.g., you are in the field watching unmarked animals), you should do your best not to resample subjects (e.g., by varying the geographic location), and you should not sample multiple subjects in the same group. This is because a subject's behavior could be influenced by the behavior of other group members. If a subject's behavior is influenced by other individuals, it is said to be not independent of others. Imagine a group of primates with a large dominant male who terrorizes younger males. Assume that this group had a lot of younger, subordinate males. If you wanted to understand something about male behavior, you would not want to base it solely on the behavior of the younger males in this group. Ideally, you would want to collect data from different groups and thus increase your "inference space" to describe males in general and not be biased by the males in one particular group who might be living in fear.

By "inference space" we mean identifying the degree of inference we would like to draw. Sometimes you care deeply about one social group. In this case, you would sample randomly (or in a systematically balanced fashion) within that social group. For instance, if you are a zoo biologist and are studying the effect of an environmental enrichment (e.g., a new tire swing) on chimpanzee behavior, you will want to know exactly what your group of chimpanzees did before and after the environmental enrichment. Thus, by focusing on all the members of the group, you will be able to draw conclusions about the effect of the tire swing on your chimpanzees. Importantly, however, you cannot logically draw inferences to other chimpanzees in other zoos. To do that, you would have to randomly sample chimpanzees across zoos. Analogously, if we are interested in the rates at which boys fall off jungle gyms, we would not want to focus only on children playing at the UCLA daycare facility, but would rather want to observe children at different daycare facilities, schools, and playgrounds (ideally around the world). The degree to which we randomly sample across space defines the inferences we can draw from a particular study.

### Select a Way to Acquire Data

When you are conducting focal observations with continuous recording, you have three options for acquiring data. There are benefits and costs to each of these methods that should be considered before initiating data collection.

First, using *JWatcher*, you can score behavior live, directly into your computer. In the field, or when studying captive animals, you can sit quietly with a laptop computer or a PDA. The main advantage of this method is that it is very time efficient. After finishing collecting the data, you can edit your focal observation immediately and then go on to the next observation. No additional laboratory work is required until you elect to analyze your data.

Second, you can observe behavior and dictate your observations into a tape recorder or other recording device. Later, ideally later the same day, you can score the recorded focal using *JWatcher*. There are at least two important advantages of this method. First, you can focus your attention exclusively on your focal subject while conducting the focal. If you are using binoculars or a spotting scope to observe your subject, it might be difficult to move those and to score a "live" focal. Second, you can rescore a focal observation until you "get it right." Sometimes when scoring live you may make a mistake and know that you made a mistake but you cannot go back and fix the mistake. Whenever you are scoring from a recording, you can go back and rescore the focal if necessary. The downside of any method that requires you to first record and then score the focal is that it takes at least twice the amount of time to collect data. Additionally, if you do not score your focal soon after collecting it, it is very possible to lose the tape or rerecord over the tape. Thus you are more likely to lose data using this technique unless you are very careful. Another downside is that narrating a focal observation into a microphone could change the behavior of your focal subjects.

Third, you can video record and later score the focal using *JWatcher*. There are many advantages of video recording your focal samples. One is that you can focus entirely on capturing the video and not worry about describing or scoring the focal observation. Later, in the comfort of your laboratory, tent, or neighborhood coffee shop, you can then score the video recorded focal. Sometimes your mere presence influences the behavior of your focal subjects. In this case, videorecording is essential. If you are conducting a series of experiments in the lab, you might be able to set up a series of video cameras and record the behavior of many individuals simultaneously. Later, you can systematically go through the videos and score behavior. If you are observing transitions that occur very quickly (imagine studying the foraging behavior of a hummingbird), or those that occur very slowly (imagine watching lizard behavior in which there are long intervals when the focal lizard is motionless), video may be essential to facilitate observation. Digitizing the video and using *JWatcher* to score from a QuickTime video is an optimal solution to these sorts of problems. Once a focal is video recorded, it can be used for archival purposes and for training other observers. The costs of scoring from video, as opposed to scoring live, are that this method requires at least twice the time to collect data, and the videotape could be lost, damaged, or accidentally rerecorded. Another cost is that it is relatively easy to video record animals, but it takes time to score them. Sometimes backlogs grow and it takes a long time to catch up. (In our experience, it is not uncommon for researchers to collect so many hours of videotape that it will take years to score them!)

OK, you have a focused question, a detailed ethogram, and a strategy with which to collect data. Let's score some behavior!

# An Overview of *JWatcher*

## 2.1 Installing *JWatcher*

In order to run the *JWatcher* installation program, you must have a current version of Java installed on your computer. Java is an operating system that operates within your existing operating system. We have developed *JWatcher* to work in Java for Windows and Java for the Macintosh. To reduce confusion later, we suggest first making sure that you have the specific version of Java installed on your computer. For *JWatcher* 1.0, you must have at least Java 1.4.2 installed. If it is not installed, go directly to Sun Microsystems (http://java.sun.com) and download JRE 1.4.2.

*JWatcher Video* allows you to score directly from digital movie files. The time stamp in your data file will be derived directly from the video time stamp. You will find this particularly useful if you have recorded behavior remotely as digital files and must look through a lot of the recording before finding the activity you wish to quantify (imagine going through hours of nest box videos waiting for a key feeding sequence or wading through hours of surveillance videos looking for people to interact with an object). You also may find this procedure useful if your subjects have long periods of inactivity followed by a quick sequence of behaviors (imagine watching lizards basking in the sun between display bouts). You will also find this useful if you need to slow down (those studying quickly moving subjects) or speed up (those studying sloths and koalas) the videos to facilitate scoring, or if you want to have several passes through a video file during which time you score different activities.

> **Warning:** *The Windows XP version of this works as intended, but we have encountered insurmountable obstacles in making the Macintosh OS 10.4 version work as well. If you are a Mac user, you may still find it very useful, but you will have to work around some of the bugs (the greatest problem is that we canot figure out how to get the scrub bar working properly). The issue stems from* JWatcher Video's *dependence upon four programs (the Macintosh operating system, QuickTime, QuickTime for Java, and the Java Virtual Machine), all of which are constantly evolving, seemingly independently! We share any and all frustrations you may have while using this module on a Macintosh; it has taken us far too long to try to squash these bugs, and we have elected to release* JWatcher *as is.*

System Requirements: *JWatcher Video* works while running Windows XP with security patch 2, and Macintosh OS 10.4.6 (i.e., operating systems that were functional in 2006). Because of a Java security update that was released in December 2005 and prevented *JWatcher* from running once installed, *JWatcher Video* will not work under older versions of the Macintosh OS. In addition to having one of these operating systems, you must also have QuickTime 7 installed; we do not guarantee that *JWatcher Video* will work with future versions of QuickTime. You also must be running Java 1.5.0; we do not guarantee that it will work with future versions of the Java operating system. *JWatcher Video* works with QuickTime .mov files.

If you envision using this program in the future, once you get *JWatcher Video* working, avoid updating anything on your scoring computer until you have convinced yourself that the program will work on the new platform.

If you have problems getting it to work under one of these operating systems, double-check that they are properly updated; if they are not, update them. If this does not work, uninstall and then reinstall both QuickTime and your JVM. Start with QuickTime.

**Warning:** *It may take a while to properly reinstall your JVM.*

In our experience uninstalling and reinstalling either or both of these programs ultimately gets *JWatcher Video* to work. We apologize for any difficulties, but if you need this program it is worth putting up with the effort needed to install it.

The handheld module requires a Palm OS device and is designed to capture data that will be analyzed on a desktop or laptop computer. Once the device is installed, you can transfer simple focal master files from your primary computer, score behavior on the handheld device, edit data on the handheld device, and transfer it back for analysis. Follow the installation directions explicitly.

Download the appropriate version of *JWatcher* from the *JWatcher* site (http://www.jwatcher.ucla.edu) for your operating system. Once it is downloaded, double-click on the installation icon. By default, *JWatcher* is installed into your "Applications" directory and will create an alias on your desktop. If you are running Windows, you may have to specify the JRE that *JWatcher* is to run with; be sure to select JRE 1.4.2 (or later versions).

Once you download the application, double-click on it and follow the instructions of "Install Anywhere."

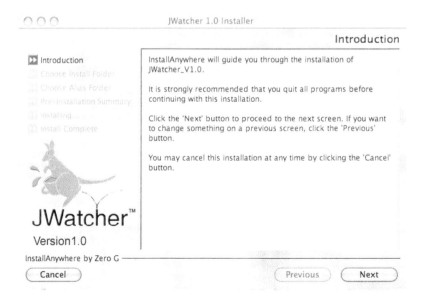

If you are using an older computer running Macintosh OS- 8.5–9.2 or Windows 95/98/NT, be sure to download *JWatcher* 0.9. This version was developed to work on the Windows Java Runtime Environment 1.1.8 and the Mac OS Runtime For Java version 2.2.3. Version 0.9 does not have all the features of 1.0, but you will be able to collect data and conduct a variety of useful analyses. It is possible to install these on computers running Microsoft Windows XP and Macintosh OS-X operating systems (only in the "Classic" mode), but you may need the help of your computer support people in getting it installed. *JWatcher* Version 1.0 only works with 2006-era machines.

## 2.2 Using *JWatcher*

To quantify behavior, you must create several types of files. The following description is an outline only, intended to illustrate the overall structure and logical relationships (see figures at the end of this section). Detailed instructions are provided in the subsequent chapters and also in a series of online help pages.

> **Note:** *The online help requires that your computer have a Web browser. If the help file does not load properly, try changing your default Web browser to Microsoft Internet Explorer.*

First, you must create a Global Definition File (*.gdf). Global definition files are a list of all the behaviors that you might possibly be interested in scoring. The *.gdf file is your ethogram—the list of behaviors that you are interested in studying. Additionally, you can specify modifiers that may follow certain behaviors. A modifier can be anything that has a logical connection to a behavior (e.g., the identity of the other individual in a dyadic social interaction, the location where a behavior was performed, or a variable component of a display). The total number of behaviors and modifiers in a *.gdf file cannot exceed the number of alphanumeric characters on a keyboard.

When asking a focused behavioral question, however, you are typically interested in a subset of behaviors and modifiers. You must specify the duration of a focal observation and any question with which you are to be prompted before beginning a focal observation (e.g., subject identity, date, time, etc.).

To do this, you will have to create a Focal Master File (*.fmf). The focal master file first inherits a preexisting global definition file (*.gdf) to which you can add or subtract behaviors or modifiers. Additionally, the *.fmf requires you to specify questions to be prompted with before scoring behavior, to specify a focal duration, to choose whether you want the event recorder's clock to count up or count down, and to choose whether the end-of-file sound should be played when scoring behavior.

To score behavior, you must specify a focal master file (*.fmf). The "Data Capture" routine allows you to score behavior and then creates a data file (*.dat) that contains a log of the key presses scored to the millisecond.

For basic analysis, and before analyzing a data file (a .dat file), you must create a Focal Analysis Master File (an *.faf file). The focal analysis master file is the "guts" of *JWatcher* and specifies which behaviors are to be treated as states and which are to be treated as events. It also allows you to "time window" a single longer focal observation and summarize behavior in each time window. It allows you to specify which behaviors are mutually exclusive, to exclude or modify certain behaviors, and to perform a variety of other specific functions. Once an *.faf file is created, *JWatcher* can analyze a single data file or it can batch process all data files contained in a folder. *JWatcher* results files (.res) are comma-delimited text files that are opened easily in spreadsheet programs for subsequent postprocessing and analysis. (See Chapter 9 on analyzing data for the difference between *.cd.res and *.tr.res files.)

Sometimes you may wish to score behavior in some detail and later combine detailed key codes into a single behavior type. For instance, a subject may "look" in a variety of postures—it can stand and look, crouch and look, or rear-up and look. *JWatcher* contains a routine to combine these different key codes into a single key code–look. To do so, a Combinations Master File (*.cmf) must be created. Once a *.cmf is created, *JWatcher* can combine the codes in a single file or else it can batch process many files. The files resulting from combination (c.dat files) are analyzed by a modified *.fmf and a new *.faf. Both of these files are based on the new key codes defined in the *.cmf.

Once you have analyzed a number of focal data files, you will probably want to combine your results files into one summary file and calculate some summary statistics. *JWatcher's* Summarize Results algorithms will help you with this. Importantly, this will also create a file that can be exported into other spreadsheet or statistical analysis programs for subsequent analyses. Note that only *.cd.res files can be summarized.

One more important tool allows you to calculate inter- or intra-observer reliability. *JWatcher's* reliability routine, located in the Analysis menu, enables you to compare the sequence of two data files. Reliability result files (*.rel.res) cannot be summarized with the "Summarize Results" routine.

For sequential analysis you must first create a global definition file (*.gdf) and a focal master file (*.fmf) and then score data files (*.dat) with the data capture routine. Sequential analysis functions independently from basic analysis and does not require a focal analysis master file (*.faf). The "General" tab enables you to specify which behaviors are to be modified or ignored, and also has several other settings. Unlike basic analysis, sequential analysis assumes that all key codes represent a simple sequence and does not take into account the times that these codes were logged. There can be no simultaneously occurring behaviors for this type of analysis, so data files must be scored accordingly. Note that the "General" tab specifications apply to all "Sequential Analysis" tabs except for the "Runs Test." The "Runs Test" examines whether a sequence of dichotomous behaviors is random, and it requires that data files be composed of no more than two behaviors. Sequential analysis results files (*.run.res, *.lag.res, *.seq.res, *.mar.res, *.com.res) cannot be summarized with the "Summarize Results" routine.

We hope by now that you have developed a basic understanding of what *JWatcher* can do for you and that you have some understanding of the process by which you score behavior. The following figures illustrate the logical relationships among files and should serve as a valuable reference as you begin to learn to use *JWatcher*. Now, let's take a step-by-step march through the tabs, each of which has a specific function.

A taxonomy of *JWatcher* files and their relationships for basic analysis:

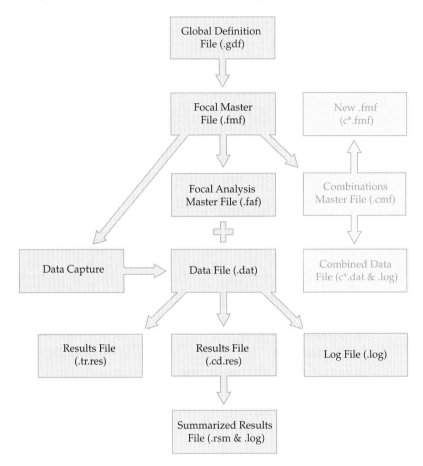

A taxonomy of *JWatcher* files and their relationships for reliability analysis:

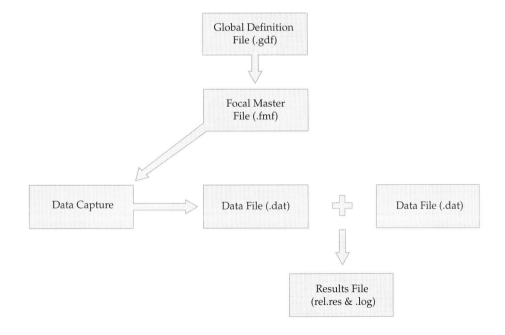

A taxonomy of *JWatcher* files and their relationships for sequential analysis:

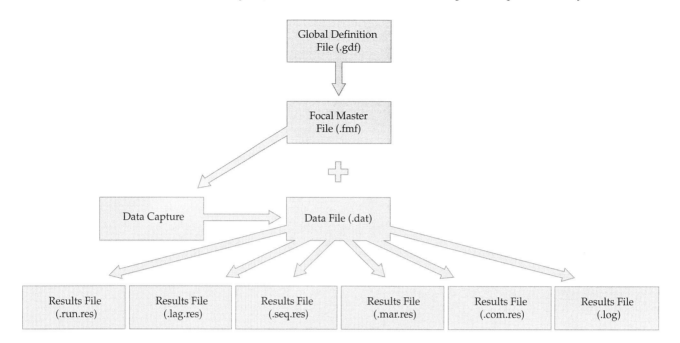

# CHAPTER 3

# Creating a Global Definition File

## 3.1 Scoring Behavior: An Overview

To score behavior, you must define the behaviors of interest and create a Global Definition File (*.gdf). As mentioned previously, a global definition files is a list of all the behaviors that you might possibly be interested in scoring. The *.gdf file could be regarded as an ethogram—a catalog of behavior. It could be a comprehensive ethogram for a given study. Or it could simply be the list of behaviors needed for a given study. Additionally, you can specify modifiers that may follow certain behaviors. A modifier can be anything that has a logical connection to a behavior (e.g., the identity of the other individual in a dyadic social interaction, the location where a behavior was performed, a variable component of a display). For instance, if you are studying play behavior, the list of modifiers might be a list of individuals with whom the subject could play. Thus you would score "p" for play and then "1" to indicate that the focal subject is playing with individual 1.

To create a Global Definition File, click on the "Global Definition File" tab in the main *JWatcher* window.

You will see a window like this (the arrangement of the tabs may differ slightly among computers and according to the overall window size of the program):

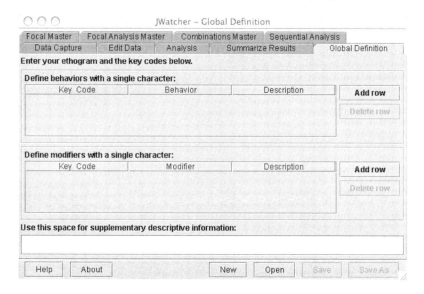

Click [Add row] to activate the window. To view or modify an existing *.gdf, click [Open].

## Behaviors

Use [Add row] to add rows. Specify a single alphanumeric keystroke for each behavior, define it, and describe it. Below we illustrate the kangaroo and wallaby *.gdf.

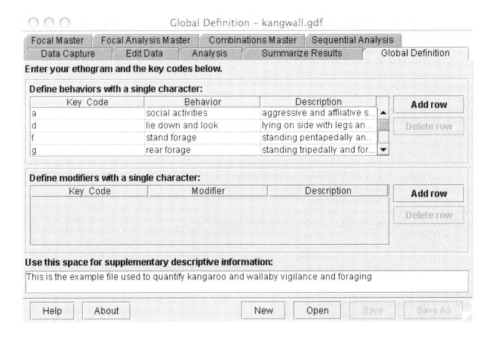

*JWatcher* is case sensitive: uppercase and lowercase key codes are treated separately. Numbers and most punctuation key codes are permissible, but the space bar, backslash (\), colon (:), period (.), equals (=), given ( | ), comma (,), return, tab, delete, and other function keys cannot be defined.

Use [Delete row] to remove rows.

## Modifiers

Use [Add row] to add rows. Specify a single alphanumeric keystroke for each modifier, define it, and describe it.

Use [Delete row] to remove rows.

Type descriptive supplementary information into the bottom text box. Do not use the return key. In this case we noted that this is our example file used to quantify kangaroo and wallaby vigilance and foraging behavior.

Use [Save] or [Save As] to save your *.gdf file when complete.

> **Note:** *The total number of behaviors and modifiers in a *.gdf file cannot exceed the number of alphanumeric characters on a keyboard. We know that some people (those with very detailed ethograms or large lists of possible interactants) have difficulties with this constraint, but for most studies it will not be a problem.*

# CHAPTER 4

# Creating a Focal Master File

When asking a focused behavioral question, you typically are interested in a subset of behaviors and modifiers. And your recording protocol will have a specific duration. When you are recording behavior, you may have some additional contextual information you would like to record. The Focal Master File helps you to score behavior consistently.

Before you make your focal master file, you must know the duration of a focal observation as well as any question(s) with which you will be prompted before beginning a focal observation (e.g., subject identity, date, time, etc.).

To create a *.fmf file, click on the "Focal Master" tab on the main *JWatcher* window. You should see something like this:

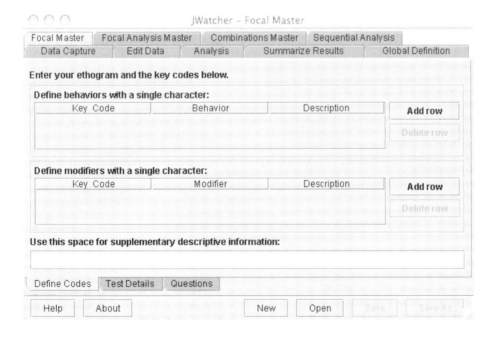

First you must define your codes. Use [New] to open a previously created *.gdf file and import the existing behaviors and modifiers. Use [Open] to open an already existing *.fmf. Clicking either button will take you into a navigation window.

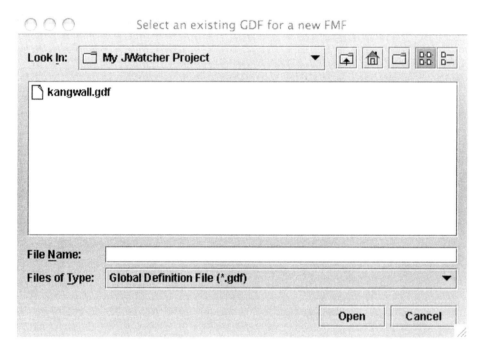

Let's import kangwall*.gdf.

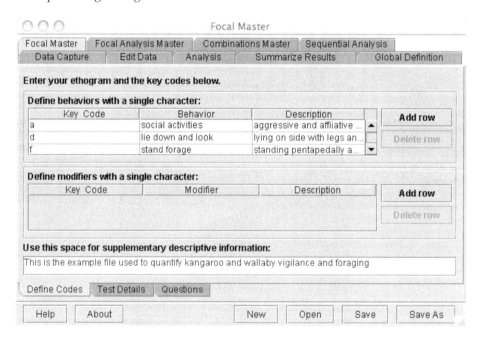

If you have imported a *.gdf file, there should be a series of already defined behaviors and modifiers. Using [Add row] or [Delete row], edit this list to include just those behaviors and modifiers you are interested in quantifying for your current project.

Click [Save] to save the file with the existing name and [Save As] to save the file with a new name. [Save] and [Save As] are activated only if you have made any changes.

Now, tab over to the "Test Details" window.

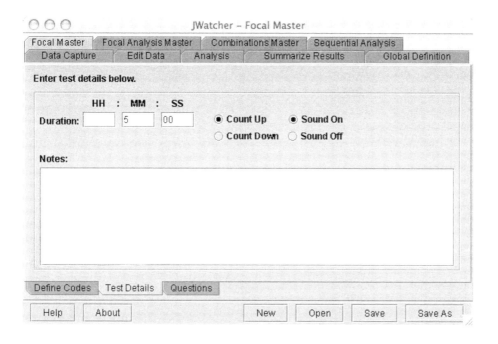

Define the observation session in hours, minutes, and seconds. When you are selecting the duration of your focal, there are two things to be concerned with: visibility of the subject and user fatigue. We have defined our focal to be 5 minutes long.

For instance, when we scored kangaroo and wallaby behavior, we conducted 5-minute focal animal samples. Five minutes does not sound like a lot of time until you realize that we often were observing the animals in pitch-black conditions and had to follow them around with an image intensifier attached to a video camera! Our work with marmots employs 2-minute focal samples. Two minutes sounds like a short amount of time until you realize that foraging marmots move, and when they move through their terrain, they disappear. Longer focals typically have much time out-of-sight. Thus, for efficiency, we elected to conduct 2-minute focal samples.

It is relatively easy to score 2- or 5-minute focal samples accurately and precisely. It is much more difficult to score 20-minute focal samples. Unless you are scoring from video and can pause during your scoring, we do not suggest long duration focal samples. JWatcher will, of course, let you score extremely long focal samples, but there is always the trade-off between duration and precision and accuracy.

When you enter your focal duration, note that it is sufficient to fill in only one box (e.g., "1" in the minutes box will create a 60-second focal). If no session duration is specified, data capture will continue until stopped.

Select "count up" or "count down" to specify whether you want the timer in "Data Capture" to be increasing to the time limit, or decreasing toward 0.

Select "sound on" or "sound off" to specify whether you would like *JWatcher* to produce a sound signifying the end of a focal session.

Add any notes to the text box. You might want to include notes on the type of experiment this *.fmf is being used for, or the date on which you initially made this *.fmf.

Now, tab over to the "Questions" tab.

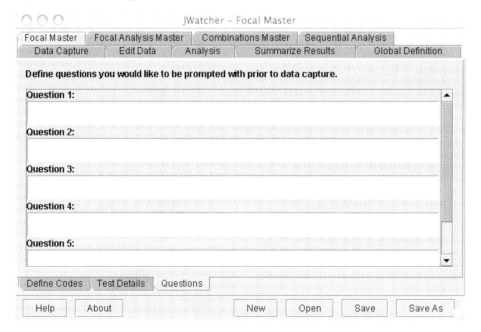

Define up to six questions with which you will be prompted prior to capturing data. For example, you might want to note the identity of the focal subject, its age, its sex, the time of day, the weather, and so on.

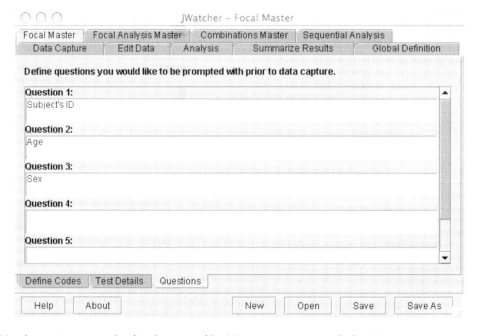

You have just created a focal master file. Now you can score behavior.

# CHAPTER 5

# Scoring Behavior Using Data Capture

"Data Capture" is *JWatcher's* event-recording program. Use this to record the onset of behavioral states (e.g., the onset of a bout of foraging or climbing on a jungle gym) or the occurrence of behavioral events (e.g., the occurrence of an alarm call or the sound of the school's bell signaling the end of recess). "Data Capture" logs any and all definable key presses (see Chapter 3), whether or not they are defined in the *.fmf file.

Note that each behavior is assumed to continue until a key defined as turning the former key off is pressed. All key codes by default turn one another off. The relationships among key codes are defined in the focal analysis master file. Unlike some event recorders, *JWatcher* does not record the durations of continuously depressed keys.

## 5.1 Basic Functionality

Tab over to the "Data Capture" tab. To score behavior, you must specify a focal master file (*.fmf). The data capture routine allows you to score behavior and then creates a data file (*.dat) that contains a log of the key presses scored to the millisecond.

In this window, you will have to both name your data file and select an *.fmf used for data capture using the file navigation tool. This example shows the "Data Capture" tab with *JWatcher's* video feature. If you are not using the video version, you will not see the "Video" file text box or the "Capture Data From Video" tab.

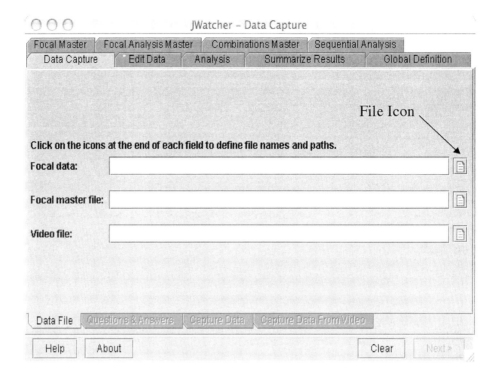

In the "Focal" data field, select the path where the data file will be stored by clicking on the file icon.

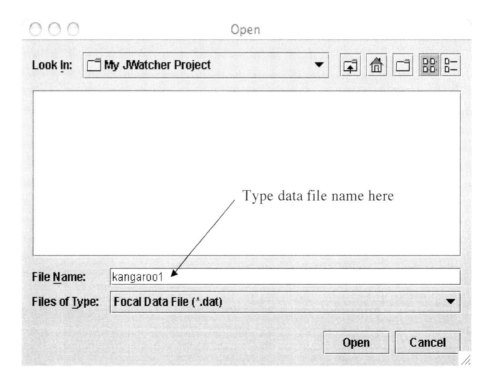

Using the pull-down directory in the navigation window, specify the location where you want to store the data file. Type the name of your new data file in the "File Name" text box, and then click [Open]. If you select an existing *.dat file, you will overwrite it.

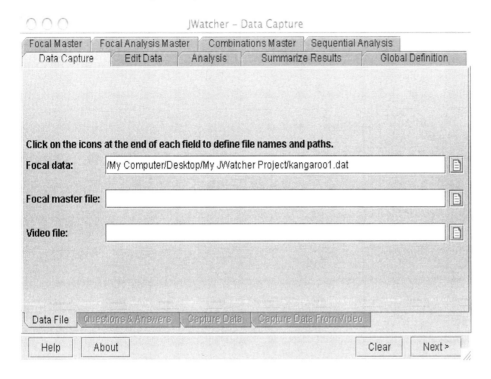

The pathway and data file name will now be shown in the "Focal" data text box. You may directly edit the file name within this text box, if you so desire.

If you do not select a pathway, and simply type a file name into the "Focal" data text box, the data file will be stored in the default location—in the "Application" folder where *JWatcher* is installed. This is shown below. For example, if you simply type "kangaroo1" into the text box and you are using the video version, this file will be saved in the *JWatcher* application folder "*JWatcher* V1.0+VIDEO."

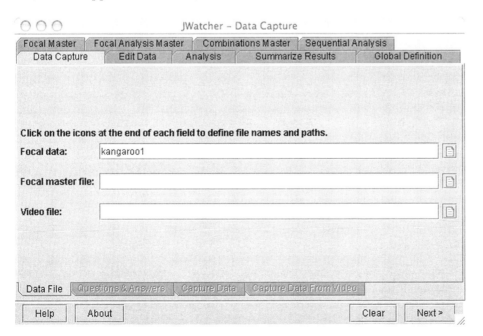

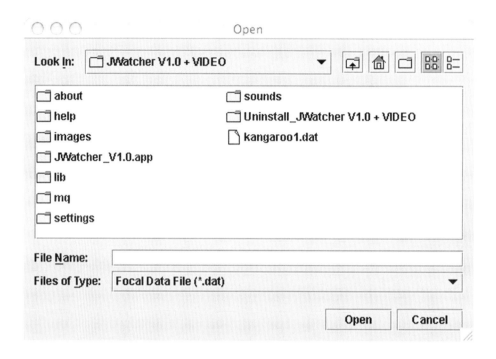

In the focal master field, select a focal master file (*.fmf) that you want to use while scoring behavior by clicking on the file icon and using the navigation box to select an *.fmf.

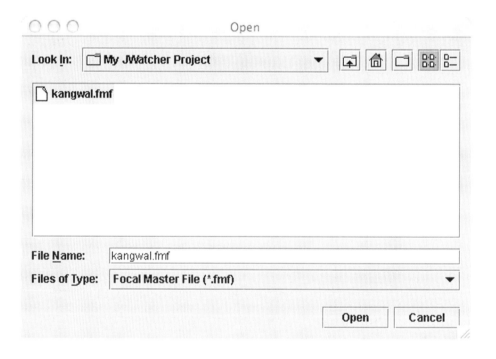

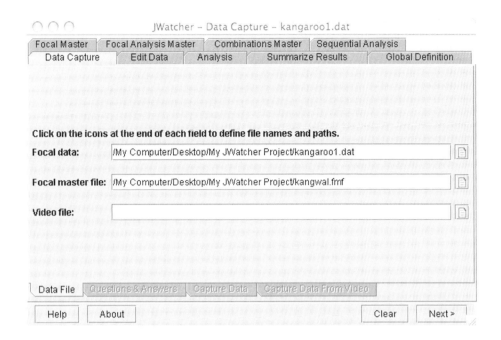

Although it is possible to score data files without specifying an *.fmf, data files scored without an associated *.fmf cannot be analyzed with sequential analysis. For basic analysis, however, scoring with an *.fmf file is not an absolute requirement.

> **Note:** *The first time you open* JWatcher *after it has been shut down,* JWatcher *will automatically revert to the default pathway (the location where you initially installed it). Once you select a path,* JWatcher *will save that path (until changed) to facilitate subsequent scoring sessions. However, this path will be lost when* JWatcher *is closed.*

If you are planning to use *JWatcher's* video feature, select a video file to score using the file browser button (see section 5.2 for additional instructions). If you are not using the video feature, leave the "Video" file box blank (if it is present) and continue below.

When you have named your data file and selected an *.fmf file, click [Next].

In this window, answer the questions that have been specified in the *.fmf file. Do not use the return key.

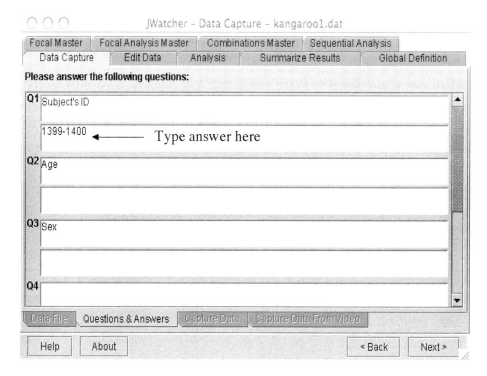

Answers should be saved from one data file to the next (although this is not always the case).

Answers will be displayed in results files for basic analysis (*.cd.res files) but will not be displayed in sequential analysis or reliability result files.

When you are finished, click [Next] to advance to the "Capture Data" tab.

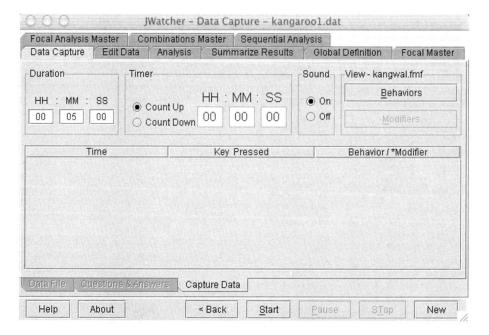

If you are not using video, you are ready to score behavior.

Using the mouse, click [Start] to begin scoring behavior. *JWatcher* will log your key presses as you score behavior and the clock will keep track of the time. Either the session will time out at the end, or you can click [Stop] to end an observation session before the predetermined time.

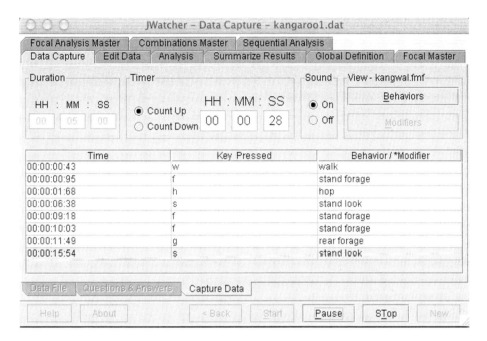

Alternatively, you can move the cursor around using the tab key. Ensure that the "focus" is on one of the duration boxes (i.e., that there is a blinking cursor) and tab until [Start] is highlighted. Depressing the space bar will now start the scoring process.

Hitting the tab key followed by the space bar will stop the session before the predetermined time.

You may also start the session by depressing Alt + s, or stop the session by depressing Alt + t.

To temporarily pause during an observation session, click [Pause] or depress the space bar (or Alt + p). The clock will stop running until data capture is resumed. To resume, either click [Pause] again or depress the space bar (or Alt + p). Stopping an observation session while data capture is paused will terminate the session at the time of the last pause.

If no session duration is specified, the data can be recorded until stopped.

You can select whether you want the clock to count up to the predetermined focal duration or count down. You can also turn the sound signifying the end of the focal on or off.

The "View [Behaviors]" button places a list of behaviors and their key codes into a separate window. Doing so may facilitate scoring.

The "View [Modifiers]" button places a list of modifiers and their key codes into a separate window.

When finished, the file is automatically saved to the location specified. Click [New] to score the next focal session.

A note on modifiers: If your behaviors are modified (e.g., you have a key code for a particular social behavior and you want to be able to determine who the social behavior was with), the key entry for the modifier must directly follow the key entry of the modified behavior. Thus, if you are scoring aggression (a) and looking (l), and you are interested in the individual the aggression was with (1, 2, 3, etc.), the sequence of key presses in your data file must look like:

| Elapsed(ms) | Time | Key Pressed | Behavior / *Modifier |
| --- | --- | --- | --- |
| 841 | 00:00:00:84 | a | aggression |
| 1010 | 00:00:01:01 | 1 | *Fred |
| 7080 | 00:00:07:08 | a | aggression |
| 7950 | 00:00:07:95 | 2 | *Sam |
| 9837 | 00:00:09:83 | l | look |
| 10728 | 00:00:10:72 | l | look |
| 11490 | 00:00:11:49 | a | aggression |
| 12090 | 00:00:12:09 | 3 | *Cindy |
| 13787 | 00:00:13:78 | l | look |
| 14478 | 00:00:14:47 | a | aggression |
| 14847 | 00:00:14:84 | 1 | *Fred |
| 17345 | 00:00:17:34 | EOF | |

When analyzing this focal, *JWatcher* will look only to the key entry immediately following a modified behavior for the modifier. If two modifiers occur in a row (such as aggression, *Sam, *Cindy), then the second modifier (*Cindy) will be ignored. However, a modifier does not always need to follow a modified behavior (e.g., aggression [no modifier], look, aggression, *Cindy).

A note on initializing a focal: Some event recorders require you to initialize behavioral states before scoring behavior. We elected to allow you to begin capturing data immediately. Therefore, to initialize a behavioral state, you have two options:

1. Quickly hit a key after starting *JWatcher*. The time delay between starting *JWatcher* and hitting the first key may be unimportant if the focal duration is relatively long.
2. In cases in which the time delay may influence later analyses, use the "Edit Data" function (see Chapter 6) to edit the data set to begin at time = 0.

## 5.2 Additional Instructions for *JWatcher Video*

If you are using video, you will have additional options and abilities.

### *Video File Formats*

To prepare your video files for scoring using *JWatcher Video*, we recommend purchasing QuickTime Pro, a US$29.99 upgrade (www.apple.com) from the freely available QuickTime Player.

Video files are encoded using various "CODEC" algorithms, which encode and decode video files. They combine intraframe and interframe (or delta) compression algorithms. Some CODEC are compatible with *JWatcher Video* while others are not. *The key element that makes a CODEC compatible with* JWatcher Video *is the way the time code is encoded*. You can open videos with unreadable time codes and play them in *JWatcher Video*, but you will not be able to associate times with keystrokes. Thus, you may have to experiment with file formats, because all do not contain time codes that *JWatcher* can read. When *JWatcher Video* is functioning properly, you will see a clock (hh:mm:ss:ms) beneath the video in the video window. When you play the video, the clock will run appropriately and key presses will register corresponding times. If the format is unsupported, you may receive a message to this effect when you open the video file.

Video files are large! You probably will save them in a compressed form for analysis using *JWatcher Video*. There are a number of decisions that you will have to make when compressing and saving your digital video files. Importantly, you will have to decide on a keyframe frequency. Every *n*th frame is saved intact (typically as a JPEG); successive frames are encoded using delta-compression that tracks only changing pixels. Since the full frames can be large (approximately 1 MB), these account for a disproportionate share of total file size, particularly when there is little action in the scene (e.g., file of small animal moving against static background, recorded with a tripod-mounted camera). Increasing the keyframe rate can be an effective tactic for reducing total file size. The optimal value will be the product of an interaction between CODEC chosen and the nature of the video footage, so experimentation is always wise. For example, someone doing behavioral neuroscience with a rat in a radial-arm maze could use a very large value, while those studying something that moves rapidly will require a smaller one.

For instance, in QuickTime Pro, you can take a raw *.dv file (a file format not supported in *JWatcher Video*) and compress it using the following routine:

1. Open a video file
2. File, Export
3. Select "Movie to QuickTime Movie"
4. Click on options
5. Video Settings:
   - Compression type H.264
   - Frame rage = current
   - Key frames (keep it set at every 24 frames with frame reordering selected)
   - Compressor Quality = medium
   - Encoding: faster encode (single pass)
6. Deselect "Prepare for Internet Streaming"

These settings took a 39 MB original raw *.dv file and turned it into an 8.7 MB file that works well with *JWatcher Video*.

### *Using* JWatcher Video

Remember, *JWatcher Video* is an easy to use addition to *JWatcher* 1.0. The programs are essentially identical, except that *JWatcher Video* provides the additional option of linking a video directly to the data capture routine. If you do not specify a video file, the data capture routine will be identical to *JWatcher* 1.0.

To use *JWatcher Video*, you must name your data file, select an *.fmf (if you wish), and select a video file. All can be selected using the file browser in the main "Data Capture" screen.

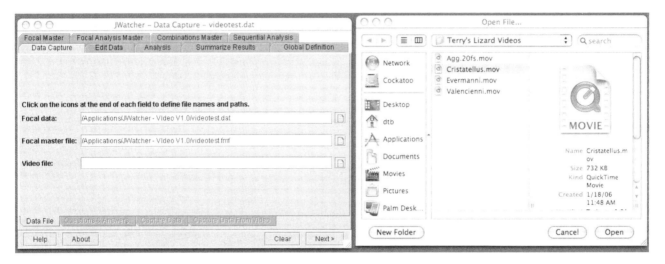

Once a video is selected, click [Next], answer any questions, and click [Next] again to enter the "Capture Data From Video" screen.

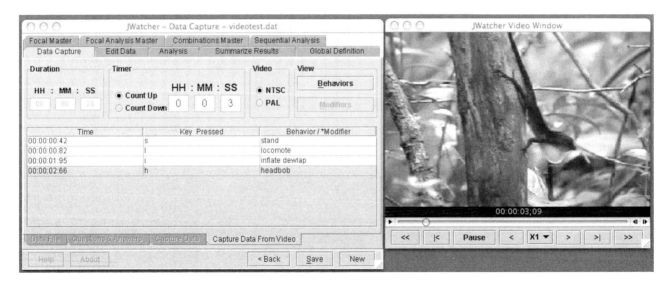

First, select NTSC or PAL, according to which type of video you digitized.

Second, decide on the speed at which you wish to view the video by clicking on the X1 button and changing the setting.

To begin scoring, click on the > icon in the video screen. Use [Pause] to pause the video. Use the scrub bar (if running Windows XP) to move back and forth through the video.

Use the >| icon to move forward frame by frame, and use the <| icon to move backward frame by frame. Use the << or >> icons to move to the beginning of the file or the end of the file.

You will note that the duration of the video is set automatically; if the duration is 0, your CODEC is incompatible with *JWatcher Video*. You will also note that the elapsed time is shown in the "Timer" window.

To end your video session, click [Save] to save your file. Once you save your file, you can edit the key codes and times using the "Edit" routine (which does not link to video). You cannot reopen the file linked to video once it is saved.

Click [New] to return to the initial screen and select another video for scoring.

> **Warning:** *You must click [Save] when you are finished with a data file. Clicking [Save] inserts the EOF (end-of-focal) time to the last line of your file and also sorts your file chronologically. If you click [New] without first saving, then you will not be able to analyze your data file with basic analysis, and you may produce erroneous results for sequential analysis.*

"Edit" and "Save As" functions work as they normally do in *JWatcher* 1.0.

> **Note:** *Mac OS X Bug #1: The scrub bar does not work in* JWatcher Video.

> **Note:** *Mac OS X Bug #2: You will need to close and reopen the program after scoring each data file with* JWatcher Video.

# CHAPTER 6

# Cleaning Up Your Act: Editing Data Following Data Capture

We all make data entry mistakes. You might hit a key twice by accident, or you might hit one key when you absolutely know that you should have hit another key. "Edit Data" allows you to modify the keystrokes and times created in "Data Capture."

It is always good practice to edit your focal samples immediately after scoring them. And it is always good practice to score focal samples as soon as possible after you have collected them if you have recorded them on audio- or videotape.

Tab over to the "Edit Data" tab.

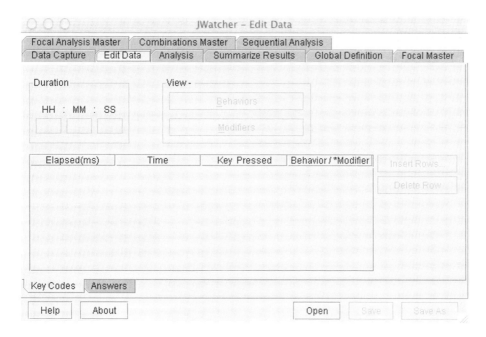

Use [Open] to open a data file (data files have the *.dat suffix).

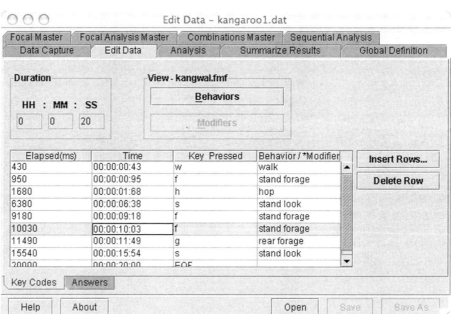

Use [Insert Row] to add rows, [Delete Row] to delete rows, and [Save] or [Save As] to save changes.

Type or edit the time in either the "Elapsed (ms)" column or the "Time (hh:mm:ss:ms)" column. Changes to one column will automatically update the other.

Make sure that new entries are chronological. For basic analysis, nonchronological entries will be treated as errors and no results files will be produced (see Chapters 8 and 9). However, for sequential analysis, time entries are irrelevant and hence need not be chronological (see Chapter 13).

Change or add key codes in the "Key Pressed" column. The "Behavior/*Modifier" column will update accordingly. If the corresponding "Behavior/*Modifier" cell remains blank, then this key code was not defined in the *.fmf associated with the data file.

You may view the behaviors and modifiers defined in the *.fmf by clicking on the "Behaviors" and "Modifiers" boxes, respectively.

You may receive the following message when opening a data file:

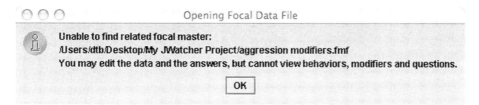

The *.fmf must be in the same directory as the data file, or in the same location as it was when the data file was scored. To solve this problem, locate the *.fmf and place it in one of the above locations.

To modify answers, tab to the "Answers" window. Do not use the return key.

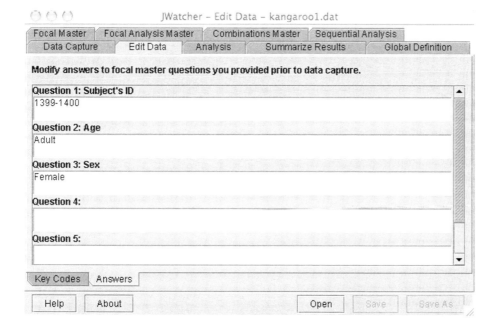

# CHAPTER 7

# Checking Your Reliability

As we have said, *JWatcher* can help train you so that you have a high degree of intra-observer reliability as well as train others so that there is a high degree of inter-observer reliability. Reliability is essential if you are to have robust results. To begin, score the same data file two times (be sure to name them differently).

Tab over to the "Reliability" tab located in the "Analysis" menu.

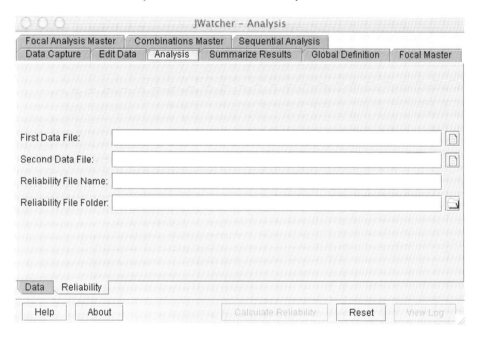

The "Reliability" algorithms calculate the percent agreement between the two files and a kappa coefficient. They also provide a "confusion" matrix and a line-by-line comparison of the two files.

Essentially, the percent agreement is a statistic that compares the sequence of key codes in two data files without respect to the times that they occur. It is simply the number of positions in the sequence at which the codes agree (e.g., are the same), divided by the total number of available positions, multiplied by 100. Cohen's kappa is a modification of the percent agreement statistic that adjusts for agreements due to chance alone. Martin and Bateson (1993) and Bakeman and Gottman (1997) both provide good descriptions of the uses and limitations of these statistics.

To calculate reliability:

1. Select the two data files you wish to compare using the file selection tools.
2. Name the reliability output file. The suffix of this comma-delimited text file will automatically be *.rel.res

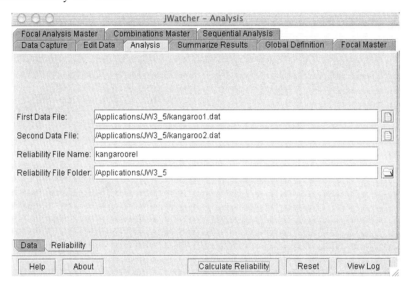

3. Click [Calculate Reliability] to perform calculations.
4. Use a spreadsheet program to open the comma-delimited text result file (*.rel.res).

When opened in a spreadsheet program, the results look like this:

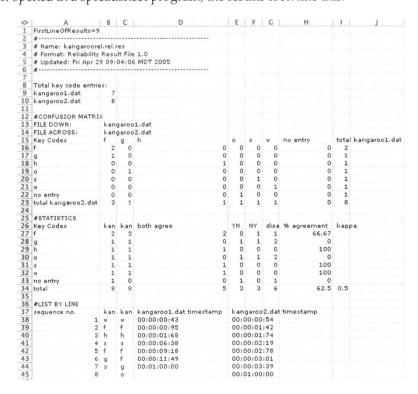

The confusion matrix tabulates the number of agreements between two data files, broken down by key code. The confusion matrix enables you to easily look for patterns of discrepancy between the sequences of two files.

Essentially, the confusion matrix shows you how many times each code from the first file occurs at the same position in the sequence as each code from the second file. If all codes match at every position in the sequence, you should see non-zero counts along the main diagonal only, with the rest of the cells containing zeros. Relatively large values found in an off-diagonal cell may indicate some systematic bias. For example, one observer may have a slightly different interpretation of a code compared to another observer.

In the example above, the codes for kangaroo1.dat are listed down (in column A), and the codes for kangaroo2.dat are listed across (in row 15). Along the main diagonal, we see that foraging (f) was scored in the same position in the sequence of both files twice, whereas hop (h), stand look (s), and walk (w) were scored in the same position once. In the off-diagonal cells, we see that there was one case in which groom (g) was scored in kangaroo1.dat but forage (f) was scored in kangaroo2.dat, and that there was one case in which out-of-sight (o) was scored in kangaroo1.dat but groom (g) was scored in kangaroo2.dat.

The list of codes in the matrix is derived from the codes that occur within the two data files. When one file has more entries than the other, some codes will occur with no corresponding entry in the other file. In this case, the category "no entry" will be added to the matrix. In our example above, there was one case in which out-of-sight occurred in kangaroo2.dat but there was no entry at that position in kangaroo1.dat.

The statistics section tabulates results from the confusion matrix. The table includes the percent agreement and kappa coefficient described above. In addition, a variation of the percent agreement statistic is given for each code separately, enabling you to quickly visually inspect whether systematic biases exist for specific codes.

> **Column A ("key codes")** lists the codes that occur within the two data files, including the category "no entry," where relevant.
>
> **Column B ("filename1.dat")** reports the number of times that each code occurred in the first file, kangaroo1.dat. The counts are derived from the row totals of the confusion matrix.
>
> **Column C ("filename2.dat")** reports the number of times that each code occurred in the second file, kangaroo2.dat. These counts are derived from the column totals of the matrix.
>
> **Column D ("both agree")** reports the number of positions in the sequence for which both files contained the same code. The counts are derived from the matrix diagonal.
>
> **Column E ("YN")** reports the number of times that a code occurred in the first file but did not occur in the second file.
>
> **Column F ("NY")** reports the number of times that a code did not occur in the first file but did occur in the second file.
>
> **Column G ("disagree")** reports the total number of disagreements for each code, which is the sum of "YN" and "NY."
>
> **Column H ("% agreement")** is calculated as the total agreements for a code divided by the sum of the total agreements and the total disagreements, times 100, for each code.

For the total, the "% agreement" is the total agreements divided by the total number of entries (based upon the longer file).

Cohen's kappa adjusts the percent agreement to incorporate agreement due to chance. Kappa is given only for the total and is calculated as follows: Kappa = (O–C)/(1–C), where O = the observed proportion of agreements (which is the same as the total percent agreement calculated above, but not multiplied by 100) and C = the proportion of agreements that are expected by chance alone. C is based upon the frequency of occurrence of the codes in each data file. It is the sum of the row total times the column total for each code, divided by the total number of entries (based upon the longer file), squared. In other words, it is the sum of the joint probabilities of occurrence of each code.

The list-by-line section juxtaposes the sequence of codes in the two data files to facilitate direct comparison of the two files. The sequence number is simply the position in the sequence. The time associated with each key press is also listed for each data file, but it is not used for any calculations described above. In our example, we may easily see that the discrepancies in the sequences of the two files are entirely due to an additional "f" scored at position 6 in kangaroo2.dat.

Generally, it makes sense to test the reliability of your final statistic(s) of interest, in addition to carrying out the point-by-point comparison of sequences described above. For example, if you are interested in time budgets, you might wish to compare two or more files for the proportion of time spent foraging or looking. Although *JWatcher's* reliability routine is not specifically designed to do this, you may use the data derived from basic analysis result files (*.cd.res) to calculate correlations or intraclass correlation coefficients (Sokal and Rohlf 1995). If the correlation between the time budget estimates for pairs of focals scored twice by an observer is high, then the observer is scoring things consistently. An intraclass correlation coefficient would distinguish variation attributable to observers from that attributable to differences between samples. Thus, an observer could score each of 10 focals five times and calculate the intraclass correlation coefficient for these 50 observations. Ideally, these would be nonsignificant within focal effects and significant between focal effects.

# CHAPTER 8

# Basic Analysis: Creating a Focal Analysis Master File

## 8.1 Focal Analysis Master: An Overview

Once you have scored some files, you are probably eager to calculate some time budgets. Remember our question: how does group size influence time allocated to foraging and vigilance? To answer this question, we have to calculate time budgets: breakdowns of time allocated to each behavior. We will use basic analysis (as opposed to sequential analysis) to accomplish this.

First you will have to create a Focal Analysis Master File (*.faf). A focal analysis master file specifies the types of analyses you are going to conduct. *JWatcher's* "score once, analyze many times" philosophy is embedded in the focal analysis master file. A single data file can be analyzed differently by changing definitions in a focal analysis master file. You may wish to modify time bins, subtract or ignore certain behaviors, redefine mutually exclusive behaviors, modify how incomplete time bins are handled, or explore the differences between state and event analyses.

**Note:** *When we designed* JWatcher, *we envisioned people scoring behavior once and analyzing it many times. However, it is also true that there will always be certain decisions you will need to make in advance of scoring. The types of analyses you wish to run ultimately will dictate the best way to score behavior. You should pay particular attention to the relationships between behaviors, that is, which behaviors turn each other off. You will need to decide in advance whether you will be analyzing simultaneous streams of behavior, or whether all behaviors will be mutually exclusive. You should also consider carefully which behaviors are to be scored as events (those which formally have no duration) or as states (those which persist through time). Although you may modify these relationships in the focal analysis master at any time and rerun analyses, the relationships must be carefully thought through in advance. If they are not, you may produce erroneous or unintended results, or find that you cannot analyze your data in the way you want. You should also decide whether you want to score repeated key codes (e.g., scoring "look" every time a subject moves its head while continuing to look), as these decisions will influence how some statistics will be calculated.*

Tab over to "Focal Analysis Master."

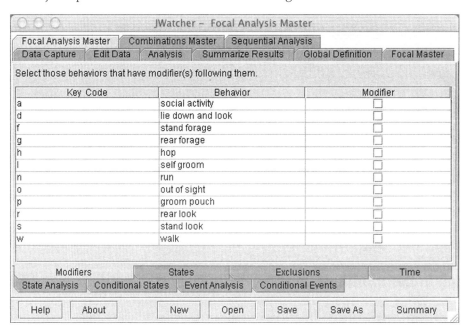

Use [New] to select a focal master file (*.fmf file) that contains the key codes to be analyzed.

Use [Open] to open a preexisting focal analysis master file (*.faf file).

We have just opened a new *.faf based on an existing *.fmf.

Make sure that you use the same *.fmf to score behavior and to analyze behavior. The analysis routine will later check whether the same *.fmf was used to capture data and to create the *.faf for analysis. If not, *JWatcher* will inform you that different *.fmf files were used. However, analysis will proceed even if the *.fmf files do not match.

## 8.2 Focal Analysis Master: Modifiers

Specify behaviors that may have modifiers following them. For instance, aggression (a) may be directed to different individuals (e.g., 1, 2, or 3). The default is that no modifiers follow any behaviors.

Since none of our behaviors have modifiers for our question, we will go onto the next tab. However, if you do have modifiers (or are considering whether they will be useful to you), continue reading below.

To view the list of modifiers associated with this file, click on [Summary]. Or, open your focal master file in the "Focal Master" tab.

When modifiers are specified to follow a behavior, results will be reported both for each behavior/modifier combination separately and for the behavior in its entirety. For example, if a count is requested in the above example involving aggression, a separate count would be reported for each "a1," "a2," and "a3." The count for "a" would also be reported, where count "a" = count "a1" + count "a2" + count "a3" + count "a" (no modifier follows). Results will be broken down as such for all statistics requested.

| Behavior | Behavior name | Modifier | Modifier name | StateAllDur N | StateAllDur Prop |
|---|---|---|---|---|---|
| a | aggression | | | 12 | 0.6159 |
| a | aggression | 1 | Fred | 8 | 0.3281 |
| a | aggression | 2 | Sam | 2 | 0.1581 |
| a | aggression | 3 | Cindy | 2 | 0.1298 |
| l | look | | | 4 | 0.3789 |

In the above example, "StateAllDur N" refers to the count, and "StateAllDur Prop" refers to the proportion of time that each behavior or behavior/modifier combination was on. More explanation of the result file headings will follow in Chapter 10 in a discussion on how to interpret *.cd.res files. Notice that the top line for aggression is the sum of aggression toward Fred, aggression toward Sam, and aggression toward Cindy.

> **Note:** Only modifier key codes that immediately follow a behavior specified as having modifiers will be reported in the results files. Any modifier key codes that do not follow a modified behavior will be recorded in the .dat file but will be ignored during analysis.

## 8.3 Focal Analysis Master: States

States are behaviors that occur over time. For instance, a subject may forage for two minutes. The onset of the bout of foraging could be noted by hitting "f" in data capture. Some behaviors may be incompatible with foraging (e.g., locomotion, abbreviated "l"), whereas others may not be (e.g., chewing, abbreviated "c"). Mutually incompatible behaviors signal the termination of a state and are used to calculate durations of states. Thus, a bout of foraging begins when "f" is hit and ends when a key code for an incompatible behavior is hit—in this case "l." This window allows you to specify precisely which behaviors are mutually exclusive, that is, which behaviors turn each other off.

Tab over to the "States" tab:

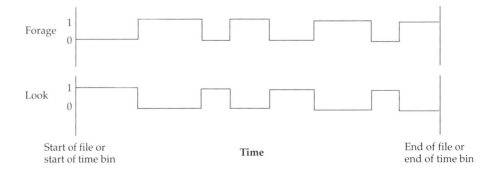

The default is that all behaviors are mutually exclusive; the onset of one behavior turns off another behavior (as shown above for our kangaroo-wallaby ethogram). You may create various combinations of mutually and nonmutually exclusive codes by selecting and deselecting boxes within the matrix. However, each code is always mutually exclusive with itself.

**Note:** *If you have nonmutually exclusive states, make sure that you specify the relationships carefully. Failure to do so may produce unintended or erroneous results. See section 8.7 on conditional states for an example using nonmutually exclusive states.*

To envision mutually exclusive states, examine the following traces of two mutually exclusive behaviors. These "traces" illustrate the onset, signified by "1," or offset, signified by "0," of a particular behavior. Note that the onset of foraging turns off looking, and vice versa. Thus, these are mutually exclusive behaviors.

The following traces illustrate two sets of behaviors. The individual behaviors within each set (stand, rear, look, forage) are mutually exclusive, an individual behavior from one set does not exclude an individual behavior from another set.

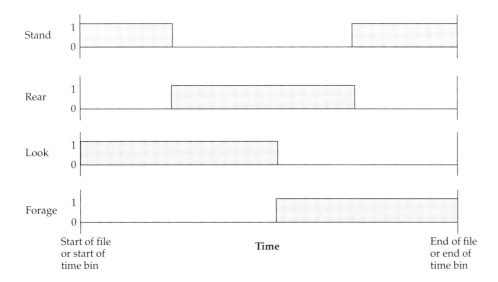

In this example, "stand" and "rear" are mutually exclusive, and "look" and "forage" are mutually exclusive, but "stand" or "rear" may occur simultaneously with "look" or "forage." Conditional state analysis may be used to generate statistics such as the conditional proportion of time (e.g., the time that a subject is standing, given that it is looking), or the number of bouts, total time, average bout duration, standard deviation of bouts, or proportion of time that two or more nonmutually exclusive states are simultaneously on (for example, the time that the subject is simultaneously standing and looking).

It is possible, and in some cases desirable, to hit the same key successively.

In State Analysis, repeated key strokes lead to intervals with no duration

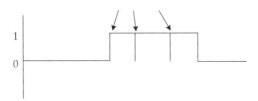

For instance, if you are interested in studying bouts of vigilance behavior, a bout begins every time a subject moves its head. In this case, because a code is mutually exclusive with itself, the duration of each bout is measured as the time between each keystroke. The interval between bouts is 0. The number of events of vigilance is the number (N) of keystrokes. The average duration of each bout of vigilance is the total duration divided by N – 1 keystrokes.

You should consider carefully whether you wish to score repeated keystrokes for a given behavior. In our example, we elected to score repeated keystrokes for vigilance, but not for other behaviors. Repeated keystrokes will affect the definition of a "bout" of behavior. In the example in the figure above, there are three bouts of vigilance. If you wish to consider the three contiguous bouts as one bout, you should not score repeated keystrokes. Or consider using a different key code to designate subsequent head movements after the initial onset of vigilance. Because repeated keystrokes affect the number of bouts, by extension, the use of repeated keystrokes will also affect the average bout duration and standard deviation of bout duration; however, the total time and proportion of time statistics will be unaffected.

## 8.4 Focal Analysis Master: Time

Tab over to the "Time" tab. We will come back to the "Exclusions" tab later.

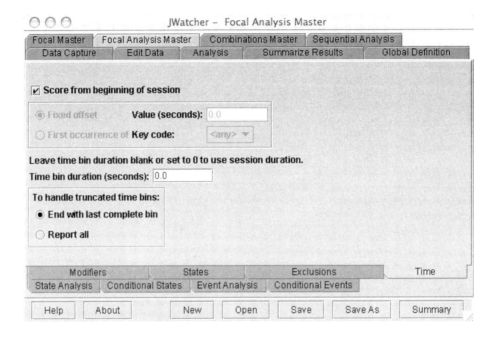

Decisions made in this window influence the time during which behavior is analyzed. The default setting is for the entire data file (*.dat file) to be analyzed, and that is what we will do for our kangaroo-wallaby example. However, there are cases in which you may wish to modify this in several ways.

You may specify at what point to begin analyzing a file (see the figure below).

Deselecting the "Score from beginning of session" box allows modifications.

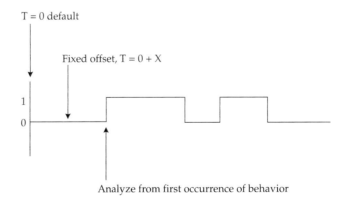

"Fixed offset" specifies the number of seconds from the beginning of the data file that should be ignored in analysis.

---

**Note:** *All key codes hit before the fixed offset time will be ignored. This means that analysis will begin at the first key code that occurs after the offset time. In an extreme example, if you have only one code in your data file and this code occurs prior to the offset value, then no behaviors will be reported as having occurred.*

---

"First occurrence" defines which, if any, behavior will trigger the onset of analysis. When a specific code has been designated, all key codes hit before this code will be ignored. You may also analyze from the onset of any key code, regardless of its identity. Choose the <any> option from the pull-down menu. You may wish to use this option to get around the problem of the time lag between the pressing of the start button and the first keystroke.

---

**Note:** *Using the <any> option will begin analysis at the first recorded keystroke regardless of whether it is defined in your *.fmf or whether it has been "ignored." In the latter case, a warning will be given during analysis, but analysis will proceed.*

---

"Time bin duration" specifies how the data file (*.dat file) is subdivided for analysis. For instance, you may wish to score a five-minute focal sample but summarize behavior in one-minute blocks of time. Specifying the time bin duration in 60-second blocks will take a five-minute focal and generate five different 60-second blocks of results. Time windowing like this is particularly useful when you are studying the response over time to an experimental treatment.

---

**Note:** *"0" time bin duration is the default and specifies that the entire focal will be analyzed in one time bin.*

---

Various combinations of time bin duration and offset times may lead to a situation in which the last time bin is truncated (i.e., it is shorter than previous time bins). Choose "End with last complete time bin" in order to report only results for complete time bins; choose "Report all" to report results for all time bins. For example, if you take a five-minute focal and specify your time bin duration to be three minutes, you will end up with one complete time bin of three minutes followed by one truncated time bin of two minutes. If you choose "End with last complete time bin," only the first time bin of three minutes will be reported. If you choose "Report all," both time bins will be reported.

## 8.5 Focal Analysis Master: State Analysis

Tab over to the "State Analysis" tab.

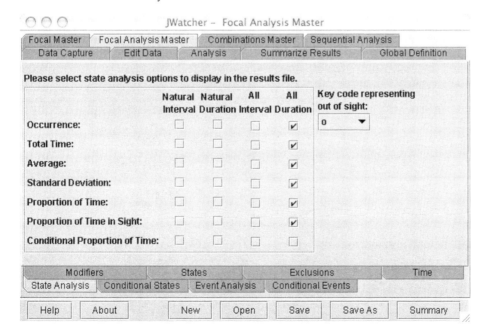

For each behavioral state, *JWatcher* calculates the number of bouts, the total time summed over all bouts, the average bout duration, the standard deviation of bout duration, and the proportion of time a focal subject engages in a given behavior calculated over the entire time bin.

If modifiers follow a behavior, the above statistics will be reported both for each behavior/modifier combination separately and also for that behavior in its entirety (globally). For example, assume that behavior "a" may be modified by "1," "2," or "3." If "Occurrence" is selected, a separate count would be reported for each of "a1," "a2," and "a3." The count for "a" would also be reported, where count "a" = count "a1" + count "a2" + count "a3" + count "a"(no modifier follows).

Subjects are not always in view. You may wish to specify a key code used when the subject is out-of-sight (e.g., "o"). The proportion of time allocated to each behavior as a function of time in-sight can also be calculated. In this case, the out-of-sight time is subtracted from the denominator of the proportion-of-time statistic.

> **Note:** *It is important to remember the following about proportion-of-time calculations: The total observation period is derived from EOF ("end of focal") time in each \*.dat file and not the focal duration specified in the \*.fmf. In other words, if you specified the focal duration in the \*.fmf to be 5 minutes, but you only scored behaviors for 1 minute, 34 seconds for a particular data file, then the total observation period for that file would be 1 minute, 34 seconds. If you calculate proportion of time (without time windowing), then the denominator used will be 1 minute, 34 seconds, and not 5 minutes. If you time window, then the denominator used to calculate proportion of time will be the time-bin duration. For example, if you scored behavior for 1 minute, 34 seconds for a particular data file, and specified a time bin duration of 60 seconds, then the denominator of the proportion-of-time statistic for the first complete time bin will be 60 seconds, and the denominator for the second truncated time bin will be 34 seconds (see section 8.4 for more on time windowing).*

A behavioral state has a duration, and there is an interval of time between bouts of behavior. These durations and intervals may be either "natural" (i.e., they start and end within a time bin), or they may be truncated by either a time-bin border or the end of a file. Selecting "natural" interval and "natural" duration reports statistics only on those intervals and state durations not truncated; that is, complete information exists about the onset and offset of all intervals and state durations included in the analysis. By selecting "all" interval and "all" duration, statistics are reported on all occurrences of interval and state durations regardless of whether they are truncated.

The duration of behavior may influence both your choice of focal duration and your selection of "natural" versus "all." To estimate time allocated to rare, relatively long-duration activities (e.g., a whale song, bouts of which may go on for hours), you may wish to analyze with "all," whereas your estimations of bout duration of more common and shorter-length activities might be better estimated by selecting "natural."

> **Note:** *The onset and termination of "out-of-sight" truncates intervals and durations. Scoring "out-of-sight" implies that you are unsure about what behavior(s) the focal subject is engaged in. If you are interested in natural durations or natural intervals, any bout of behavior adjacent to a bout of "out-of-sight" is, by definition, truncated.*

How "out-of-sight" truncates natural durations:

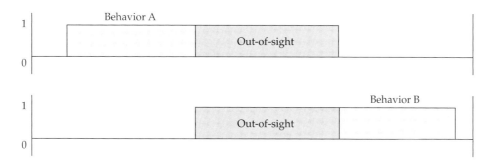

In the top line of the figure, behavior A is truncated by the onset of out-of-sight. In the bottom line, behavior B is truncated by the termination of out-of-sight. Truncated bouts of behavior will not be included in "natural" calculations.

Interval and duration definitions:

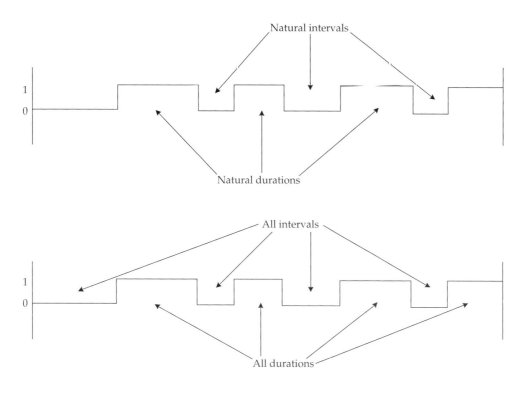

---

**Note:** *For durations only, the beginning of the focal does not truncate a duration. However, the beginning of subsequent time bins when time windowing is employed would do so. Thus, if you are interested in natural durations, we suggest that you begin your focal at the true onset of a behavior.*

For "all" interval analysis, if a behavior does not occur during a time bin, the interval is considered to occur once (i.e., N = 1), with a total duration equal to the time bin.

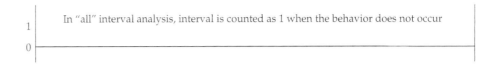

For "natural" interval analysis, if a behavior does not occur during a time bin, the interval count would be 0, because the interval is truncated by both the beginning and end of the time bin.

"Out-of-sight" has an additional consequence for "all" interval analysis.

Consider the following traces:

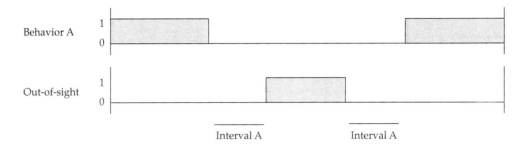

For "all" interval analysis, the count for interval A would be 2. "Out-of-sight" divides the interval into two because we do not know that behavior A did not occur during this time. "Out-of-sight" terminates the interval but does not truncate it. For "natural" interval analysis, the count for interval A would be 0. In this case, "out-of-sight" truncates both intervals on either side of it, and so these intervals are excluded from analysis.

**Note:** *If you are interested in calculating time budgets, you should be aware that statistics for proportion of time (and proportion of time in-sight) are calculated using the duration of the entire time bin as the denominator (or the duration of the entire time bin minus the time out-of-sight). This applies to both "all" and "natural" duration calculations. Thus, for "natural" duration calculations, the time associated with any truncated states is not removed from the denominator, but the time associated with truncated states will be removed from the numerator (which may not make sense for your analysis). We therefore recommend that time budgets involving proportions be calculated using "all" duration statistics, rather than "natural" duration statistics.*

For example, consider the following trace:

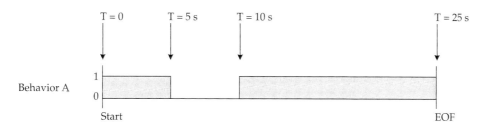

For "all" proportion of time, the numerator includes both bouts of behavior A (5 s + 15 s), and the denominator is the focal length (25 s). The proportion is 20/25 = 0.8.

For "natural" proportion of time, the numerator is composed of the first bout of behavior A only (5 s), with the denominator remaining as the focal length (25 s). The proportion is 5/25 = 0.2, which may be misleading. Remember that the first bout of behavior A is included because the start of the focal is a special case that does not truncate durations of behavior.

If you are interested in the average duration and standard deviation of bouts, then "natural" statistics may be appropriate If you wish to include only those bouts for which you have complete information about their onset and offset.

For example, consider the following trace:

If the first bout of behavior B is more representative of bout length than the second truncated piece, then removing this piece from calculations may improve your estimates of average or standard deviation of bout lengths.

"Conditional" proportion of time generates statistics for up to four streams of simultaneously occurring behaviors. To generate these statistics, the specific behavioral combinations to be analyzed must also be specified in the "Conditional States" tab (see section 8.7). For example, if B | A (B given A) is specified for analysis, then the conditional proportion of time will be reported as the following: given that a subject is engaged in behavior A, what proportion of time is it simultaneously engaged in behavior B, where A and B are nonmutually exclusive states? The number of bouts, total time, average bout duration, standard deviation of bouts, proportion of time, and proportion of time-in-sight will be reported for bouts of A and B occurring simultaneously, when those statistics are also selected above.

Conditional proportion of time may be calculated for "natural" or "all" durations, and also for "natural" or "all" intervals.

Consider the following traces where "Stand" and "Look" are nonmutually exclusive behaviors. The durations included in the numerator and denominator for "All" duration conditional proportion of time for "Stand given Look" are shown.

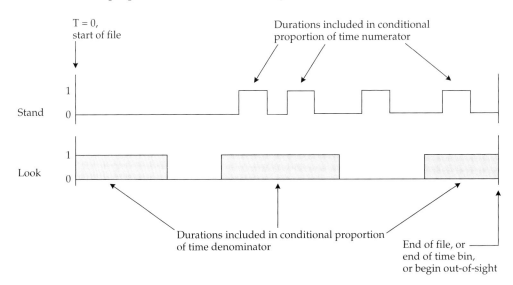

The following traces show the durations included in the numerator and denominator for "Natural" duration conditional proportion of time for "Stand given Look," where "Stand" and "Look" are nonmutually exclusive behaviors.

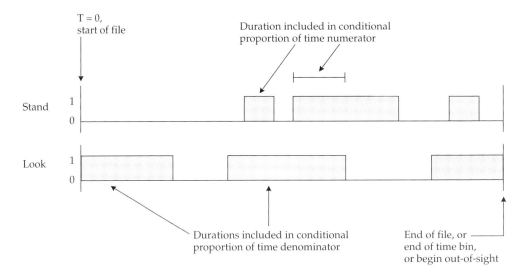

Note that the beginning of the focal (T = 0) does not truncate state durations, but the end of the focal, the beginning and end of a time bin, and the beginning and end of out-of-sight do truncate state durations.

If B | A (B given A) is specified for interval analysis, the conditional proportion of time will report the proportion of time that a subject is not engaged in B, given that it is not engaged in A (i.e., the proportion of time that interval B occurs, given that interval A is occurring).

The following traces show the intervals included in the numerator and denominator for "All" interval conditional proportion of time for B | A, where B and A are nonmutually exclusive behaviors.

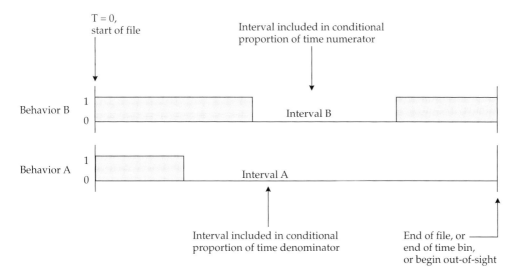

Note that for "natural" interval analysis, the conditional proportion of time = 0 in the above example, because interval A is truncated by the end of focal (or end of time bin or beginning of out-of-sight). Unlike durations, intervals are truncated by the beginning of a focal (T = 0) as well.

See "Conditional States," below (section 8.7), for more details about conditional state analysis.

We now return to our question about whether group size influences time allocated to foraging and vigilance in kangaroos and wallabies. For this question, we are interested in time budgets, the proportion of time allocated to each behavior. Our subjects are not always visible for the entire focal observation session. We thus calculate the proportion of time in-sight for "all" durations.

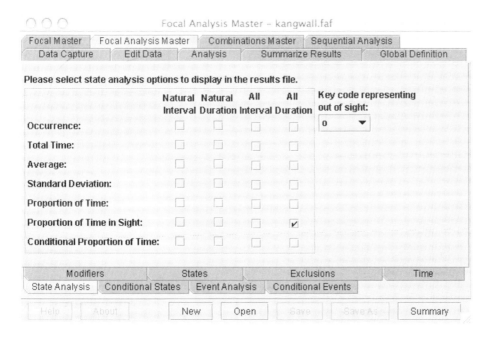

## 8.6 Focal Analysis Master: Exclusions

Tab back to the "Exclusions" tab.

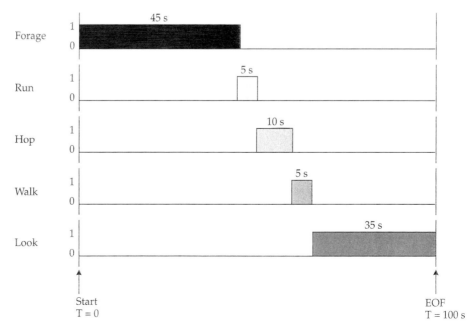

The "subtract" function subtracts the total time for a specified state from the total duration of a time bin when calculating time budgets. For example, you might wish to calculate the time allocated to running as a function of total locomotion. In this case, behaviors other than those involved in locomotion could be subtracted. The proportion of time and proportion of time-in-sight statistics reported for each behavior in the results will be adjusted accordingly.

For example, consider the following trace representing a subject who foraged for 45 s, ran for 5 s, hopped for 10 s, walked for 5 s, and then ended by looking for 35 s. We will use a slightly modified version of our kangaroo-wallaby ethogram for this particular example, in which all postures associated with foraging or looking are combined into one category of forage or look, respectively.

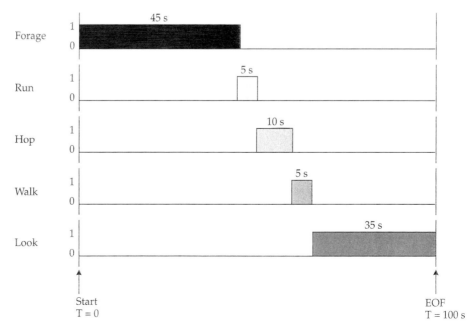

A time budget for this subject using the proportion-of-time statistic would be as follows:

| | |
|---|---|
| Forage | = 45 s /100 s = 0.45 |
| Look | = 35 s /100 s = 0.35 |
| Hop | = 10 s /100 s = 0.10 |
| Run | = 5 s /100 s = 0.05 |
| Walk | = 5 s /100 s = 0.05 |

If you were interested in the proportion of time that the subject ran, given that it was engaged in locomotion, you could subtract the time spent foraging (45 s) and looking (35 s) from the denominator.

$$Run = 5 \text{ s} / (100 \text{ s} - 45 \text{ s} - 35 \text{ s}) = 5 \text{ s} / 20 \text{ s} = 0.25$$

"Subtract" only influences duration statistics, but not interval statistics.

"Subtract" only influences the statistics for proportion of time and proportion of time in-sight.

"Subtract" does not affect the logical relationships with other behaviors. Time is removed, but subtracted behaviors still terminate bouts of mutually exclusive behaviors.

"Subtract" is best used with "all" duration statistics, rather than "natural" duration statistics. This is true when calculating time budgets in general. That is, time budgets are best calculated with "all" duration statistics, and not "natural" duration statistics. (See section 8.5 on state analysis for a more detailed explanation.) Essentially, truncated states are removed from the numerator but not the denominator of "natural" proportion-of-time statistics.

When you subtract a behavior, you will still see results reported for that behavior. However, for subtracted behaviors only, the proportion of time and proportion of time in-sight will continue to be calculated as the total time for the subtracted behavior divided by the total duration of the time bin. The total time for the subtracted behavior is not subtracted from the denominator in this case.

Going back to the question of the time allocated to running as a function of locomotion, we might find the following results for a different subject:

Results before subtracting "forage" and "look":

| Behavior | Behavior name | StateAllDur N | StateAllDur Prop |
|---|---|---|---|
| f | Forage | 12 | 0.4353 |
| l | Look | 8 | 0.3654 |
| p | Hop | 2 | 0.1269 |
| r | Run | 1 | 0.0341 |
| w | Walk | 1 | 0.0383 |

Results after subtracting "forage" and "look":

| Behavior | Behavior name | StateAllDur N | StateAllDur Prop |
|----------|---------------|---------------|------------------|
| f | Forage | 12 | 0.4353 |
| l | Look | 8 | 0.3654 |
| p | Hop | 2 | 0.6367 |
| r | Run | 1 | 0.1711 |
| w | Walk | 1 | 0.1922 |

**Note:** *"StateAllDur" refers to "all" duration statistics. "N" is count and "Prop" is proportion of time. More explanation of the result file headings will follow in Chapter 10 on how to interpret \*.cd.res files.*

We see that the time allocated to running as a function of locomotion (hop, run, or walk), is 0.1711. Note that the sum of the proportion of times for hop, run, and walk is 1.000 after the other behaviors (look, forage) have been subtracted. Also note that the proportion of time did not change for the subtracted behaviors (look, forage) after subtraction.

There are two ways you could conceivably use *JWatcher* to calculate the proportion of time in-sight. One way is to subtract the behavior that represents out-of-sight and then examine the proportion of time statistics, as described above. The other way is to specify an out-of-sight key in the "State Analysis" tab and examine the statistics for proportion of time in-sight. For "all" duration statistics, the results will be identical.

**Note:** *Remember that if you are interested in "natural" duration statistics, or either "natural" or "all" intervals statistics, then specifying an out-of-sight key in the "State Analysis" tab will have additional consequences beyond the calculation of proportion of time in-sight. See section 8.5 for more information on out-of-sight and its effects.*

"Ignore" literally ignores selected behaviors when calculating states. Ignored behaviors, therefore, do not turn off mutually exclusive behaviors; it is as if the key code were never pressed.

Note that nonsensical output potentially can result if some behaviors in a related set are ignored while others are retained for analysis.

"Ignore" has precedence over "subtract." The default situation is that no behaviors are either subtracted or ignored. Ignored behaviors are not reported in the results, while subtracted behaviors are.

## 8.7 Focal Analysis Master: Conditional States

Use this window to specify the combinations of behaviors to be analyzed as simultaneous streams. Up to four streams of simultaneously occurring behaviors may be analyzed.

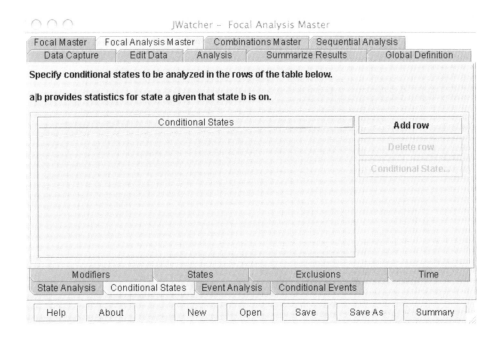

Conditional states analysis can be performed only when at least two behaviors are non-mutually exclusive (or at least one behavior is modified—see the special case below). The relationships among behaviors are defined in the "States" tab.

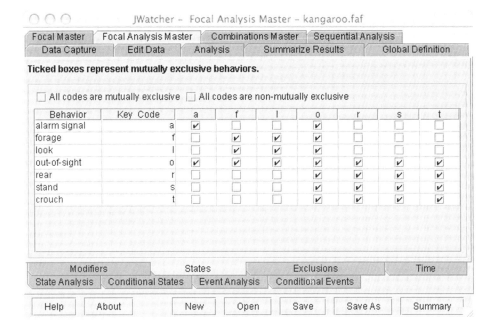

In the example above, we have defined two sets of mutually exclusive behaviors. The actions forage and look make up one set, and the postures rear, stand, and crouch make up the second set. We have also defined an event—alarm signal—which does not exclude and is not excluded by any other behavior. By definition, out-of-sight must exclude everything else.

The statistics to be reported are specified in the "State Analysis" section above (section 8.5).

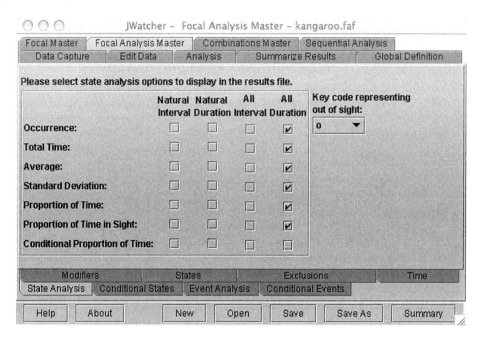

The number of bouts, total time, average bout duration, standard deviation of bouts, proportion of time, and proportion of time in-sight can be reported for bouts of up to four simultaneously occurring behaviors. For example, if A | B is specified, then the above statistics will be reported for all bouts of A and B taking place simultaneously. If A | B | C is specified, then statistics will be generated for all simultaneous bouts of A, B, and C simultaneously. Likewise, if A | B | C | D is specified, then calculations will be based upon all simultaneous bouts of A, B, C, and D.

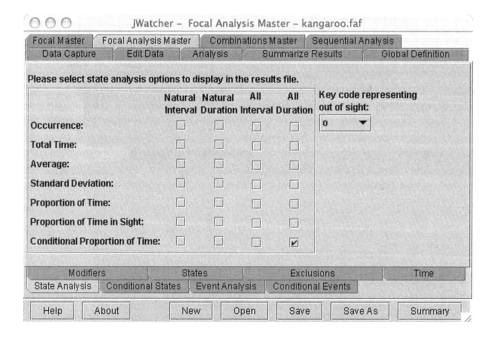

In addition, the conditional proportion of time can be reported for behaviors A | B, A | B | C, or A | B | C | D. For A | B, this statistic calculates the proportion of time that A is on, given that B is also on.

When A | B | C is specified for analysis, two separate conditional proportion-of-time statistics will be generated automatically: A | BC calculates the proportion of time that A is on, given that B and C are on simultaneously, and AB | C calculates the proportion of time that A and B are on simultaneously, given that C is on. These are not necessarily the same. Consider the following traces:

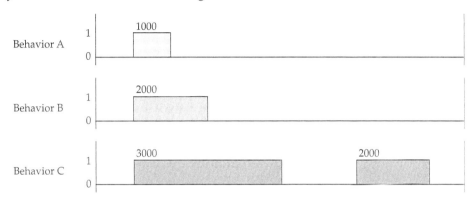

In the above figure, behavior A is on for one bout of 1000 ms, behavior B is on for one bout of 2000 ms, and behavior C is on for two bouts of 3000 ms and 2000 ms, respectively. A | BC = time that A is on/time that B and C are simultaneously on = 1000/2000 = 0.5000. AB | C = time that A and B are simultaneously on/time that C is on = 1000/5000 = 0.2000.

Which statistic is most appropriate? It depends upon your question. For example, just say that you are interested in comparing time budgets when a predator is present versus when there is no predator present. Specifically, you might be interested in comparing the time allocated to rear looking under the two circumstances. If behavior A is rear (a posture), behavior B is look (an action), and behavior C is predator present, then you might be interested in the proportion of time that the subject is simultaneously rearing and looking, given that there is a predator present (AB | C). You probably would also want to calculate, for comparison, the proportion of time that the subject is simultaneously rearing and looking, given that predators are absent. A question with a slightly different focus would be how the presence of a predator affects the postures associated with looking. In other words, given that the subject is looking, what proportion of time is spent engaged in the various postures (rear, stand, crouch, etc.) when a predator is present compared to when predators are absent. Here you might calculate the time allocated to rearing, given that the subject is simultaneously looking and in the presence of a predator (A | BC), and compare this with the time allocated to rearing, given that the subject is simultaneously looking and not in the presence of a predator.

For A | B | C | D, four conditional proportion-of-time statistics are automatically generated: A | BCD calculates the proportion of time that A is on, given that B, C, and D are simultaneously on. AB | CD calculates the proportion of time that A and B are simultaneously on, given that C and D are simultaneously on. AC | BD calculates the proportion of time that A and C are simultaneously on, given that B and D are simultaneously on. And ABC | D calculates the proportion of time that A, B, and C are simultaneously on, given that D is on.

Once again, the relevant conditional proportion-of-time statistic(s) will depend upon your question of interest.

To generate statistics for simultaneous streams of behavior, you must specify the behavioral combinations of interest in the "Conditional States" tab.

Click [Add row] to begin.

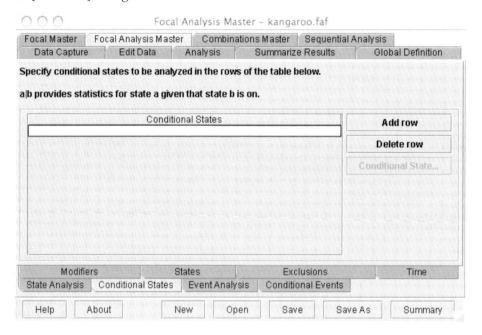

Click [Conditional State] to select a pair of behaviors for conditional analysis (e.g., A | B).

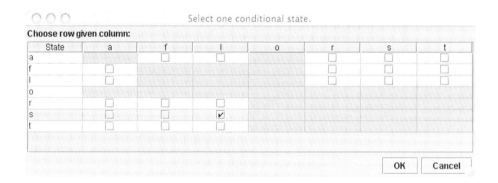

In this case, we have selected "stand given look" (s | l). Note that you will only be able to choose pairs of behaviors that are nonmutually exclusive. The rest of the options will be grayed out. Click [OK].

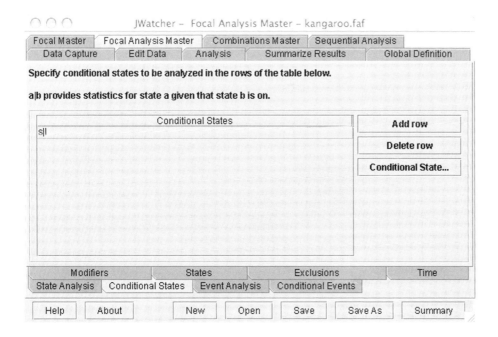

The appropriate pair will now be entered for you. You may also enter behavioral combinations directly into the text field, separating each key code with the given symbol ( | ).

To add a third behavior (e.g., to specify A | B | C), place cursor back within the cell containing the pair (e.g., A | B), and click on [Conditional State] again. Select third behavior.

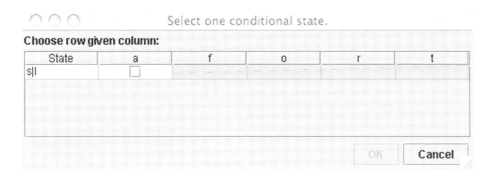

Only behaviors that are not mutually exclusive with both of the behaviors in the previously defined pair will be displayed. In this case, the only behavior that is available is "alarm signal."

Repeat the process above to add up to four behaviors.

Click [Add row] to specify another combination of behaviors for analysis.

Modified behaviors may also be included within the combination of behaviors to be analyzed. These will be treated according to the description above for regular, unmodified behaviors. For example, if behaviors A and B are followed by modifiers 1 or 2, then combinations such as A1 | B2 or A | B1 | C | D may be analyzed.

*Note:* *There is a special case involving modifiers: It is also possible to analyze A1|A or A2|A with conditional states analysis, where A is a behavior modified by 1, 2, or 3. The conditional proportion of time for A1|A would be the proportion of time that A1 is on, given that any A is on, where "any A" includes A1, A2, A3, or A alone not followed by a modifier.*

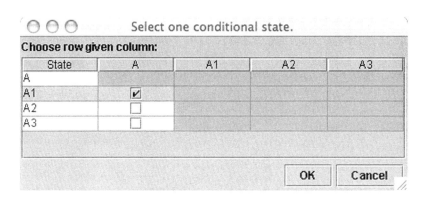

You also could achieve the identical analysis by subtracting all of the behaviors other than A (not shown above) and examining the proportion of time statistics for A1, A2, and A3.

## 8.8 Focal Analysis Master: Event Analysis

Tab over to "Event Analysis."

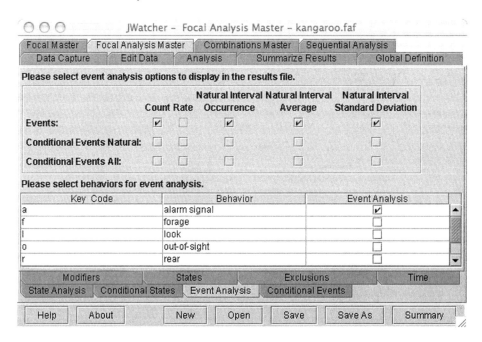

Events are behaviors that are treated as instantaneous and therefore have no duration. Thus, they can be counted and intervals between them can be quantified. For event analysis, *JWatcher* quantifies only "natural" intervals.

In Event Analysis, repeated key strokes are scored as events

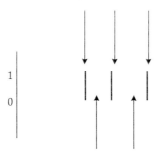

In Event Analysis, natural intervals are between events

*JWatcher* permits behaviors to be analyzed as both events and states. This is in keeping with our "score once, analyze many times" philosophy.

Select those behaviors for which event analysis is requested and select the output required.

The first row ("Events") reports results for standard event analysis. Event count is a tally of the number of times an event occurred, while the natural interval count is the number of natural intervals between events. "Average interval between" and "standard deviation" are based on natural intervals. Remember that if you specified an out-of-sight key in the "State Analysis" window, out-of-sight will truncate any natural intervals, including those in event analysis. If a modifier follows a behavior that is analyzed as an event, then the above statistics will be reported both for each behavior/modifier combination separately, and also for each behavior in its entirety (globally).

The second and third rows ("Conditional Events Natural" and "Conditional Events All") report statistics for conditional event analysis. Conditional event analysis tallies the number of events that occur while a specified state is on (or while up to three simultaneously occurring states are on). Statistics for natural intervals occurring between those events are also reported. The rate is the number of events that occur while the state is on, divided by the total time (in milliseconds) that the state is on. "Natural" conditional event analysis does not tally events occurring during truncated states. Once again, remember that if you specified an out-of-sight key in the "State Analysis" window, out-of-sight will truncate state durations. "All" conditional event analysis tallies events occurring during states regardless of whether states are truncated.

The following figures illustrate "Conditional Events All" analysis:

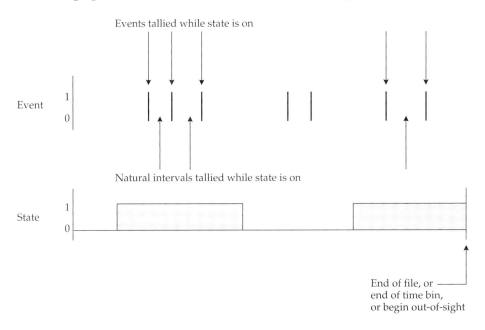

The following figure illustrates "Conditional Events Natural" analysis:

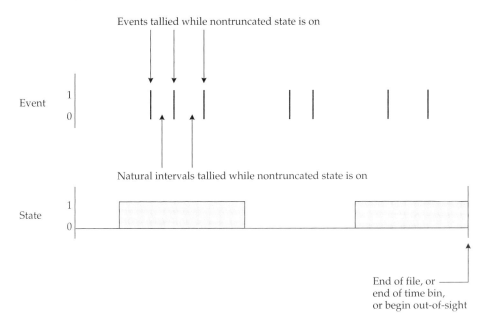

The combination of events and states to be analyzed must be specified in the "Conditional Events" tab (see section 8.9).

> **Warning:** *For each combination of event and state(s) to be analyzed with conditional event analysis, the event must be made nonmutually exclusive with the state(s) in the "States" tab. Otherwise, each occurrence of the event will turn off the state(s) of interest, and thus produce potentially unintended results. The program does not currently provide any error checking or warnings with respect to this issue.*

## 8.9 Focal Analysis Master: Conditional Events

Use this window to specify the combinations of events and states to be analyzed as a conditional event. Conditional event analysis calculates statistics for events that occur while a specified state is on. Events occurring during up to three streams of simultaneously occurring states may be analyzed.

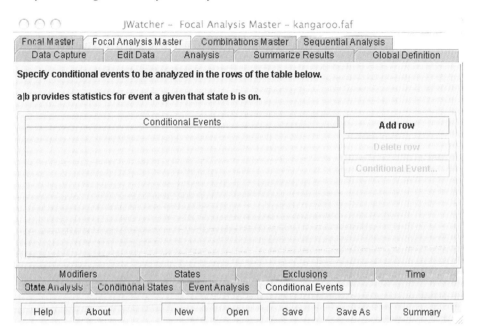

To begin, you must specify the behaviors to be analyzed as events in the "Event Analysis" tab (see section 8.8). For conditional event analysis, behaviors are considered to be either events or states, but not both. All behaviors not specified as an event in the "Event Analysis" tab will be considered as states for this analysis.

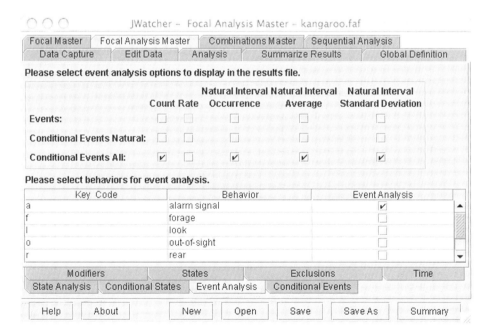

In this example, we have specified alarm signal (a) to be an event. We are interested in the number of alarm signals that are given by a subject while it is simultaneously looking and rearing. We are also interested in the number, average, and standard deviation of the natural intervals between those alarm signals as they occur when the subject is simultaneously looking and rearing. Those statistics are selected above.

> **Warning:** *Events must be made nonmutually exclusive with state(s) in the "States" tab for this analysis to proceed correctly. Otherwise, each occurrence of the event will turn off the state(s) of interest, and thus produce potentially unintended results. The program does not currently provide any error checking or warnings with respect to this issue.*

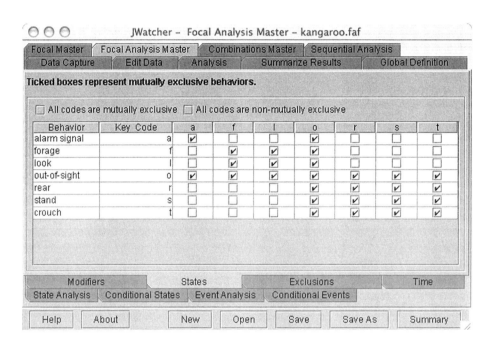

Notice that we ensured that alarm signal is nonmutually exclusive with both look and rear. Also, look and rear must themselves be nonmutually exclusive.

As mentioned previously, the statistics to be reported are specified in the "Event Analysis" tab. For A | B, statistics will be reported for event A, given that state B is occurring. For A | B | C, statistics will be reported for event A, given that states B and C are simultaneously occurring. For A | B | C | D, statistics will be reported for event A, given that states B, C, and D are simultaneously occurring. See section 8.8 for more details about particular statistics.

Remember that if you specified an out-of-sight key in the "States Analysis" tab, then out-of-sight truncates natural durations of states (for "Conditional Events Natural" analysis only). Out-of-sight may not be included as part of a conditional event.

Modified behaviors may also be included within the combination of behaviors to be analyzed, and they will be treated as previously described for regular, unmodified behaviors. For example, if behaviors A and B are followed by modifiers 1 or 2, then combinations such as A1 | B2 or A | B1 | C | D may be analyzed.

Go back to the conditional events tab, and click [Add row] to begin.

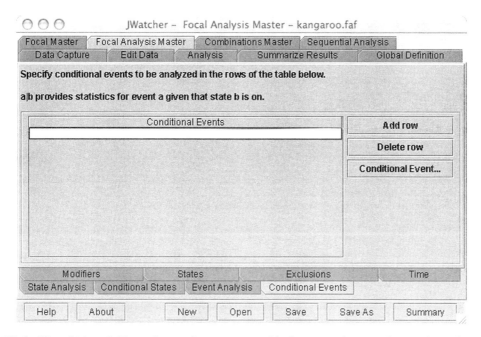

Click [Conditional Event] to select a pair of behaviors for conditional analysis (e.g., A | B).

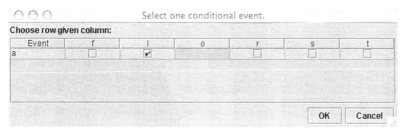

You will be given a list of those behaviors specified as events in the left column (representing rows). In this case, we have just one event, alarm signal (a). Behaviors not specified as events are considered to be states and will be listed in subsequent columns (forage, look, rear, stand, crouch). In this case, we begin by selecting the event, alarm signal (a), given that the subject is engaged in the state, look (l). Click [OK].

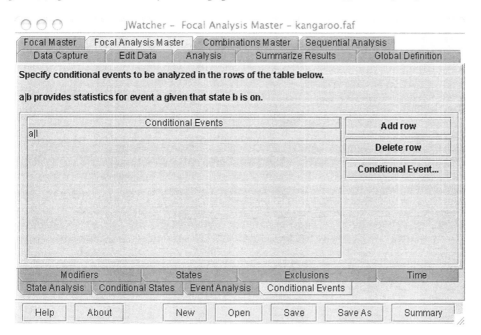

The conditional event combination will be entered into the table for you. You may also type conditional event combinations directly into the table yourself, ensuring that each behavior is separated by the given symbol ( | ).

To add a third behavior (e.g., to specify A | B | C), place the cursor back within the cell containing the pair (e.g., A | B), and click on [Conditional Event] again. Select the third behavior.

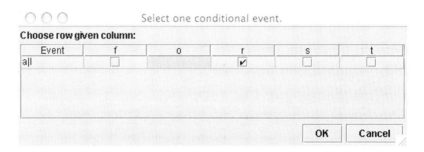

In this case, we will be calculating the number of alarm signals (a) given that the subject is simultaneously looking (l) and rearing (r). Click [OK].

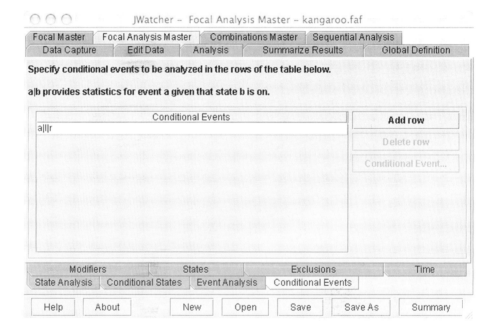

Repeat the process to add up to four behaviors.

Click [Add row] to specify another combination of behaviors for analysis.

## 8.10 Saving Your Focal Analysis Master File

Once you have selected analysis options, save changes using [Save], or create a new file name using [Save As].

> **Note:** *You may notice that it takes a very long time to save an \*.faf file the very first time the program is opened. Simply wait and the file will eventually be saved. This problem should not occur for subsequent saves. It is due to the \*.faf validation process described below, and it is more likely to occur when using a computer with limited RAM.*

> **Note:** *When JWatcher is run on a PC, you may be asked if you want to save changes, even when no changes were made to your file.*

Every time that you save an \*.faf, the program will check for logical inconsistencies among the selections made within the file. For example, out-of-sight may not be subtracted lest meaningless statistics be generated. If such inconsistencies exist, a pop-up window will list the problems and propose solutions. You may either accept the proposed changes or cancel the save.

## 8.11 What Constitutes a Valid \*.faf?

In order for an \*.faf to be saved, the \*.faf must be considered to be valid (internally consistent). That is, it should not contain requests for logically inconsistent analyses.

The following error checking will occur when saving the \*.faf:

1. Key code representing "out-of-sight" must be mutually exclusive with all other behaviors.
2. Key code representing "out-of-sight" cannot be a modified behavior.
3. Key code representing "out-of-sight" cannot be subtracted or ignored.

4. Key code representing "out-of-sight" cannot be part of a conditional state or event.
5. A subtracted or ignored behavior cannot be part of a conditional state or event, except that the first key (event) in a conditional event may be subtracted.
6. The first key code in a conditional event must be selected as an event in the "Event Analysis" tab.
7. The second, third, and fourth key codes in a conditional event cannot contain mutually exclusive behaviors
8. Conditional states cannot contain mutually exclusive behaviors.
9. Conditional states or events cannot contain key codes that are not defined in the *.fmf.
10. Conditional states or events cannot contain modifiers that are not associated with a behavior selected to be modified in the "Modifiers" tab.

If any of the above conditions are not met, you will be given a choice: to either cancel the save or to proceed with the save. If you elect to save, then the program will automatically correct the above problems in a predetermined manner (described below). If you cancel the save, then no changes will be made, allowing you to go back and fix any inconsistencies in the manner you find most appropriate.

The following fixes will be made automatically upon saving the *.faf:

1. Key code representing "out-of-sight" will be made mutually exclusive with all other behaviors in the "States" table.
2. Key code representing "out-of-sight" will be deselected in the "Modifiers" tab.
3. Key code representing "out-of-sight" will be deselected in the "Exclusions" tab.
4. Conditional states or events containing the key code representing "out-of-sight" will be removed.
5. Conditional states or events containing subtracted or ignored behaviors will be removed (except as described above).
6. Conditional events not containing an event as the first key code will be removed.
7. Conditional events containing mutually exclusive states will be removed.
8. Conditional states containing mutually exclusive behaviors will be removed.
9. Conditional states or events containing key codes not defined in the *.fmf will be removed.
10. Conditional states or events containing modifiers associated with unmodified behaviors will be removed.

## 8.12 Other Tools Related to Your Focal Analysis Master File

[Summary] opens a text window containing all the specifications in the current focal analysis master file (*.faf). Select the text using a mouse, and copy the contents ("Ctrl + c") of the text window. The contents can now be pasted into a word processor and printed.

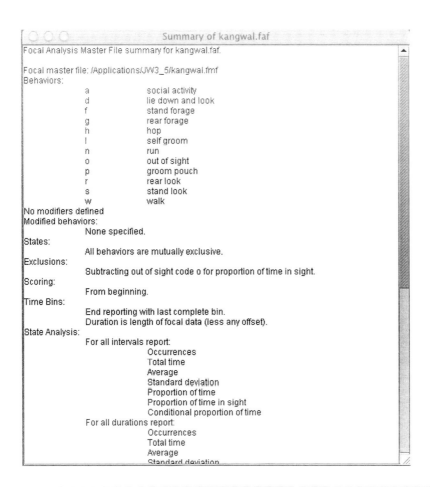

**Note:** *The section under the heading "warnings" in the summary will list some potential problems that may arise during analysis.*

# CHAPTER 9

# Basic Analysis: Analyzing Your Data

*JWatcher* allows you to analyze files one at a time or in batch processing mode. Batch processing mode fits nicely with our "score once, analyze many times" philosophy. For instance, you can analyze a set of files without exclusions and then go back later and modify your focal analysis master file and rerun all the analyses with certain exclusions.

Tab over to "Analysis > Data."

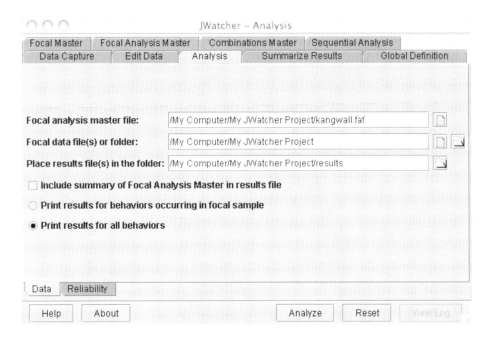

You must have a focal analysis master file (*.faf file) and at least one data file (*.dat file) to run the "Analysis" routine.

Click on the file icon to specify the *.faf file used to analyze the data. We have selected our kangwall.faf.

Click on either the file icon or the folder icon to specify a *.dat file or a folder with one or more *.dat files to be analyzed. All *.dat files in a folder will be analyzed if the folder option is selected. In this case, we selected the folder in which all of our files are contained.

Use the folder icon to specify a folder in which the results file(s) will later be placed. *JWatcher* will create a new folder if one does not already exist.

> **Note:** JWatcher *names the results files by changing the suffix of the original .dat file name. For example, the results file generated by analyzing a data file named "test.dat" will be "test.cd.res" and "test.tr.res." (See below for the distinction between *.cd.res and *.tr.res.) If you modify the *.faf file and rerun an analysis, be sure to specify a different folder for the results; the default is to write over existing results files. JWatcher will ask if it is OK to overwrite files before doing so.*

There are two types of results files output; both are comma-delimited text files. To view results files, open them in a word-processing or spreadsheet program.

"*.cd.res" is a "codes down" results file suitable for importing into a spreadsheet or word-processing program. After a specified header, each row of results summarizes a behavior or a behavior and modifier. Each column in the results file contains a summary statistic specified when creating the focal analysis master file (*.faf file).

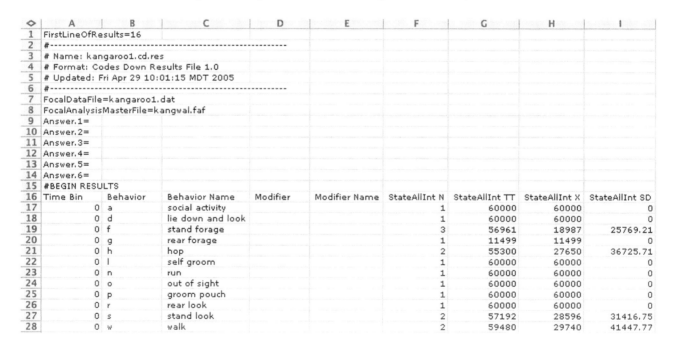

| ◇ | A | B | C | D | E | F | G | H | I |
|---|---|---|---|---|---|---|---|---|---|
| 1 | FirstLineOfResults=16 | | | | | | | | |
| 2 | #----------------------------------------------------- | | | | | | | | |
| 3 | # Name: kangaroo1.cd.res | | | | | | | | |
| 4 | # Format: Codes Down Results File 1.0 | | | | | | | | |
| 5 | # Updated: Fri Apr 29 10:01:15 MDT 2005 | | | | | | | | |
| 6 | #----------------------------------------------------- | | | | | | | | |
| 7 | FocalDataFile=kangaroo1.dat | | | | | | | | |
| 8 | FocalAnalysisMasterFile=kangwal.faf | | | | | | | | |
| 9 | Answer.1= | | | | | | | | |
| 10 | Answer.2= | | | | | | | | |
| 11 | Answer.3= | | | | | | | | |
| 12 | Answer.4= | | | | | | | | |
| 13 | Answer.5= | | | | | | | | |
| 14 | Answer.6= | | | | | | | | |
| 15 | #BEGIN RESULTS | | | | | | | | |
| 16 | Time Bin | Behavior | Behavior Name | Modifier | Modifier Name | StateAllInt N | StateAllInt TT | StateAllInt X | StateAllInt SD |
| 17 | 0 | a | social activity | | | 1 | 60000 | 60000 | 0 |
| 18 | 0 | d | lie down and look | | | 1 | 60000 | 60000 | 0 |
| 19 | 0 | f | stand forage | | | 3 | 56961 | 18987 | 25769.21 |
| 20 | 0 | g | rear forage | | | 1 | 11499 | 11499 | 0 |
| 21 | 0 | h | hop | | | 2 | 55300 | 27650 | 36725.71 |
| 22 | 0 | l | self groom | | | 1 | 60000 | 60000 | 0 |
| 23 | 0 | n | run | | | 1 | 60000 | 60000 | 0 |
| 24 | 0 | o | out of sight | | | 1 | 60000 | 60000 | 0 |
| 25 | 0 | p | groom pouch | | | 1 | 60000 | 60000 | 0 |
| 26 | 0 | r | rear look | | | 1 | 60000 | 60000 | 0 |
| 27 | 0 | s | stand look | | | 2 | 57192 | 28596 | 31416.75 |
| 28 | 0 | w | walk | | | 2 | 59480 | 29740 | 41447.77 |

"*.tr.res" provides a way to graph "traces" of behavior over time using a spreadsheet or graphics program. Import the comma-delimited text file into your program to graph the trace. All 0–1 and 1–0 "transitions" along with the transition times are specified for each behavior.

> **Warning:** *When the number of columns in your *.tr.res file is greater than 256, you may not be able to open the file in Excel. In this case, you may receive a message stating that the file is incompletely opened. This has no impact on the validity of the associated *.cd.res file.*

```
 1  FirstLineOfResults=16
 2  #-------------------------------------------------------
 3  # Name: kangaroo1.tr.res
 4  # Format: Behaviour Trace Results File 1.0
 5  # Updated: Fri Apr 29 10:01:15 MDT 2005
 6  #-------------------------------------------------------
 7  FocalDataFile=kangaroo1.dat
 8  FocalAnalysisMasterFile=kangwal.faf
 9  Answer.1=
10  Answer.2=
11  Answer.3=
12  Answer.4=
13  Answer.5=
14  Answer.6=
15  #BEGIN RESULTS
16  Bin            0  Offset    0    60000   60000   300000
17  Trace    a        State     0        0      -1       -1
18
19  Bin            0  Offset    0    60000   60000   300000
20  Trace    d        State     0        0      -1       -1
21
22  Bin            0  Offset    0      952     952     1681    1681    9189    9189   11499
23  Trace    f        State     0        0       1        1       0       0       1       1
24
25  Bin            0  Offset    0    11499   11499    60000   60000  300000
26  Trace    g        State     0        0       1        1      -1      -1
27
28  Bin            0  Offset    0     1681    1681     6381    6381   60000   60000  300000
29  Trace    h        State     0        0       1        1       0       0      -1      -1
30
31  Bin            0  Offset    0    60000   60000   300000
32  Trace    l        State     0        0      -1       -1
33
34  Bin            0  Offset    0    60000   60000   300000
35  Trace    n        State     0        0      -1       -1
36
37  Bin            0  Offset    0    60000   60000   300000
38  Trace    o        State     0        0       1        1
39
40  Bin            0  Offset    0    60000   60000   300000
41  Trace    p        State     0        0      -1       -1
42
43  Bin            0  Offset    0    60000   60000   300000
44  Trace    r        State     0        0      -1       -1
45
46  Bin            0  Offset    0     6381    6381     9189    9189   60000   60000  300000
47  Trace    s        State     0        0       1        1       0       0      -1      -1
48
49  Bin            0  Offset    0      432     432      952     952   60000   60000  300000
50  Trace    w        State     0        0       1        1       0       0      -1      -1
```

Checking the box "Include summary of the focal analysis master in the results file" will do just that.

Selecting the appropriate radio button will determine whether the results for all behaviors and modifiers will be reported in the focal analysis master file, or only those that occurred in a data file.

> **Note:** *If you wish to later summarize all your results files into a single summary sheet using the "Summarize Results" routine, then you* must *print results for all behaviors.*

Select [Analyze] to run the program. A progress box is updated each time a data file is analyzed. A text box provides an option to examine a file that contains a list of any errors or warnings. If an "error" occurs, no results files will be produced. However, in the case of a "warning," the *.dat file will be processed. This log file (*.log file) is saved into the active directory with a unique date/time-based name.

Select [Reset] to clear the text fields, but note that the pathways and file names are editable.

Select [View Log] to view the log file created when analyzing data.

# CHAPTER 10

# Basic Analysis: Interpreting Your Output

*JWatcher's* abbreviations can be a bit intimidating the first time you run an analysis. Your output will be a function of what, specifically, you have selected in your focal analysis master file. Here are the abbreviations that *JWatcher* uses in your *.cd.res results file.

**StateNatInt** refers to "State Analysis, Natural, Interval" statistics. See the first column in "State Analysis" tab with heading "Natural Interval." The statistics are calculated for the intervals between each state that begin and end completely within a time bin and are not truncated by the onset or termination of the out-of-sight key. Statistics are calculated based upon those intervals only for which "complete information" exists about when they begin and end.

**StateNatDur** refers to "State Analysis, Natural, Duration" statistics. See the second column in the "State Analysis" tab with the heading "Natural Duration." The statistics are calculated for the durations of states that begin and end completely within a time bin and are not truncated by the onset or termination of the out-of-sight key. Statistics are calculated based upon those durations only for which "complete information" exists about when they begin and end. Note that for natural duration statistics, unlike natural interval statistics, the duration of a behavioral bout that begins at the very beginning of a focal will be included in the calculations.

**StateAllInt** refers to "State Analysis, All, Interval" statistics. See the third column in "State Analysis" tab with heading "All Interval." The statistics are calculated for the intervals between states, regardless of whether they begin and end completely within a time bin. Note that the out-of-sight key will affect "all" interval statistics—see section 8.5.

**StateAllDur** refers to "State Analysis, All, Duration" statistics. See the fourth column in the "State Analysis" tab with the heading "All Duration." The statistics are calculated for the durations of states. All durations of a behavioral state are included in the calculations, regardless of whether they begin and end completely within a time bin, and regardless of whether they occur adjacent to the onset or termination of the out-of-sight key. In this case, the out-of-sight key affects the proportion of time-in-sight statistic only.

| N | Occurrence |
|---|---|
| TT | Total time (milliseconds) |
| X | Average (milliseconds) |
| SD | Standard deviation (milliseconds) |
| Prop | Proportion of time |
| PropIS | Proportion of time in sight |
| Cond Prop | Conditional proportion of time |

For "State Analysis" statistics, results will be reported for all behaviors in your list, except the proportion of time in sight will not be reported for the out-of-sight key and the conditional proportion of time will be reported only for those key code combinations specified in the "Conditional States" tab.

```
#BEGIN RESULTS
Time Bin    Behavior    Behavior Name  StateAllDur N  StateAllDur TT  StateAllDur Prop  StateAllDur PropIS  StateAllDur Cond Prop
       0 A              Forage                     2            4066            0.1722              0.2364
       0 B              Look                       2            2896            0.1226              0.1684
       0 C              Hop                        2            2332            0.0988              0.1356
       0 a              Stand                      3            5464            0.2314              0.3176
       0 b              Rear                       3            3840            0.1626              0.2232
       0 c              Lie down                   3            4018            0.1702              0.2336
       0 o              Out-of-sight               4            6412            0.2715
       0 A|a                                       1            1724            0.0730              0.1002                 0.3155
```

In the example output file above, the conditional state combination A | a (Forage given Stand) was specified in the "Conditional States" tab. Behavior and modifier names are not given for conditional state combinations.

Remember that if you selected "End with last complete bin" when time windowing, then the duration of every time bin reported will be equal to the time bin duration that you specified. If you selected "Report all," then the last time bin may be shorter than the rest.

**Time Bins**

| 0 | 1st time bin, or whole focal if no time windowing used |
|---|---|
| 1 | 2nd time bin |
| 2 | 3rd time bin |
| etc . . . | |

The statistics you selected in the "Focal Analysis Master > Event Analysis" tab will be abbreviated in the results file (*.cd.res) as follows:

**Events**

| Event N | Event count |
|---|---|
| EventNatInt N | Natural interval count (milliseconds) |
| EventNatInt X | Natural interval average (milliseconds) |
| EventNatInt SD | Natural interval standard deviation (milliseconds) |

For Events statistics (first row in "Event Analysis" tab), results will be reported only for those behaviors specified to be events (in the "Event Analysis" column of the "Event Analysis" tab). The rest of the cells will be blank.

Remember that "Events" statistics tabulate events and the intervals between them across the entire time bin.

In the following example output file, "Look" and "Alarm Signal" were specified as events, but "Forage," "Hop," "Stand," "Rear," "Lie Down," and "out-of-sight" were not.

| #BEGIN RESULTS | | | | | | | |
|---|---|---|---|---|---|---|---|
| Time Bin | Behavior | Behavior Name | StateAllDur N | Event N | EventNatInt N | CondEventNat N | CondEventNatIntN |
| 0 | A | Forage | 2 | | | | |
| 0 | B | Look | 2 | 2 | 1 | | |
| 0 | C | Hop | 2 | | | | |
| 0 | a | Stand | 3 | | | | |
| 0 | b | Rear | 3 | | | | |
| 0 | c | Lie down | 3 | | | | |
| 0 | s | Alarm signal | 5 | 5 | 4 | | |
| 0 | o | out-of-sight | 4 | | | | |
| 0 | s\|C | | | | | 3 | 1 |

Note that the "Event N" and "StateAllDur N" statistics are identical. Each will tabulate the number of times that a key code was pressed.

The last line in the output file reports results for the conditional event s|C ("Alarm Signal given Hopping"), described below.

### Conditional Events Natural

| | |
|---|---|
| CondEventNat N | Event count, given natural state is on |
| CondEventNat Rate | Event count per millisecond that natural state is on |
| CondEventNatInt N | Natural interval count, given natural state is on |
| CondEventNatInt X | Natural interval average, given natural state is on (milliseconds) |
| CondEventNatInt SD | Natural interval standard deviation, given natural state is on (milliseconds) |

For "Conditional Events Natural" statistics (second row in "Event Analysis" tab), results will be reported only for those combinations specified in the "Conditional Events" tab. The rest of the cells will be blank.

"Conditional Events Natural" statistics tabulate events and the intervals between them while up to three specified natural states are on. Natural states begin and end completely within a time bin, and do not occur adjacent to the onset or termination of the out-of-sight key. However, a state that begins at the very beginning of the focal will be included in the calculations.

In the example output file shown above, the conditional event combination s|C (Alarm Signal while Hopping) was specified in the "Conditional Events" tab.

Behavior and modifier names are not given for conditional event combinations.

| Conditional Events All | |
| --- | --- |
| CondEventAll N | Event count, given state is on |
| CondEventAll Rate | Event count per millisecond that state is on |
| CondEventAllInt N | Natural interval count, given state is on |
| CondEventAllInt X | Natural interval average, given state is on (milliseconds) |
| CondEventAllInt SD | Natural interval standard deviation, given state is on (milliseconds) |

For "Conditional Events All" statistics (third row in "Event Analysis" tab), results will be reported only for those combinations specified in the "Conditional Events" tab. The rest of the cells will be blank. See example output file above.

"Conditional Events All" statistics tabulate events and the intervals between them while up to three specified states are on. Events occurring during the specified states will be tabulated, regardless of whether the states begin and end completely within a time bin, or occur adjacent to the onset or termination of the out-of-sight key.

# CHAPTER 11

# Basic Analysis: Summarizing Your Results

Each data file that you analyze produces one *.cd.res result file. Once you have analyzed a number of data files, you will probably want to combine your *.cd.res results files into one summary file and calculate some summary statistics. *JWatcher's* "Summarize Results" algorithms will help you with this. Importantly, this will also create a file that can be exported into other spreadsheet or statistical analysis programs for subsequent analyses.

Tab over to "Summarize Results."

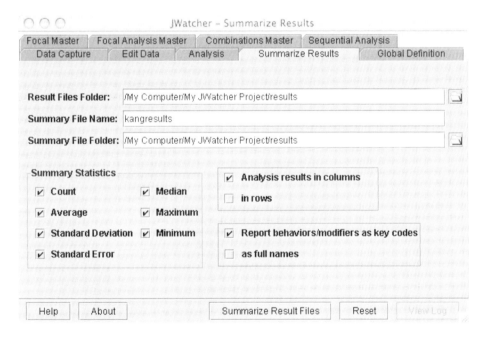

1.  Select the folder containing your results files (*.cd.res files) using the folder selection tool. All results files must have been analyzed using the same *.faf. In addition, you must have selected the "Print results for all behaviors" button in the "Analysis > Data" tab. The summarize routine will compare all results files to the first file in the results files folder to ensure matching settings.

2. Type in the name for your new summary file in the "Summary File Name" text field. Do not enter the directory in this field. The output file will be a comma-delimited text file with the suffix *.rsm.
3. Modify, if necessary, the location where you wish to save your new summary file, using the folder selection icon to the right of the "Summary File Folder" text field.
4. Specify which summary statistics you would like to calculate from the set of results files. All summary statistics are calculated for each behavior and every statistic in the results file.
5. Select whether you would like your summary statistics in columns or in rows. Some spreadsheet programs limit the number of columns able to be imported. If you have many behaviors and/or statistics in your results files, and you encounter this problem, try "Analysis results in rows."
6. Select whether you would like the behaviors/modifiers reported as key codes (to save space) or as full names. Conditional states and conditional events will always be reported as key codes.
7. Click on [Summarize Results Files] to summarize your results.

Your comma delimited *.rsm file is located in the results file that you specified. If you did not specify a summary file folder, then the *.rsm file will be placed by default in the result files folder.

This *.rsm file contains a list of results from every *.cd.res file in the result file folder, followed by the requested summary statistics calculated across all those *.cd.res files.

FirstLineOfResults=10

\#----------------------------------------------------------

\# Name: wallaby.rsm
\# Format: Summary Result File 1.0
\# Updated: Thu Jul 27 12:20:40 MDT 2006

\#----------------------------------------------------------

cd.resFilesFolder=/My Computer/My JWatcher Project/results

#BEGIN RESULTS

| cd.res file | faf file | Answer 1 | Answer 2 | Answer 3 | An: | An: | An: | StateAllDur TT-0-d | StateAllDur TT-0-f |
|---|---|---|---|---|---|---|---|---|---|
| wallaby1.cd.res | wallaby.faf | 0001 | Adult | Female | | | | 10513 | 28753 |
| wallaby2.cd.res | wallaby.faf | 0002 | Yearling | Male | | | | 0 | 6646 |
| wallaby3.cd.res | wallaby.faf | 0003 | Young-at-foot | Female | | | | 0 | 18389 |

#STATISTICS

| | | | | | | | | | |
|---|---|---|---|---|---|---|---|---|---|
| Count | | | | | | | | 3 | 3 |
| Average | | | | | | | | 3504.3333 | 17929.3333 |
| Max | | | | | | | | 10513 | 28753 |
| Min | | | | | | | | 0 | 6646 |
| Median | | | | | | | | 0 | 18389 |
| Std | | | | | | | | 6069.6834 | 11060.666 |
| Sterr | | | | | | | | 3504.3333 | 6385.8785 |

When you select "Analysis results in columns," your summary file will be organized as shown above. Note that the lines beneath the #BEGIN RESULTS contain the actual results of each file. This is a very "wide" file. The results go far to the right of this screen shot and illustrate the results for each behavior in the focal master file and for each statistic requested. There are three *.cd.res result files shown above. Supposing we had 100 files; the set of 100 rows following the #BEGIN RESULTS would contain the actual raw results, one row per result file.

Following #STATISTICS, we see the summary statistics calculated from each of the files included in this run. If you wished, you could run the analysis for males only, or females only, or have a folder for all animals observed foraging alone, all those foraging in groups of two, etc. Then your summary statistics would allow you to begin to see if males had different foraging patterns from those of females or if group size influenced time allocated to foraging time.

---

**Note:** *Remember that a considerable part of careful data analysis is careful data management. You must name your files clearly and keep careful notes about which files reflect certain conditions. In the Macintosh OS, you are limited in the number of characters you can use for each file name. JWatcher appends suffixes to many file names, and by doing so, you may lose some descriptive names. We often adopt an animal, date, time naming protocol. For instance, 0001-01may05-1236 is shorthand for "animal 0001, studied on 1 May 2005, at 12:36." Importantly, with such a naming protocol, it is relatively easy to put all the data files or results files from animal 0001 into one folder for subsequent analyses.*

---

When you select "Analysis results in rows," your summary file will be organized as follows:

```
FirstLineOfResults=10
#------------------------------------------------------------
# Name: wallaby2.rsm
# Format: Summary Result File 1.0
# Updated: Thu Jul 27 12:47:19 MDT 2006
#------------------------------------------------------------
cd.resFilesFolder=/My Computer/My JWatcher Project/results
```

| #BEGIN RESULTS | | | | #STATISTICS | | | | |
|---|---|---|---|---|---|---|---|---|
| cd.res file | wallaby1.cd.res | wallaby2.cd.res | wallaby3.cd.res | Count | Average | Max | Min | Median |
| faf file | wallaby.faf | wallaby.faf | wallaby.faf | | | | | |
| Answer 1 | 0001 | 0002 | 0003 | | | | | |
| Answer 2 | Adult | Yearling | Young-at-foot | | | | | |
| Answer 3 | Female | Male | Female | | | | | |
| Answer 4 | | | | | | | | |
| Answer 5 | | | | | | | | |
| Answer 6 | | | | | | | | |
| StateAllDur N-0-a | 0 | 0 | 0 | 3 | 0 | 0 | 0 | 0 |
| StateAllDur N-0-d | 1 | 0 | 0 | 3 | 0.3333 | 1 | 0 | 0 |
| StateAllDur N-0-f | 2 | 1 | 6 | 3 | 3 | 6 | 1 | 2 |
| StateAllDur N-0-g | 0 | 0 | 0 | 3 | 0 | 0 | 0 | 0 |
| StateAllDur N-0-h | 0 | 1 | 1 | 3 | 0.6667 | 1 | 0 | 1 |
| StateAllDur N-0-l | 0 | 0 | 2 | 3 | 0.6667 | 2 | 0 | 0 |
| StateAllDur N-0-n | 0 | 0 | 0 | 3 | 0 | 0 | 0 | 0 |
| StateAllDur N-0-o | 0 | 1 | 1 | 3 | 0.6667 | 1 | 0 | 1 |
| StateAllDur N-0-p | 0 | 0 | 0 | 3 | 0 | 0 | 0 | 0 |
| StateAllDur N-0-r | 2 | 1 | 0 | 3 | 1 | 2 | 0 | 1 |
| StateAllDur N-0-s | 3 | 1 | 6 | 3 | 3.3333 | 6 | 1 | 3 |
| StateAllDur N-0-w | 0 | 0 | 0 | 3 | 0 | 0 | 0 | 0 |
| StateAllDur TT-0-a | 0 | 0 | 0 | 3 | 0 | 0 | 0 | 0 |
| StateAllDur TT-0-d | 10513 | 0 | 0 | 3 | 3504.33 | 10513 | 0 | 0 |
| StateAllDur TT-0-f | 28753 | 6646 | 18389 | 3 | 17929.3 | 28753 | 6646 | 18389 |
| StateAllDur TT-0-g | 0 | 0 | 0 | 3 | 0 | 0 | 0 | 0 |
| StateAllDur TT-0-h | 0 | 3981 | 1429 | 3 | 1803.33 | 3981 | 0 | 1429 |
| StateAllDur TT-0-l | 0 | 0 | 5276 | 3 | 1758.67 | 5276 | 0 | 0 |
| StateAllDur TT-0-n | 0 | 0 | 0 | 3 | 0 | 0 | 0 | 0 |
| StateAllDur TT-0-o | 0 | 44464 | 8348 | 3 | 17604 | 44464 | 0 | 8348 |

In this case, the analysis headings are listed in the rows under #BEGIN RESULTS, whereas the raw results from each of the three *.cd.res file are listed in the subsequent three columns. Summary statistics follow in the columns to the right.

Each analysis heading is composed of the statistic name (as reported in the *.cd.res file), followed by the time bin (as reported in the *.cd.res file), followed by the key code or behavior name. For example, "StateAllDur N-0-f" refers to "State Analysis for 'All' Durations, Count, for time bin zero, for key code f." See Chapter 10 on how to interpret *.cd.res files for a complete list of statistic abbreviations.

In some circumstances, analysis headings will be generated without any associated data. That is, some columns (or rows) may be blank. This occurs whenever the *.cd.res files have blank cells within the result matrix. For example, whenever statistics for conditional proportion of time have been selected, blank cells will be produced for the list of regular behaviors. Or, whenever regular event analysis statistics have been selected, blank cells will be generated for those behaviors not specified to be events. These blank columns (or rows) in the summary file are essentially irrelevant. You will need to delete them yourself in your word-processing or spreadsheet program. If you are uncertain as to why specific columns (or rows) are blank, we suggest examining the original *.cd.res files for clarification.

For example, consider the following *.cd.res file:

```
#BEGIN RESULTS
Time Bin    Behavior  Behavior Name       StateAllDur TT  StateAllDur Cond Prop
       0  a           alarm signal                79300
       0  f           forage                      25885
       0  h           locomotion                      0
       0  l           look                        74115
       0  o           out-of-sight                    0
       0  p           PREDATOR PRESENT            60000
       0  q           PREDATOR ABSENT             40000
       0  r           rear                        52811
       0  s           stand                       19189
       0  t           crouch                      28000
       0  r||q                                     2536          0.0634
       0  r|| q                                    2536          0.1797
       0  r||p                                    50275          0.8379
       0  r|| p                                   50275          0.8379
```

Notice the blank cells under "StateAllDur Cond Prop" (for conditional proportion of time) for the list of regular behaviors.

The summarized files will look like this when "Analysis results in rows" is selected:

| #BEGIN RESULTS | | | |
|---|---|---|---|
| cd.res file | file1.cd.res | file2.cd.res | file3.cd.res |
| faf file | example.faf | example.faf | example.faf |
| Answer 1 | | | |
| Answer 2 | | | |
| Answer 3 | | | |
| Answer 4 | | | |
| Answer 5 | | | |
| Answer 6 | | | |
| StateAllDur TT-0-a | 79300 | 28511 | 57960 |
| StateAllDur TT-0-f | 25885 | 52975 | 44985 |
| StateAllDur TT-0-h | 0 | 4396 | 0 |
| StateAllDur TT-0-l | 74115 | 55591 | 55692 |
| StateAllDur TT-0-o | 0 | 1969 | 0 |
| StateAllDur TT-0-p | 60000 | 52511 | 29467 |
| StateAllDur TT-0-q | 40000 | 60451 | 71210 |
| StateAllDur TT-0-r | 52811 | 25057 | 16177 |
| StateAllDur TT-0-s | 19189 | 27566 | 19252 |
| StateAllDur TT-0-t | 28000 | 55943 | 65248 |
| StateAllDur TT-0-r l\|q | 2536 | 0 | 6445 |
| StateAllDur TT-0-r\|l q | 2536 | 0 | 6445 |
| StateAllDur TT-0-r l\|p | 50275 | 25057 | 9732 |
| StateAllDur TT-0-r\|l p | 50275 | 25057 | 9732 |
| StateAllDur Cond Prop-0-a | | | |
| StateAllDur Cond Prop-0-f | | | |
| StateAllDur Cond Prop-0-h | | | |
| StateAllDur Cond Prop-0-l | | | |
| StateAllDur Cond Prop-0-o | | | |
| StateAllDur Cond Prop-0-p | | | |
| StateAllDur Cond Prop-0-q | | | |
| StateAllDur Cond Prop-0-r | | | |
| StateAllDur Cond Prop-0-s | | | |
| StateAllDur Cond Prop-0-t | | | |
| StateAllDur Cond Prop-0-r l\|q | 0.0634 | 0 | 0.0905 |
| StateAllDur Cond Prop-0-r\|l q | 0.1797 | 0 | 0.2411 |
| StateAllDur Cond Prop-0-r l\|p | 0.8379 | 0.4772 | 0.3303 |
| StateAllDur Cond Prop-0-r\|l p | 0.8379 | 0.5802 | 0.3361 |

Notice that the blank cells in the *.cd.res files are translated into blank cells in the summarized file. Simply delete these extraneous cells to clean up your summary file.

Your *.cd.res files (and hence summary file) may contain many more statistics than you need for your final analysis. For example, in the files shown above, for total time (StateAllDur TT), you may be interested only in the total time that rear, look, and predator present (or predator absent) are simultaneously on. However, the program automatically generates values for total time for the entire list of regular behaviors. If these are not useful to you, simply delete them.

In addition, whenever you specify three or more conditional states (A|B|C or A|B|C|D), you will get redundant lines whenever you also select statistics such as count, total time, average duration, standard deviation, and proportion of time. The program automatically generates two versions of A|B|C, or four versions of A|B|C|D. (See section 8.7 on conditional states for further explanation.) In the example file above, although the values for the two conditional proportion-of-time statistics (r l|q and r|l q) may differ, these are identical for total time. Once again, simply delete these extraneous cells to make working with your file more manageable.

**Note 1:** *Please note in regard to error checking that* JWatcher *derives the analysis headings from the first* \*.cd.res *file in your result files folder.* JWatcher *will then compare each subsequent* \*.cd.res *file in the folder with this first file to ensure that the same* \*.faf *file was used. In addition,* JWatcher *tests whether the number of rows and columns of the result matrix for each* \*.cd.res *file is the same as the first file. This is why you must choose "Print results for all behaviors" when generating* \*.cd.res *files. Note that if your time window and the session duration (EOF time) vary drastically among data files, you could potentially generate* \*.cd.res *files with a different number of time bins (and hence a different number of rows and columns). In this case, you will not be able to summarize this collection of files.*

**Note 2:** *A known issue is that if you type the name of a nonexistent folder into the "Result Files Folder" text field, nothing will happen when you click on [Summarize Result Files]. No warning message or output will be generated. The log will not be updated, and it will continue to display the previous analysis. You may be asked if it is OK to overwrite the existing file, when relevant, but the file will not be overwritten, as no analysis will occur.*

# CHAPTER 12

# Substituting or Combining Key Codes

"Combinations Master" allows you to substitute key codes in data files (*.dat files). You may replace one or more existing key codes with another different code that you specify. The routine will generate a new set of data files with the substituted codes, preserving the original data files intact for reference or future use.

The combinations routine was initially conceived to deal with the following problem. Let's say that you are interested in foraging, vigilance, and locomotion. However, in your ethogram, you have broken down each of these larger categories into subcategories such as forage on berries, forage on leaves, rear look, stand look, hop, walk, etc. If you used separate key codes for each subcategory (defined to be mutually exclusive) then you will not automatically generate results for the larger category. The combinations routine enables you to combine these subcategories into a more global category that you specify. Specifically, rather than getting detailed results on the occurrences of each type of foraging (forage on berries, forage on leaves, etc.) or each type of vigilance (rear look, stand look, etc.), or each type of locomotion (hop, walk, etc.), you could combine them into one omnibus measure for each category (all forage, all vigilance, all locomotion).

> **Warning:** *By combining key codes, you may generate a series of repeated key codes. Repeated key codes will affect some state statistics (such as count, average duration, and standard deviations of bouts) but not others (such as total time and proportion of time). Repeated key codes will affect how a "bout" is defined. For example, say you originally scored rear look, stand look, rear look. If you combined "rear and stand look" into a single code for all vigilance, you will end up with three separate, contiguous bouts of vigilance. The sequence will not be translated into one bout of continuous vigilance regardless of posture. This may or may not be desirable or consequential depending upon your needs. If your analysis does require that such sequences be considered one continuous bout, then you should consider scoring simultaneous streams of behaviors, as opposed to mutually exclusive subcategories.*

To run this routine, you must first specify the key codes to be substituted. To do this, you will create a combinations master file (*.cmf) in the "Define Combinations" window. Next, you will use the "Combine Key Codes" routine to generate a new set of "combined" data files containing the substituted codes.

Tab over to "Combinations Master."

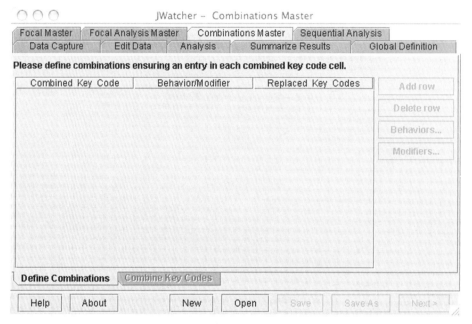

To create a combinations master file, click [New]. Using the navigator box, select a pre-existing focal master file (*.fmf). This inherits a set of key codes that can now be combined. You will not see these codes at this point. However, [Add row] should now be enabled.

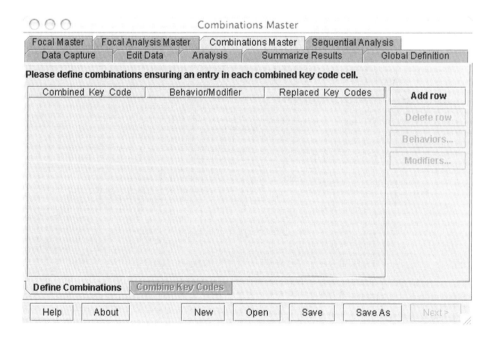

Use [Add row] to add a row.

---

**Note:** *A hint to remember is that you may want to have a printout of the \*.fmf file you are modifying next to you when creating a \*.cmf file. To print it, open the file in a word-processing or text-editing program. Alternatively, you could view your \*.fmf by opening it in the "Focal Master" window and tabbing between windows.*

---

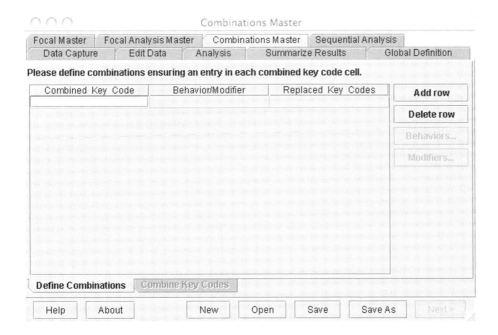

Type a key code into the "Combined Key Code" cell. This is the key code that will replace one or more existing codes. You must enter a code into this cell before continuing. You cannot use a code already defined in your *.fmf. For example, "x" (meaning, all forage) may be used to replace a series of scored foraging behaviors (f and g), "y" (all look) may be used to replace a series of scored looking behaviors (d, s, and r), and "z" (all locomotion) may be used to replace a series of scored locomotion behaviors (w, h, and n).

Define the newly created key code in the "Behavior/Modifier" text box.

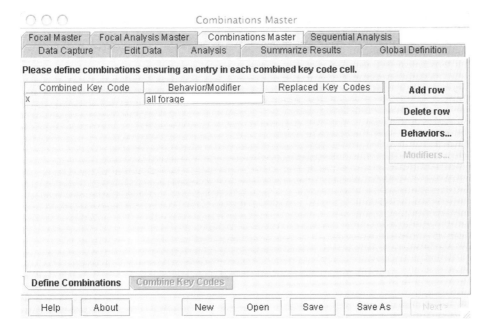

Click on the "Replaced Key Codes" text box and either type the key codes (separated by a comma) to be replaced, or click on the now highlighted [Behaviors . . .] button to see a list of the key codes. Use the control key to select multiple key codes to be combined. Clicking [OK] places those key codes into the "Replaced Key Codes" text field.

If you have modifiers defined in your *.fmf, then [Modifiers . . .] will be enabled as well. You can replace one or more existing behaviors with a new behavior, or you can replace one or more existing modifiers with a new modifier. You may not replace a mix of behaviors and modifiers with a new code.

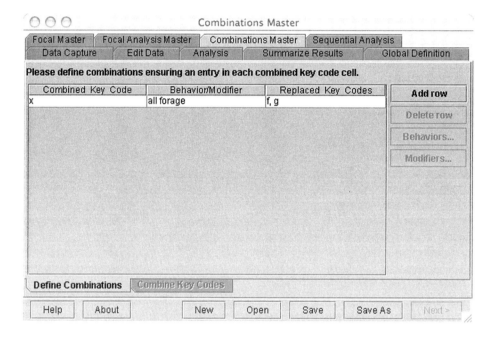

Click [Add row] to add more codes. You may not enter key codes in the "Combined Key Code" cells that are already used.

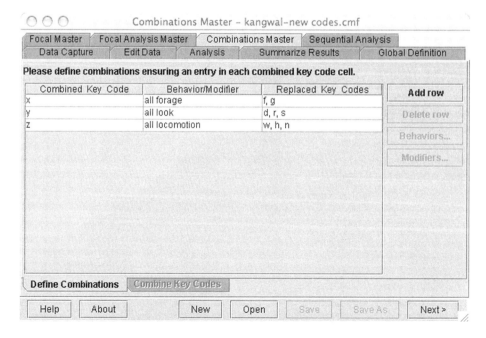

Save this file by clicking [Save] or [Save As].

[Next] will become enabled once you save the file. Click [Next] to shift to the "Combine Key Codes" window.

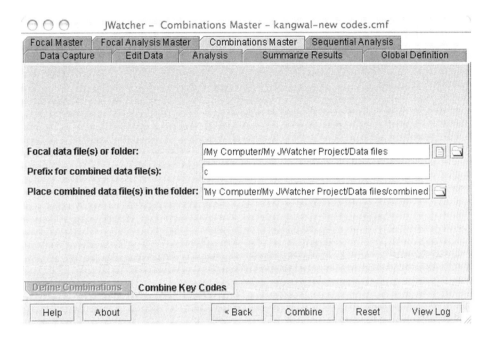

Select the focal data file(s) or folder that you wish to combine. The default prefix for combined data files is "c"; change this if you wish. You can also modify the default location where the combined files will be placed if you wish.

Click [Combine] to combine key codes.

> **Note:** *When your newly created \*.cmf file is saved, a new \*.fmf file with the replaced key codes is automatically created and placed in the same folder as your \*.cmf file. By default, it is named c\*.fmf, where \* = the name you gave the .cmf. You may view the newly created "combined" data file(s) in "Edit Data." The \*.fmf displayed (along with associated behaviors and modifiers) will be the c\*.fmf. Before analyzing combined files, you will have to create a new \*.faf which is based on the c\*.fmf. To create an \*.faf, see Chapter 8.*

For example, consider the following original data file (before combining) called "wallaby1.dat." Note that the *.fmf associated with this data file is called "kangwal.fmf."

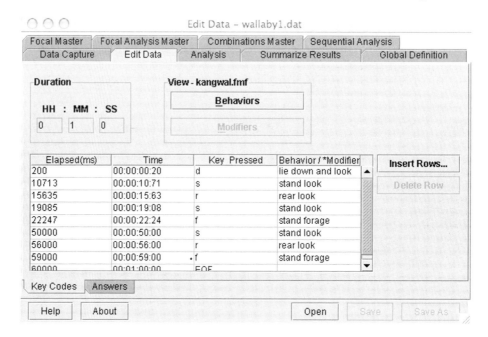

After running the combinations routine using "ckangwal-new codes.cmf" as shown above, the new combined data file will be called "cwallaby1.dat" and will look like this:

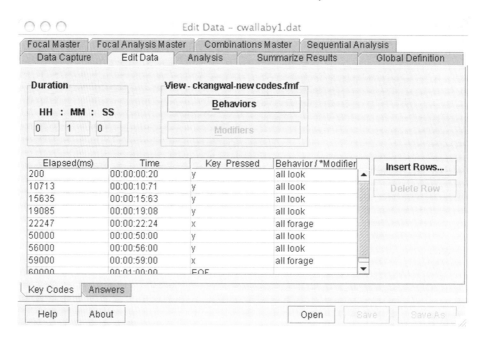

Note that the *.fmf associated with this file is called "ckangwal-new codes.fmf."

To analyze the old data file (wallaby1.dat), you will need to create a focal analysis master (*.faf) using the codes defined in kangwal.fmf. That is, you must use the same *.fmf associated with the data file when creating your *.faf. The *.faf shown below was created doing exactly this, by clicking [New] and selecting "kangwal.fmf."

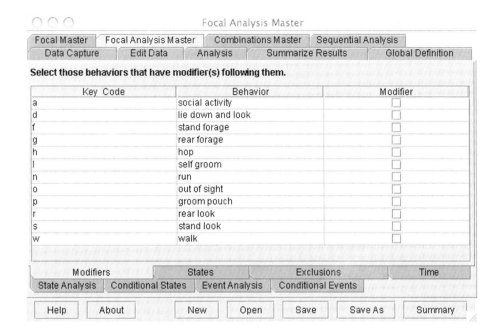

To analyze the new combined data file (cwallaby1.dat), you will need to create a focal analysis master file (*.faf) using the codes defined in "ckanwal-new codes.fmf." Again, you must use the same *.fmf associated with the new combined data file to create the focal analysis master file to analyze it. This *.faf file was created by clicking [New] and selecting "ckangwal-new codes.fmf."

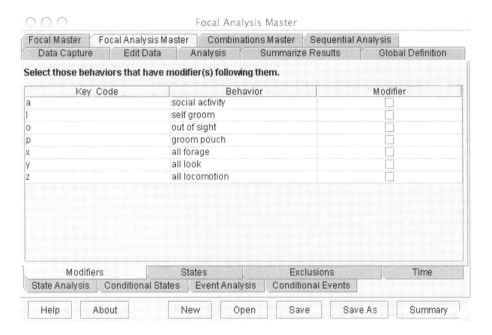

# CHAPTER 13

# Sequential Analysis

For many behavioral questions it is sufficient to calculate time budgets or to study the frequency or relative frequency of events. However, time budgets do not tell us about the *structure* of behavior. Thus, another important way to study behavior is to look for temporal patterns in a sequence of behaviors and by doing so, to describe its structure. For example, animals often engage in a series of behaviors that are quite stereotyped, such that behaviors follow a prescribed and repeatable pattern. One example that many of us are familiar with is the "play bow" given by dogs (Bekoff 1975). Before dogs play, one typically "invites" the other to play with a play bow (the dog's front legs are collapsed, its rump is in the air, it wags its tail and may bark). Play bows almost always precede play but typically not other behaviors. In many cases a larger category of behavior may always consist of a repeatable pattern of component behaviors. For example, incubating Greylag geese occasionally need to retrieve an egg that has rolled away from their ground nest. The egg retrieval behavior usually consists of the goose extending its neck forward, tucking the egg under its bill, and rolling the egg back into the nest (Tinbergen 1951). Birdsong often involves stereotypical sequences of notes, and courtship behavior is also often very stereotyped. Human behavior may also be remarkably structured. Some of the best writings about how to conduct sequential analyses have been written by psychologists. Specifically, Bakeman and Gottman's (1997) "Observing interaction: an introduction to sequential analysis" is required reading if you want to learn more about sequential analyses, and we have implemented many of their algorithms in *JWatcher*.

*JWatcher's* sequential analysis routines provide you with several options for describing patterns in a sequence of behaviors. We begin with a brief overview of some of the analyses calculated by *JWatcher* and then we have specific sections on implementing each algorithm. We use several different examples to illustrate these routines because depending upon your specific question, it may not be logical to conduct every possible sequential analysis. By seeing how others have used sequential analyses, and by working through our examples, you may see that you can develop a focused question that can be answered using sequential analyses. By doing so, we hope that you will increase the depth of your understanding of the phenomena you study.

All calculations are based upon the sequence of key codes in a data file, without respect to the specific times that the key codes were pressed. Thus, these analyses assume a single stream of events. Some analyses require long sequences of behavior in order to confidently describe patterns; in some cases you may wish to combine different files to obtain a sufficiently long behavioral stream.

## 13.1 Sequence Analysis Tab

The number of transitions between each pair of events found within your sequence is calculated and reported in this tab, along with associated probabilities of occurrence. Two types of probabilities are reported. The simple probability is the probability that an event pair occurs in the sequence. The transition probability is the probability that one event follows another in the sequence.

Barbara Clucas helped us develop a laboratory exercise based on her dissertation research which focuses on a fascinating behavior engaged in by some species of ground squirrels. The squirrels chew on the shed skins of rattlesnakes (one of their important predators) and apply the scent to their fur by licking their bodies; this behavior is called "snake scent application" (Clucas et al. in press; Owings et al. 2001; Kobayashi and Watanabe 1986). Clucas and others were very interested in the function of this behavior and its evolution. Thus she needed to compare the structure of snake scent application in several different related species.

To do so, we might look at the order of body parts in which the squirrel applies the scent. For instance, a squirrel may begin applying scent to its arms, followed by its head, and then it may continue by anointing its flank, upper tail, mid tail, and then end with its lower tail. The sequence may be completely stereotyped (i.e., always following an exact pattern) or it may be completely unpredictable. A first step in describing this pattern might be to calculate the number of transitions between each body section and the corresponding transition probabilities. *JWatcher* will report these values for you in matrix form, which shows the frequency of all possible transitions.

Clucas developed the following ethogram identifying the sections of the body groomed by the squirrel.

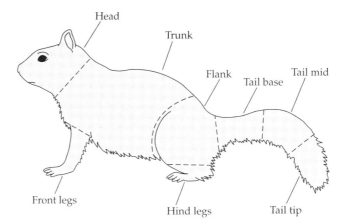

Below we deviate from Clucas's data and have generated hypothetical data to illustrate sequence analysis.

After scoring behavior, we first calculate the observed frequencies for transitions between immediately adjacent events.

**Observed Matrix**

| | | | | Behaviors that follow | | | | | | |
|---|---|---|---|---|---|---|---|---|---|---|
| | Head | Front legs | Trunk | Flank | Hind legs | Tail base | Tail mid | Tail tip | End | Row total |
| Start | 35 | 0 | 0 | 0 | 0 | 0 | 0 | 0 | 0 | 35 |
| Head | 0 | 21 | 39 | 0 | 0 | 0 | 0 | 0 | 0 | 60 |
| Front legs | 14 | 0 | 0 | 0 | 0 | 0 | 0 | 0 | 6 | 20 |
| Trunk | 14 | 0 | 0 | 42 | 0 | 0 | 0 | 0 | 0 | 56 |
| Flank | 0 | 0 | 0 | 0 | 20 | 25 | 0 | 0 | 0 | 45 |
| Hind legs | 0 | 0 | 0 | 4 | 0 | 0 | 0 | 0 | 12 | 16 |
| Tail base | 0 | 0 | 0 | 0 | 0 | 0 | 20 | 2 | 0 | 22 |
| Tail mid | 0 | 0 | 0 | 0 | 0 | 2 | 0 | 18 | 0 | 20 |
| Tail tip | 0 | 0 | 0 | 0 | 0 | 0 | 0 | 0 | 17 | 17 |
| Column total | 63 | 41 | 39 | 46 | 0 | 27 | 20 | 20 | 35 | 291 |

The above matrix shows hypothetical frequencies. It lists the first behavior in rows and the subsequent behavior in columns. Thus "Head" follows "Start" 35 times, "Front legs" follows "Head" 21 times, and "Trunk" follows "Head" 39 times, etc.

*JWatcher* uses overlapped sampling to tabulate these frequencies. Overlapped sampling means that you slide your sampling "window" from the first code, to the second code, to the third code, and so forth, through the entire sequence. You are moving from one position in the sequence to the next. For example, for the sequence {A B C D E}, overlapped sampling for adjacent events would produce the following series: AB, BC, CD, DE. If you are interested in other ways of sampling (non-overlapped), you may use *JWatcher's* complex sequences tab, described later.

In the sequence analysis tab, you may also calculate the simple probability that each event pair occurs in the sequence. The simple probability is calculated as the frequency of occurrence for each event pair divided by the total number of event pairs in the sequence. For example, the simple probability for the event pair "Head-Front legs" is 21/291 = 0.07.

## Simple Probability Matrix

| | Behaviors that follow | | | | | | | | | |
| | Head | Front legs | Trunk | Flank | Hind legs | Tail base | Tail mid | Tail tip | End | Row total |
|---|---|---|---|---|---|---|---|---|---|---|
| Start | 0.12 | 0 | 0 | 0 | 0 | 0 | 0 | 0 | 0 | 0.12 |
| Head | 0 | 0.07 | 0.13 | 0 | 0 | 0 | 0 | 0 | 0 | 0.22 |
| Front legs | 0.05 | 0 | 0 | 0 | 0 | 0 | 0 | 0 | 0.03 | 0.07 |
| Trunk | 0.05 | 0 | 0 | 0.14 | 0 | 0 | 0 | 0 | 0 | 0.19 |
| Flank | 0 | 0 | 0 | 0 | 0.08 | 0.09 | 0 | 0 | 0 | 0.15 |
| Hind legs | 0 | 0 | 0 | 0.01 | 0 | 0 | 0 | 0 | 0.04 | 0.05 |
| Tail base | 0 | 0 | 0 | 0 | 0 | 0 | 0.07 | 0.01 | 0 | 0.08 |
| Tail mid | 0 | 0 | 0 | 0 | 0 | 0.01 | 0 | 0.06 | 0 | 0.07 |
| Tail tip | 0 | 0 | 0 | 0 | 0 | 0 | 0 | 0 | 0.06 | 0.06 |
| Column total | 0.22 | 0.14 | 0.13 | 0.16 | 0 | 0.09 | 0.07 | 0.07 | 0.12 | 1 |

Transition probabilities are derived by dividing the observed frequency for an event pair by the number of times the first behavior occurred as part of any event pair in the sequence (the row total for that behavior). For example, the transition probability for "Front legs" following "Head" is 21/60 = 0.35.

## Transitional Probability Matrix

| | Behaviors that follow | | | | | | | | | |
| | Head | Front legs | Trunk | Flank | Hind legs | Tail base | Tail mid | Tail tip | End | Row total |
|---|---|---|---|---|---|---|---|---|---|---|
| Start | 1.0 | 0 | 0 | 0 | 0 | 0 | 0 | 0 | 0 | 1.0 |
| Head | 0 | 0.35 | 0.65 | 0 | 0 | 0 | 0 | 0 | 0 | 1.0 |
| Front legs | 0.70 | 0 | 0 | 0 | 0 | 0 | 0 | 0 | 0.3 | 1.0 |
| Trunk | 0.25 | 0 | 0 | 0.75 | 0 | 0 | 0 | 0 | 0 | 1.0 |
| Flank | 0 | 0 | 0 | 0 | 0.44 | 0.56 | 0 | 0 | 0 | 1.0 |
| Hind legs | 0 | 0 | 0 | 0.25 | 0 | 0 | 0 | 0 | 0.75 | 1.0 |
| Tail base | 0 | 0 | 0 | 0 | 0 | 0 | 0.91 | 0.09 | 0 | 1.0 |
| Tail mid | 0 | 0 | 0 | 0 | 0 | 0.10 | 0 | 0.90 | 0 | 1.0 |
| Tail tip | 0 | 0 | 0 | 0 | 0 | 0 | 0 | 0 | 1.0 | 1.0 |

Once you have a list (or matrix) of transition frequencies, you will probably want to summarize them in some way to better understand the patterns that they describe. One way is to make a series of graphs, one for each behavior, that plot the transition frequencies to every other behavior of interest. However, depending upon your question and the number of behaviors that you have, this may not be very efficient. We illustrate one such graph below, made in Excel, for behaviors that follow "Head."

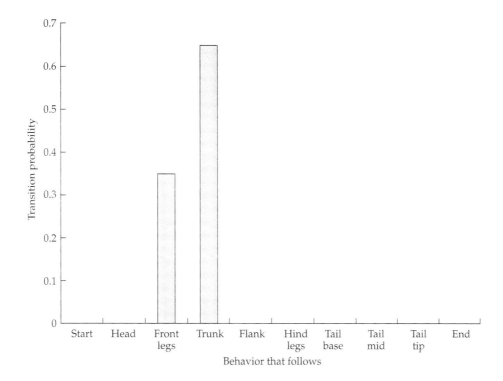

Perhaps a more common way to summarize such information would be to create a transition diagram (also called a kinematic graph). A transition diagram is a visual depiction of the transition probabilities between events. Arrows are drawn between behaviors, with the thickness of the arrow reflecting the frequency of the transition. *JWatcher* does not automatically draw this; you must draw this in a graphics program of your choice.

For our hypothetical squirrel grooming data, we calculated the following transition diagram.

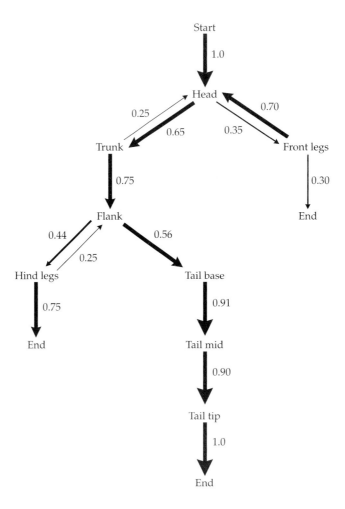

From this hypothetical transition diagram, we see that the squirrels always begin by anointing their heads. They are then most likely to anoint their trunk, followed by flank, tail base, and mid tail, and ending with tail tip. To increase clarity, probabilities less than 0.10 are not shown on the graph. Many people also illustrate the overall frequencies of occurrence of each behavior in the sequence by modifying the relative size of the behaviors on the graph. We do not illustrate this here.

Once you have described the pattern of transitions, you may wish to know whether particular transitions are more likely to occur than would be expected by chance alone. To do so, *JWatcher* calculates *z*-scores (these are also referred to as adjusted residuals) and their associated *p*-values, and reports them in matrix form (the formula we use for *z*-scores comes from Equation 7.2 in Bakeman and Gottman 1997). *JWatcher* currently does not compute more elaborate log-linear models or omnibus tests (as suggested by Bakeman and Quera 1995).

The following matrix shows hypothetical values for *z*-scores that might be derived from an analysis of squirrel anointment behavior.

**Z-scores**

| | Head | Front legs | Trunk | Flank | Hind legs | Tail base | Tail mid | Tail tip | End |
|---|---|---|---|---|---|---|---|---|---|
| | | | | Behaviors that follow | | | | | |
| Start | **12.00** | −2.55 | −2.48 | −2.73 | −1.71 | −2.01 | −1.71 | −1.71 | −2.33 |
| Head | −4.57 | **5.23** | **13.16** | −3.76 | −2.36 | −2.78 | −2.36 | −2.36 | −3.21 |
| Front legs | **5.44** | −1.87 | −1.82 | −2.00 | −1.25 | −1.48 | −1.25 | −1.25 | **2.56** |
| Trunk | 0.68 | −3.37 | −3.27 | **13.51** | −2.26 | −2.66 | −2.26 | −2.26 | −3.07 |
| Flank | −3.84 | −2.95 | −2.87 | −3.16 | **10.83** | **11.63** | −1.98 | −1.98 | −2.69 |
| Hind legs | −2.16 | −1.66 | −1.61 | 1.04 | −1.11 | −1.31 | −1.11 | −1.11 | **7.97** |
| Tail base | −2.56 | −1.97 | −1.91 | −2.11 | −1.32 | −1.56 | **16.20** | 0.43 | −1.80 |
| Tail mid | −2.43 | −1.87 | −1.82 | −2.00 | −1.25 | 0.12 | −1.25 | **15.22** | −1.71 |
| Tail tip | −2.23 | −1.72 | −1.67 | −1.84 | −1.15 | −1.35 | −1.15 | −1.15 | **11.49** |

If we set our alpha at 0.05, then *z*-scores larger than 1.96 (or smaller than −1.96) are considered to indicate transitions that occur more (or less) often than expected by chance. For example, *z*-scores > 1.96 are highlighted in bold in our table.

In the calculation of these probabilities, there is a caveat in regard to the multiple comparisons and resultant type I statistical errors that these generate. When you set your alpha to 0.05, you expect significant values for 1 out of 20 comparisons that result by chance alone. Some investigators have dealt with this problem by performing either Bonferroni or sequential Bonferroni corrections (Holm 1979; Rice 1989) to identify those significant relationships after adjusting for multiple comparisons. To perform a Bonferroni correction, you divide your alpha level of 0.05 by the number of comparisons to derive a new critical value. If you make five comparisons, your new critical value becomes 0.05/5 = 0.01. Bakeman and Quera (1995) propose log-linear methods that employ omnibus (tablewide) tests and the winnowing of results (a procedure employing stepwise deletion of cells to test for the model with the best fit) to deal with this problem. See Bakeman and Gottman (1997) for a description of the procedure and for a discussion of the applicability of these methods.

Another caveat associated with your interpretation of *z*-scores is that *JWatcher* calculates them based upon expected values that assume behaviors are allowed to repeat. For example, you may be studying the sequence of notes within birdsong, in which a particular note may be repeated multiple times. In some cases, a behavior simply does not follow the very same behavior or cannot logically do so. In the squirrel example above, anointing scent to a particular body part takes a certain amount of time, and once finished with this part, the squirrel moves on to another part. The individual behavior (the annointing of the body parts) cannot logically repeat because a "repetition" would by definition be part of the same bout. Once again, Bakeman and Quera (1995) propose log-linear methods along with an iterative process of generating expected values as a solution. Nonetheless, they do suggest that in some cases using adjusted residuals (as calculated by *JWatcher*) may provide a reasonable, although less conservative, approximation when codes are not allowed to repeat.

There are many examples of studies that illustrate the use of transition probabilities, z-scores, and/or kinematic graphs. For example, Hurt et al. (2004) compared the mating behavior of two species of Sonoran topminnows to determine whether these behaviors serve as premating barriers to reproduction. Slooten (1994) used sequence analysis to describe the behavior of Hector's dolphins. Miller and Anderson (1990) compared the courtship behavior of domestic ferrets and black-footed ferrets to determine whether the domestic ferret could act as a reasonable surrogate for reproductive behavior research on the critically endangered black-footed ferret. With the same goal of ultimately recovering the endangered black-footed ferret, Miller and Anderson (1989) compared the courtship patterns in domestic ferrets that are allowed to come into estrus naturally versus the patterns in individuals that were induced with hormone injections.

The odds ratio is another statistic that may help you decide whether a particular event is likely to follow another particular event. For example, you might be interested in knowing if chimpanzees are likely to pant hoot after climbing a tree. You may have scored a sequence of behaviors that includes such things as forage, look, walk, run, climb tree, pant hoot, groom, etc. You may then use the odds ratio to determine whether chimpanzees are more or less likely to pant hoot after climbing a tree than after other behaviors. Yule's Q is a related statistic derived from the odds ratio. Additional explanations about the odds ratio and Yule's Q are provided later in section 13.12 ("Sequence Analysis") illustrating example calculations.

So far, we have described transitions between behaviors that immediately follow each other in a sequence. But to describe structure, we are often interested in what happens at two or more positions away. For example, although a kinematic graph may show that B is likely to follow A and C is likely to follow B, it does not necessarily indicate that the pattern A, B, C occurs in the sequence, unless you can also show that C is likely to follow A two positions ahead. You might also be interested in whether two or more behaviors occur in fixed positions relative to each other, even if intervening behaviors vary randomly. For example, C may be highly likely to follow A two positions ahead, but the position in between A and C may be occupied by any number of other behaviors.

Let's define some terms. The relative position in the sequence between two behaviors is called the lag. Generally, in the lingo of sequential analysis, you begin by specifying one behavior as the "criterion" or "given" or "lag 0" event. This is the behavior for which you want to identify what follows. The behavior that follows this event is called the "target" event. "Lag 1" means that the target event is one position ahead of the given event in the sequence. "Lag 2" means that the target event is two positions ahead of the given event in the sequence. *JWatcher* calculates sequence analysis statistics from lag 1 through lag 5. For example, assume you have scored the following sequence: {A B C D E}. If A is the given event, then B occurs at lag 1, C occurs at lag 2, D occurs at lag 3, and E occurs at lag 4.

There may be situations in which you will want to identify what happens at lags greater than 5, or at negative lags. A negative lag means that the target precedes the given behavior, rather than follows it. For example, lag –2 means that the target is two positions behind the given behavior in the sequence. In this case, *JWatcher's* lag sequential tab may be useful to you.

## 13.2 Markovian Analysis Tab

Markovian analysis examines the overall structure of a series of behaviors (as opposed to specific pairs) to determine whether serial dependencies exist within the sequence.

For example, a series of behaviors may be independent; that is, previous behaviors have no influence upon the probability of occurrence of subsequent behaviors. Or behaviors may be constrained in some way or predicted by behaviors that precede them. Markovian analysis uses Shannon and Weaver (1949) information statistics to analyze these models. This method allows you to calculate increasingly higher order "Markovian models" and analyze how the "uncertainty" is reduced with each successive step. Uncertainty, in this context, is the amount of information required to predict that a particular event will occur, where amount of information is expressed as number of yes/no choices (bits). When there is zero uncertainty, no additional information is required to predict what will happen next in a sequence. Maximum uncertainty will occur when all the behaviors are equiprobable and thus are distributed randomly throughout a sequence.

A zero-order model examines whether behaviors in a sequence are independent. If so, the sequence is said to exhibit the "Markov property." When previous events entirely predict subsequent events, then this is termed a "Markov process." A first-order Markov process is one in which the next event is predicted entirely by the immediately preceding event. A second-order Markov process is one in which the next event is predicted entirely by two immediately preceding events.

Uncertainty values of zero at some order indicate that the data follow a Markov process at that order. Large drops in uncertainty between two orders suggest that the data approach a Markov process at that order. Data that strongly approach a Markov process are often called "semi-Markovian." For example, a large drop in uncertainty between zero- and first-order uncertainty values suggests that the immediately preceding event predicts the next event with a high likelihood, but not entirely.

Following Hailman and Hailman (1993), *JWatcher* calculates uncertainty statistics only up to second-order Markovian models because ethological studies are usually limited in their duration and prevent meaningful interpretation of higher-level processes.

Each time that you run an analysis, *JWatcher* will automatically report four uncertainty values: maximum, zero order, first order, and second order. Maximum uncertainty is calculated from the number of different behavior types in a sequence and assumes that these behaviors are equiprobable and distributed randomly. Zero-order uncertainty assumes that behaviors are randomly distributed but takes into account the actual frequencies of occurrence of each behavior in the sequence. When all behaviors are in fact equiprobable, then zero-order uncertainty will be the same as maximum uncertainty. However, zero-order uncertainty will be much less than maximum uncertainty when one behavior is highly likely to occur while the remaining behaviors are rare. First-order uncertainty examines serial dependencies between adjacent behaviors, and second-order uncertainty examines serial dependencies between two preceding behaviors and a subsequent behavior. *JWatcher* will also report the observed, simple probability, and transitional probabilities for first- and second-order models, upon which these uncertainty statistics are based. The first-order transition probabilities are identical to those produced in the sequence analysis tab and may be used to construct kinematic graphs, a common accompaniment to first-order analysis.

Markovian analyses assume "stationarity," which means that the probabilities of occurrences of events and their transition probabilities do not change over time. This assumption is not often tested in ethological studies (but see Lusseau 2003), and currently *JWatcher* does not provide an easy way to test this.

Markovian statistics are calculated based upon overlapped sampling of the sequence.

Markovian analyses are commonly used to describe the sequential structure and organization of communication displays. For instance, Peters and Ord (2003) wanted to describe the visual displays of Jacky dragons. A Jacky dragon is an Australian agamid lizard that has a remarkable "hand-waving" submissive display: subordinates wave their front hands slowly to signal subordination. To ask whether display components were structured, the  researchers used a Markovian analysis to examine the serial dependencies of five display components (tail flick, backward arm wave, forward arm wave, push up, and body rock). Most displays proceeded in a systematic pattern, starting with an attention-getting push-up followed by more subtle displays (Peters and Evans 2003). These could be explained by a first-order semi-Markovian model.

Many studies use Markovian analyses to describe vocal communication systems. Ficken et al. (1994) described the pattern of notes within the "chick-a-dee" call system of the Mexican Chickadee and compared this system to the closely related Black-capped Chickadee (Hailman et al. 1987). Fernández-Juricic et al. (2003) examined whether South American sea lions varied the order in which they produced vocalizations according to different social contexts (which implies syntactical structure). Suggs and Simmons (2005) analyzed the pattern of amplitude modulations in the advertisement calls of male bullfrogs.

Markovian analyses can be used as a metric of randomness to study the development or function of stereotypical movement patterns. Bekoff (1975) proposed that the amount of randomness could distinguish between two hypotheses about animal play, one of which posits that the sequence of play behaviors is different from, and more random than, the sequence of nonplay behaviors. Jander and Jander (1993) studied the ontogeny of randomness of antennal grooming in milkweed bugs. They quantified the structure of grooming movements and found that there were short-stroke and long-stroke movements that could be patterned in different ways (SS, SL, LS, LL). They found that the bugs' ordering of these movements became less random with developmental age.

## 13.3 Lag Sequential Analysis Tab

*JWatcher's* lag sequential routine enables you to quantify the frequency with which one behavior event follows or precedes another behavior event at different "distances" along the sequence (i.e., at different lags). For example, you may be interested in the relative positions of falling and crying in a sequence of behaviors derived from a young child. Maybe crying often happens two positions ahead of falling in a sequence of behaviors, or perhaps crying often precedes falling by two positions. Algorithms in this tab enable you to specify a range of lags and then examine whether some of these relative positions between behaviors are more frequent than others.

*JWatcher's* lag sequential and sequence analysis routines are similar in many respects, but they also differ in noteworthy ways. We describe these below.

Classic "lag sequential analysis," first described by Sackett (1979), allows you to look for specific patterns in sequences composed of more than two immediately adjacent behaviors. Whereas Markovian analysis provides a general idea about whether such structure exists, lag sequential analysis examines which *specific* combinations of behavior may occur. By comparing pairs of behaviors at different lags, more complicated patterns may be described without the need to tabulate all possible combinations of behavior in a sequence. For example, as previously mentioned, if you want to know whether a particular sequence of three behaviors is particularly likely (e.g., ABC), you could examine whether B is likely to follow A one position ahead, C is likely to follow

B one position ahead, and C is likely to follow A two positions ahead. Or several behaviors may occur in fixed relative positions to each other, with intervening behaviors varying randomly.

In Sackett's classic lag sequential analysis, z-scores based upon a binomial test are used to determine whether transition probabilities for pairs of behaviors are beyond those expected by chance. Douglass and Tweed (1979) described a similar analysis called the "pre-post-state histogram," which emphasizes the plotting of observed frequencies (rather than transition probabilities) and the examination of confidence intervals around expected means (rather than z-scores) to determine which observed frequencies are more likely to occur than chance. Despite these minor differences, their approach is essentially the same as Sackett's, in that they both use a binomial test to determine which transitions differ significantly from random.

Bakeman and Quera (1995) have since suggested that log-linear approaches are a more appropriate way to determine which transition probabilities differ from random, particularly when behaviors are not allowed to repeat, and also when sampling is not overlapped or contains many breaks in the sequence. However, Bakeman and Gottman (1997) suggest that classic lag sequential analysis is still appropriate when codes are allowed to repeat, when overlapped sampling is employed, and with single unbroken sequences, because both methods produce almost identical results under these conditions.

One caveat with respect to classic lag sequential analysis is that multiple comparisons of many relative positions among many different behavior pairs will generate type I errors. Nonetheless, these calculations may provide adequate estimates when only a few pairs of behaviors are examined over a relatively small range of positions, and when adjustments to control for type I error, such Bonferroni corrections, are employed. The other caveat that applies to classic lag sequential analysis (but not to *JWatcher's* sequence analysis) is that z-score calculations are not table-based (i.e., they consider single events and not event pairs—see Bakeman and Gottman 1997). However, adequate estimates may still result with sufficient sample sizes and when relatively few breaks exist in the sequence.

*JWatcher's* algorithms are based upon Douglass and Tweed (1979) and Sackett (1979). Currently we have not implemented the Allison and Liker (1982) corrected formula when calculating standard deviations, and hence confidence intervals and z-scores. The calculations of Allison and Liker (1982) are based upon empirically derived expected values rather than theoretical ones, and thus they are technically correct. That said, Sackett's (1979) calculations produce more conservative estimates of departure from random (Bakeman 1983). Additionally, unlike Sackett (1979), we calculate our z-scores employing a continuity correction (Khazanie 1996) that is typically used with the normal approximation to the binomial distribution (which is what the tests are based upon). The inclusion of the continuity correction produces more conservative results than its omission. Following Douglass and Tweed (1979), we report observed frequencies, but not transition probabilities. However, transition frequencies are very easily calculated by adding a single column to the results file in a spreadsheet program. We report results when behaviors are not allowed to repeat following the method described in Douglass and Tweed (1979) using matrix multiplication (but see caveats in Bakeman and Quera 1995 and Bakeman and Gottman 1997).

For those who wish to calculate Allison and Liker z-scores, we provide an example showing how adjustments may be easily made to your output file to include the Allison and Liker correction (see how to use lag sequential analysis, below). We also show how you may easily remove the continuity correction, if you so desire.

Please note that the *z*-score (adjusted residual) calculated by the sequence analysis tab is nearly identical to the Allison and Liker *z*-score, with the added benefit of its being a table-wise statistic instead of a score based upon single events in the sequence. Table-wise statistics apply even when there are multiple break codes in the sequence, and when non-overlapped sampling is employed. Thus, if you are only interested in lags 1 through 5, you may explore your data using the sequence analysis tab in addition to, or as a substitute for, this tab.

Like sequence analysis, lag sequential analysis is based upon overlapped sampling.

Also note that you can always use *JWatcher's* "Complex Sequences" routine to generate tabulated data for export that can be used in other general purpose log linear programs, such as SPSS (SPSS Inc., www.spss.com). See below.

We now provide a few examples to give you a feeling for how lag sequential analysis has been, and can be, used.

Lag sequential analysis has been used extensively to examine the social interactions between two individuals, when the objective is to understand how each individual influences the other. In classic work, Gottman et al. (1977) compared the communication styles of human couples in distressed and nondistressed marriages. For each couple, they scored the interactions between husbands and wives discussing a marital problem. Examples of behaviors scored included: problem description, proposing a solution, agreement, disagreement, summarizing other, and summarizing self. In one analysis the researchers examined the initial phase of the discussion, noting that most discussions began with a description of the problem. For each group (distressed versus nondistressed), they used the husband's description of the problem as the criterion or given code, and then examined which behaviors were most likely to follow at a series of lags from 1 to 6. For nondistressed couples, they found that "wife agreement" was most likely to follow at lag 1, followed by "husband problem description" at lag 2, "wife agreement" at lag 3, "husband problem description" at lag 4, and ending with "wife agreement" at lag 5, with no particular behavior departing significantly from random at lag 6. They called this process "validation." On the other hand, for distressed couples, "husband problem description" was most likely followed by "wife problem description" at lag 1, "husband problem description" at lag 2, "wife problem description" at lag 3, and so forth through lag 6. They called this process "cross-complaining." Similar patterns were observed using "wife problem description" as the criterion or given event, except in this case the "validation" process ended after lag 4. Thus they concluded that the beginning phase of discussions by nondistressed couples is characterized by a "validation" cycle of comparatively few interactions, whereas the discussions by distressed couples involved "cross-complaining" that persisted longer.

In a nonhuman example, Waas (1991) studied agonistic displays in little blue penguins, examining the relationship between the risk of performing a display (measured as the likelihood of being injured by one's opponent) and the display's effectiveness (measured by how well it deterred its opponent). The penguins were defending nest sites or temporary calling sites used for mate attraction from intruders. The interaction between two individuals was recorded as a sequence alternating between one individual's behavior and the other's response, such that the individual defending the site was defined as the actor and the intruder was defined as the opponent. Waas analyzed the opponent's behavior both immediately before and after an actor's aggressive display to obtain a measure of the display's effectiveness. In other words, for each aggressive behavior performed by the actor, he compared the distribution of frequencies of the opponent's behaviors prior to that event with the distribution subsequent to the event. He did the same thing to see how the actor reacted to the opponent's response. To see whether an actor escalated or retreated, he compared the distribution of frequencies of the actor's behaviors before and after each of the opponent's behaviors. Waas found that high-risk displays were more effective at deterring opponents than low-risk displays, and that displays could be used to predict what individuals would do next.

Many other studies have used lag sequential analysis to examine the social interactions between two individuals. We list a few more studies here to help you to decide whether this analysis might be useful to you. For example, Breithaupt and Eger (2002) studied chemical communication in fighting crayfish. Using a procedure similar to Waas (1991), they showed that the production of urine coupled with aggressive behavior is effective in deterring blindfolded opponents. Eide et al. (2003) studied physician–patient relations to examine which physician behaviors preceded and followed patients' expressions of emotional cues and concerns. Fossi et al. (2005) used lag sequential analysis to describe the interactions of victim and perpetrator during sexual assault, and identified two different styles of attack, each with potentially different implications for rape prevention strategies.

Lag sequential analysis also has been used to describe the sequence of behaviors used by single individuals (as opposed to interactions between two individuals). In one such study, Butler (2005) studied the foraging behavior of a South African chameleon to determine whether the species is an active forager or a sit-and-wait predator. To do so, she examined behaviors at a series of lags prior to the eating event to describe the foraging mode. In another study, Molles et al. (2006) used lag sequential analysis to identify repeatable song sequences within the duets of the New Zealand Kokako, a rare endemic wattlebird.

## 13.4 Runs Tab

The runs test allows you to determine whether a sequence of dichotomous events is random. For instance, if you are interested in whether an individual bird develops a search image (a perceptual bias when selecting prey) to aid foraging on cryptic prey (e.g., Tinbergen 1960; Dawkins 1971; Langley et al. 1996; Bond and Kamil 1999), you might provide a mix of equally cryptic prey and observe prey choice. If animals formed search images, we might expect them to focus quickly on one prey type and only select that type. The runs test would allow us to test whether the sequence of prey selection is random.

A "run" is a series of repeated behaviors within a longer sequence. For example, the longer sequence {A A B B B A B B} consists of four runs {A A}, {B B B}, {A}, and {B B}. The runs tests examines whether the frequency of runs in a sequence deviates from random. There are two ways in which a sequence may depart from random. A subject may tend either to repeat its behavior or alternate its behaviors. In either case, the probability of a particular event may in some way be a function of the outcome of a previous event.

Note that when calculating the runs test, behaviors must be able to repeat themselves or else the test will not make any sense. Also, you cannot score more than two behaviors in any one data file.

Sokal and Rohlf (1995) provide more examples of the runs test.

## 13.5 Complex Sequences Tab

Most of *JWatcher's* statistics are descriptive. In many cases, you may wish to perform inferential tests (or other descriptive tests) that we do not provide. In this case, you may score data files with *JWatcher* and use the complex sequences tab to tabulate a list of transitions (e.g., AB, BC, CA, where A, B, and C are behaviors), and then use this series of transitions to run tests in other programs such as SPSS (SPSS Inc., www.spss.com). For example, for sequence analysis or lag sequential analysis, you may wish to run log-linear models.

The following example illustrates the format of exported data. Assume that you have three behaviors (e.g., A, B, and C), and have scored a data file with the sequence {A A B A C A}. Overlapped sampling of adjacent codes will produce the series: AA, AB, BA, AC, CA. The list of transitions will look like this in the output file:

```
#EXPORT DATA
Sample number    Sequence        Code 1        Code 2
            1 AA                  A             A
            2 AB                  A             B
            3 BA                  B             A
            4 AC                  A             C
            5 CA                  C             A
```

The series of transitions are listed in the order in which they are sampled, accompanied by a corresponding sample number. Each sampled sequence is also broken down into separate columns containing no more than one code per column to facilitate importation into some statistical packages. If your sampled sequences contained three codes each, then there would be three columns containing a single code each.

> **Note:** *If you intend to use this routine, we strongly advise creating a test file and importing it into your program of interest (after reorganizing the file appropriately) to verify that this routine will work for you.*

As mentioned earlier, all sampling in *JWatcher* is overlapped (except for the runs test). In some cases, you may wish to analyze your data files with non-overlapped sampling. Or you may wish to sample more than two codes at a time (e.g., event trios or event quadruplets, rather than event pairs). In this case, you may create a list of transitions using the complex sequences tab and use this list to perform tests in other programs.

Using the same example above, non-overlapped sampling of event trios would produce an output file like this:

```
#EXPORT DATA
Sample number    Sequence       Code 1      Code 2      Code 3
            1 AAB               A           A           B
            2 ACA               A           C           A
```

You may also vary the lag. If you were interested in overlapped sampling of event pairs at lag 2, you would get the following output:

```
#EXPORT DATA
Sample number    Sequence         Code 1         Code 2
            1 AB               A              B
            2 AA               A              A
            3 BC               B              C
            4 AA               A              A
```

In addition to a list of transitions, the complex sequences tab will report a table of observed frequencies for whatever sampling regimen that you specify. This may be useful for exploratory purposes (although you will need to perform further analyses with other programs).

For the case of overlapped sampling of adjacent codes, the observed frequency table would look like this:

```
#OBSERVED FREQUENCY TABLE
Sequence              Count
AA                             1
AB                             1
AC                             1
BA                             1
CA                             1
Total                          5
```

For the case of non-overlapped sampling of three codes, the observed frequency table would look like this:

```
#OBSERVED FREQUENCY TABLE
Sequence              Count
AAB                            1
ACA                            1
Total                          2
```

For the case of overlapped sampling of event pairs at lag 2, the observed frequency table would look like this:

```
#OBSERVED FREQUENCY TABLE
Sequence              Count
AA                             2
AB                             1
BC                             1
Total                          4
```

See section 13.11 for more details on how to use complex sequence tab.

## 13.6 Using *JWatcher* to Calculate Sequential Analyses

To run these routines, you will need a focal master file (*.fmf) and at least one data file (*.dat).

**Warning:** *For sequential analysis, you must specify a focal master file when capturing data. Data files created without an associated focal master file cannot be analyzed with sequential analysis routines.*

Remember that all calculations are based upon the sequence of key codes in a data file, without respect to the specific times that the key codes were pressed. Thus, these analyses assume a single stream of events. There can be no simultaneously occurring behaviors for these types of analyses, so data files must be scored (or edited) accordingly.

Because large sample sizes are often required to properly estimate many sequential analysis statistics, you may wish to combine multiple observation sessions into one data file. Currently, *JWatcher* does not provide a way to combine separate data files into one analysis. You have two options to overcome this problem: (1) score all your data as one data file during one data capture session, using a break code between separate sections, or (2) combine separate data files into one large data file using a spreadsheet program. Tips on combining data files using a spreadsheet program are provided in Appendix A.

**Note:** *The times associated with key codes in data files are completely ignored during sequential analysis.*

### General Tab

Click on the "Sequential Analysis" window to open it. The "General" tab should be open; if not, click on the "General" tab.

To begin, specify the focal master file and other parameters in the "General" tab. "General" tab specifications apply to all sequential analysis tabs except for the runs test. Omit this step for the runs test, and go directly to the "Runs test" tab by clicking on it.

To specify the focal master file (*.fmf), click on the file icon to the right of the text field and use the navigation window to select the file. The focal master file specified here should be the same as the focal master file associated with your data files.

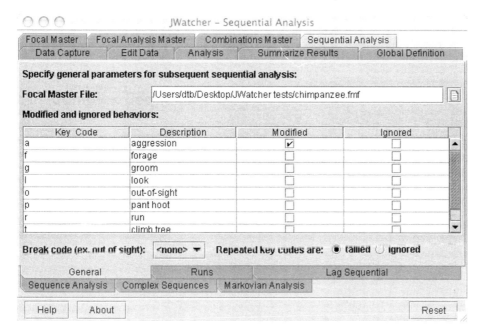

Select any behaviors that have modifiers following them. For instance, aggression (a) may be directed to different individuals (e.g., 1, 2, or 3). The default is that no modifiers follow any behaviors.

> **Note:** *Only modifiers that immediately follow a behavior specified as having modifiers will be reported in the results files. Any modifiers that do not follow a modified behavior will be recorded in the \*.dat file but will be ignored during analysis.*

When behaviors are modified, each behavior/modifier combination will be treated as a distinct event. For example, if aggression (a) is followed by individuals 1 or 2, then the behavior/modifier combinations of a1 and a2 will each be considered as an event. Thus the sequence {a1 a2 b a2 c} will consist of five entries or events. For further description of how modified behaviors are treated during analysis, see sections 13.8, 13.9, and 13.10 on how to use sequence analysis, Markovian analysis, and lag sequential, respectively.

Select any behaviors to be ignored. "Ignore" literally ignores selected behaviors within the sequence. Thus the sequence will be tabulated as if the ignored code never occurred. Default is that no behaviors are ignored.

Specify a break code from the pull-down menu. A break code can be any code that indicates a break in the sequence (i.e., when you are not certain what behavior followed or preceded other codes in the sequence). For example, a subject may go out-of-sight, or a sequence in a data file may be composed of several shorter sequences scored on different occasions. The default is that no break code is specified. See section 13.8 for specifics on how break codes affect analyses.

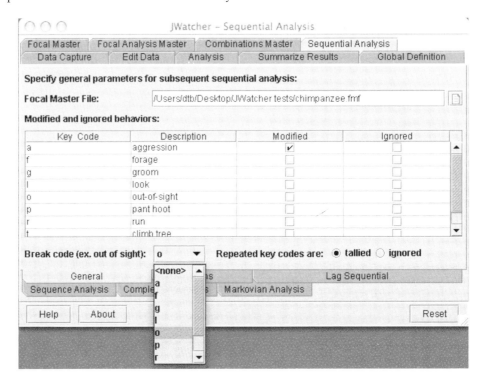

Specify whether consecutive, repeated codes are to be tallied or ignored. Depending upon your question, it may or may not make sense for a code to follow (or precede) itself. If codes cannot logically repeat, check the "ignored" button. If codes are allowed to repeat, then check the "tallied" button.

**Note:** *For repeated key codes, when "ignored" is checked, any repeated codes in your data file will be treated as if they do not exist in the sequence.*

With the exception of the output for the runs test, results files will contain a list of general tab settings in place at the time of analysis. This is illustrated in the following table.

| | |
|---|---|
| Focal master file from general tab | /my folder/data files/test.fmf |
| Number of behaviors (or behavior/modifiers) | 7 |
| Behaviors that are modified | A |
| Number of entries in data file | 30 |
| Break code | X |
| Number of break code entries | 1 |
| Number of continuous records | 2 |
| Behaviors that are ignored | None |
| Number of ignored codes | 0 |
| Consecutive repeated codes tallied | Yes |

The number of behaviors found in the data file sequence is reported, regardless of the total number of behaviors listed in the *.fmf. When behaviors are modified, each behavior/modifier combination (e.g., A1, A2, A3, where A is behavior followed by modifiers 1, 2, or 3) is reported as a distinct event. Thus a sequence consisting of A1, A2, A3, and B would be reported as containing four behaviors (or behavior/modifiers). The break code, if specified, and any ignored codes are not included.

The number of entries in the data file is the total number of times that either a behavior key code or a behavior/modifier combination has been pressed. For example, there are five entries for the sequence {A1 B A2 A1 C}, where A, B, and C are behaviors and A is modified by 1, 2, or 3. Break codes are not included, if specified and present, nor are any ignored codes.

The number of continuous records will always be 1, unless a break code is specified and present. For example, a single break code occurring in midsequence will divide a sequence into two separate, continuous records. The number of continuous records will always be 1 greater than the number of break code entries, except when those break codes occur at the very beginning or very end of the overall sequence.

All results files will also contain a list of general statistics (except for the runs test). The following table gives an example, where A, B, C, and D are behaviors and A is modified by 1, 2, or 3:

```
#GENERAL STATISTICS
Behavior/Modifier   Description        Count      Probability
A                   beh A                9          0.3000
A*                  beh A/ *none         1          0.0333
A1                  beh A/ *mod 1        4          0.1333
A2                  beh A/ *mod 2        2          0.0667
A3                  beh A/ *mod 3        2          0.0667
B                   beh B                9          0.3000
C                   beh C                7          0.2333
D                   beh D                5          0.1667
```

The count is the number of times that the behavior occurred in the sequence. The probability is the count for each behavior divided by the total number of entries in the data file. For modified behaviors, counts and probabilities are reported for each behavior/modifier combination separately (e.g., A1, A2, A3) and also for the behavior in its entirety (A). A modified behavior occurring without a modifier following it is treated as a distinct event and is reported as the behavior followed by an asterisk (e.g., A*).

### Features Common to All Tabs

Next, open the window for the type of analysis desired by clicking on it. There are five options: "Runs," "Lag Sequential," "Sequence Analysis," "Complex Sequences," and "Markovian Analysis."

For all tabs, you must specify the data file(s) to be analyzed and the folder in which result files will be placed.

For the focal data file(s) field, click on either the file icon or the folder icon to specify a data file (*.dat) or a folder with one or more *.dat files to be analyzed. All *.dat files in a folder will be analyzed if the folder option is selected.

For the results folder field, use the folder icon to specify a folder in which the results file(s) will later be placed. *JWatcher* will create a new folder if one does not already exist.

*JWatcher* names the results files by changing the suffix of the original data file (*.dat) name. For example, the results file generated by the runs test for a data file named "test.dat" will be "test.run.res." The suffixes for sequence analysis, Markovian analysis, lag sequential analysis, and complex sequences are *.seq.res, *.mar.res, *.lag.res, and *.com.res, respectively. If you rerun an analysis with different parameters, be sure to specify a different folder for the results; the default is to write over existing results files. *JWatcher* will ask if it is OK to overwrite files before doing so.

Specify the statistics you wish to be calculated.

Click [Analyze] to run the program. A progress box is updated each time a data file is analyzed. A text box provides an option to examine a file containing a list of any errors or warnings. If an "error" occurs, no results files will be produced. However, in the case of a "warning," the *.dat file will be processed. This log file (.log) is saved in the results file folder with a unique date/time-based name.

Select [Reset] to clear the text fields and restore statistics selections to default values. Note that the file and folder names within text fields are directly editable.

Select [View Log] to view the log file of the last analysis that you ran.

To view results files, open them in a word-processing or spreadsheet program. Results files are comma-delimited text.

**Note:** *Remember that one data file will generate one result file.* JWatcher *currently does not combine separate data files into one analysis, nor does* JWatcher *summarize multiple sequential analysis result files into one summary file. All data to be used in a particular analysis must be scored (or combined with a spreadsheet program) into one data file.*

## 13.7 Runs Test

The "Runs Test" examines whether a sequence of dichotomous behaviors is random. Data files must comprise no more than two behaviors. Analysis proceeds independently of any selections made in the "General" tab. Thus behaviors may not be modified, ignored, or specified to be a break code.

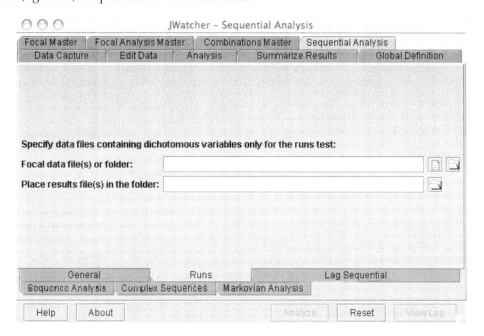

Key codes defined as modifiers in the focal master file associated with the data file(s) will be ignored.

The following statistics are reported in the results file for a sequence consisting of two behaviors, A and B:

Cases (A)

Cases (B)

Total cases

Number of runs

$z$-score

$p$-value (2-tailed)

Cases (A) and Cases (B) are the number of times behavior A and B occurred in the sequence, respectively. The total cases is total number of behaviors in the sequence (Cases A + Cases B). A "run" is a series of repeated behaviors within a longer sequence, preceded or followed by the other behavior. For example, the longer sequence {A A B B B A B B} is composed of four runs {A A}, {B B B}, {A}, and {B B}. *JWatcher* reports the $z$-score based upon a normal approximation to the expected mean and standard deviation of the distribution of the number of runs. The normal approximation assumes that the sample size of at least one of the dichotomous variables is greater than 20.

The null hypothesis for this test is that the sequence is random.

See Sokal and Rohlf (1995) for further description and examples of the runs test, including the $z$-score formula. Rohlf and Sokal (1995) provide a table of critical values for small sample sizes.

## 13.8 Sequence Analysis

Sequence analysis algorithms quantify the frequency with which one behavioral event follows another behavior event. Transition probabilities, $z$-scores, and $p$-values are reported for every possible transition in your sequence. Odds ratio and Yule's Q are reported for specific event pairs that you specify.

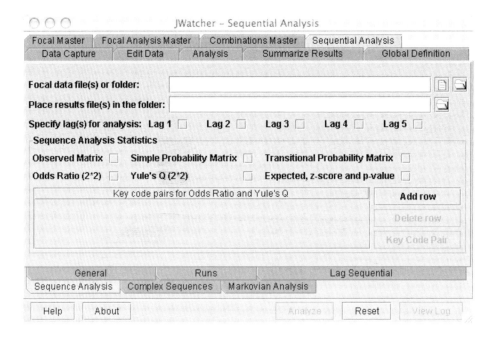

Specify the lag(s) for analysis and the statistics desired.

Remember that the settings in the "General" tab will affect sequence analysis calculations:

- When break codes are used, sampling stops at each break code and resumes at the first code immediately thereafter. For example, for the sequence {A B C X D E F} where X is the break code, overlapped sampling for lag 1 would produce the following series: AB, BC, DE, EF. For lag 2, the series would be AC, DF.

- When codes are ignored, sampling occurs as if these codes never occurred in the sequence. For example, for the sequence {A B C D E F}, the following series would be produced for lag 1 if B were ignored: AC, CD, DE, EF.

- When repeated codes are ignored, sampling occurs as if the repeated code never occurred in the sequence. For example, for the sequence {A A B B C C}, the following series would be produced for lag 1: AB, BC.

- When behaviors are modified, each behavior/modifier combination is treated as a distinct event. For example, for the sequence {A1 A2 B A1 C}, where A, B, and C are behaviors and A is modified by 1 or 2, the following series would be produced for lag 1: A1A2, A2B, BA1, A1C. If a behavior specified to have modifiers following it occurs without a modifier in the sequence, then this unmodified behavior will be treated as a distinct event and will be designated by an asterisk in the results file. For example, for the sequence {A1 A A2 B}, the following series would be produced for lag 1: A1A*, A*A2, A2B.

To specify key code pairs for Odds ratio and/or Yule's Q, click [Add row] in the key codes pairs table.

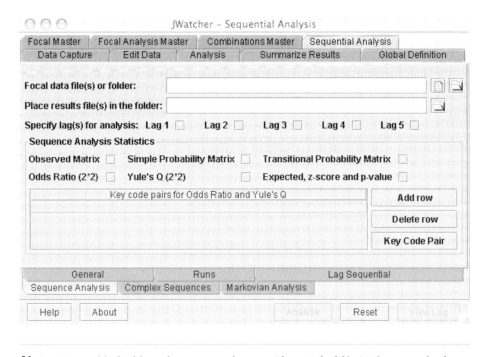

**Note:** *To enable [Add row], you must first specify an *.fmf file in the general tab.*

Click [Key Code Pair] and select key code pair in the pop-up window.

Click [OK].

Alternatively, key code pairs may be typed directly into the table such that A | B represents A given B.

Click [Add row] to add another pair. Use [Delete row] to delete one or more rows.

There are some other important things you must keep in mind when conducting sequence analysis:

To use this tab, you must first specify a focal master file (*.fmf) and other settings in the general tab. However, the results reported are based upon the key codes occurring within each data file itself, and not the *.fmf. In other words, a behavior may be listed in the *.fmf, but if it never occurs it will not be included in the result matrices. The same applies for modifiers.

**Warning 1:** *It is essential that in the general tab you specify the same focal master file that was used to create your data files. A mismatch in the list of behaviors and modifiers between these focal master files may produce erroneous results. You will be given a warning in the log when the name and pathway of the focal master files do not match. Depending upon the nature of the mismatch, your results files may contain a combination of the two lists of behaviors and modifiers and/or you may see entries of –1 in some of your observed matrices. These entries of –1 in observed matrices will lead to erroneous calculations for all other matrices (simple probabilities, transitional probabilities, etc.) because these are derived from the observed matrix. This applies to Odds Ratio and Yule's Q.*

**Warning 2:** *For specifying key code pairs for Odds ratio and Yule's Q, the available list of behaviors and modifiers will be based upon the focal master file specified in the general tab. However, it is possible to specify pairs based upon one focal master file in the general tab, and then later to change that focal master file while retaining your original selections in the key code pairs table. If you do not delete these selections, the program will report results for them. However, if there is a mismatch between the first focal master file and the focal master file used to create the data files, then erroneous results may be produced, as described above (Warning 1).*

When behaviors are modified, the matrices will include tabulations for each behavior/modifier combination separately and also tabulations for that behavior globally. For example, consider the sequence {A1 A2 B A1 B A2 B B A A1 A1 B}, where A and B are behaviors and A is modified by 1 or 2. The following observed matrix would be produced for lag 1:

|  |  | A | A* | A1 | A2 | B | Total |
|---|---|---|---|---|---|---|---|
|  |  | | | Lag 1 | | | |
| Lag 0 | A | 3 | 0 | 2 | 1 | 4 | 7 |
|  | A* | 1 | 0 | 1 | 0 | 0 | 1 |
|  | A1 | 2 | 0 | 1 | 1 | 2 | 4 |
|  | A2 | 0 | 0 | 0 | 0 | 2 | 2 |
|  | B | 3 | 1 | 1 | 1 | 1 | 4 |
|  | Total | 6 | 1 | 3 | 2 | 5 | 11 |

Note that A* represents an A followed by no modifier in the sequence, and that A* is treated as a distinct event for analysis. Also, note that in this case A refers to the global behavior A. Thus, A|A refers to "any A" followed by "any A." A1|A refers to A1 following "any A" (i.e., A1 following A*, A1, or A2). A|A1 refers to "any A" following A1 (i.e., A*, A1, or A2 following A1).

## 13.9 Markovian Analysis

Markovian analysis algorithms calculate uncertainty statistics to determine whether a series of behaviors is independent or whether events are predicted by previous events. See the overview in the introduction to sequential analysis (see section 13.1) for more detail about Markovian analysis and how to interpret uncertainty values. Also, see Bakeman and Gottman (1997) and Hailman and Hailman (1993) for further general descriptions and interpretations of Markovian analysis as applied to the study of behavior.

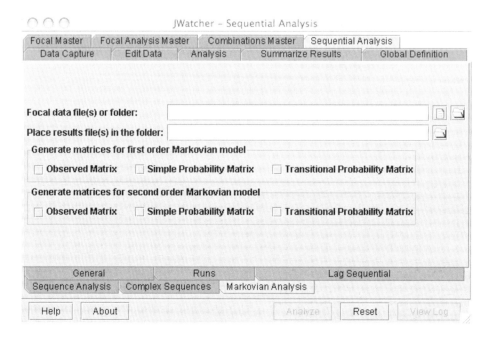

To use this tab, you must specify a focal master file (*.fmf) and other settings in the general tab. However, statistics are calculated based upon the behaviors (and modifiers) occurring in each data file only. In other words, a behavior (or modifier) that is listed in the focal master file but that does not occur in the data file will not be included in the results.

Remember that general tab settings will affect how your sequence is tabulated. See section 13.8 on how to use sequence analysis for a description.

*JWatcher's* Markovian analysis will produce the following statistics for every analysis, regardless of statistics selected in the menu:

$U_m$ (maximum uncertainty)
$U_0$ (zero-order uncertainty)
$U_1$ (first-order uncertainty)
$U_2$ (second-order uncertainty)

*JWatcher* will also produce the following statistics (when selected) for first and second order models:

Observed matrix
Simple probability matrix
Transitional probability matrix

These matrices for first-order models will be identical to the matrices generated by the sequence analysis tab with lag 1.

Markovian analysis treats each behavior/modifier combination as a distinct event. For example, if behavior A is modified by 1 and 2, then the behavior/modifier combinations A1 and A2 (or A*, if A is not followed by any modifier) are considered to be distinct events. However, unlike sequence analysis, no calculations are made with respect to the overall occurrence of behavior A.

The sample size, number of cells in the matrix, and mean sample size per cell is reported for each uncertainty statistic. The sample size is the number of entries used to calculate each statistic (matrix grand total).

```
#UNCERTAINTY STATISTICS
Order     Uncertainty  Sample size  Number of cells in matrix  Mean sample size/cell
   Max      1.5850
     0      1.5750          25                   3                     8.33
     1      1.3734          24                   9                     2.67
     2      0.8028          23                  27                     0.85
```

## 13.10 Lag Sequential Analysis

Lag sequential analysis algorithms quantify the frequency with which one behavior event follows or precedes another behavior event for a range of lags. For each event pair that you specify, *JWatcher* will report observed frequencies, expected mean frequencies, and 95% confidence intervals around these means for a series of successive lags prior to or following the focal behavior. For more details, see Douglass and Tweed (1979), Van Hooff (1982), and Bakeman and Gottman (1997).

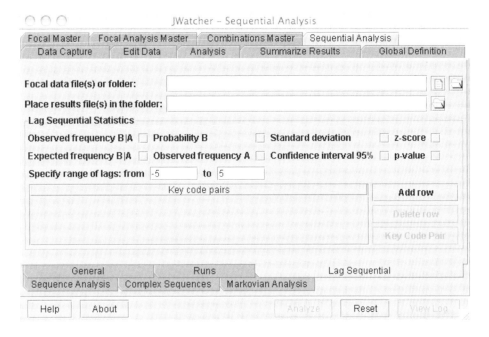

To use this tab, you must first specify a focal master file (*.fmf) and other settings in the general tab.

**Warning:** *The "Lag Sequential" tab is the only tab for which calculations differ based upon whether or not codes are allowed to repeat. Make sure that you specify properly whether repeated codes are to be tallied or ignored in the general tab. If you want probabilities and expected values based upon nonrepeating codes, check the repeated key codes "ignored" option. If you want probabilities and expected values based upon repeating codes, check the repeated key codes "tallied" option. All statistics are affected by this choice, except for "Observed frequency B|A" and "Observed frequency A." See below and section 13.12 (under "Lag Sequential Analysis") for more details on statistics.*

You must specify at least one event pair for analysis in the key code pairs table. Modified behaviors may be included within an event pair (e.g., X5 | Y may be specified, where X and Y are behaviors and X is modified by 5).

To specify key code pairs for analysis, click [Add row] in the key codes pairs table.

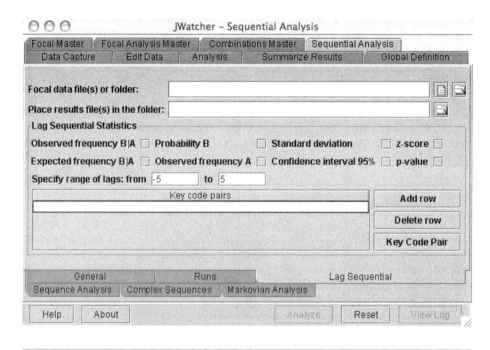

**Note:** *To enable [Add row], you must first specify an \*.fmf file in the general tab.*

Click [Key Code Pair] and select key code pair in the pop-up window.

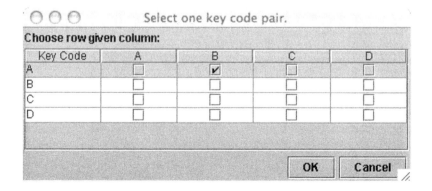

Click [OK].

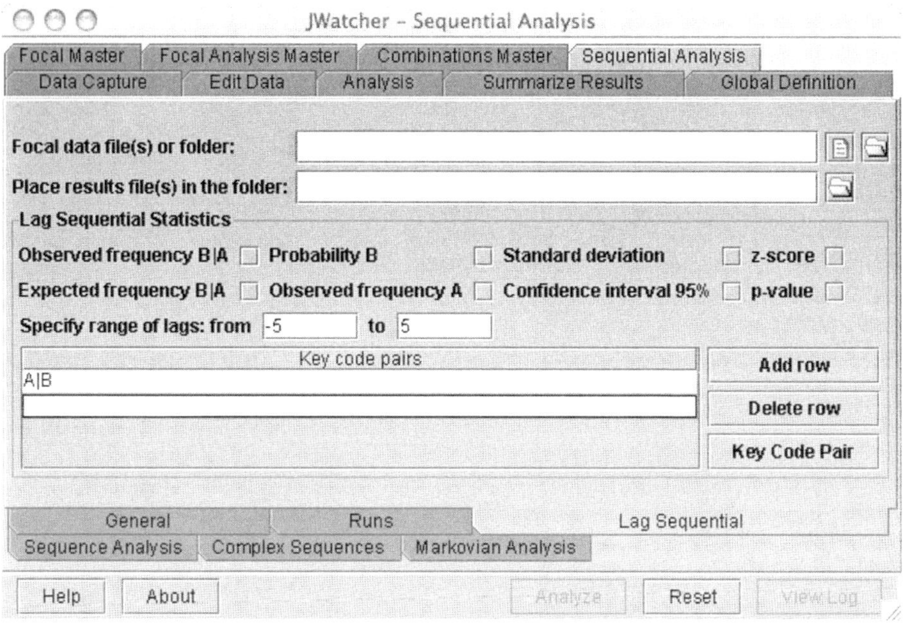

Alternatively, key code pairs may be typed directly into the table such that A | B represents A given B.

Click [Add row] to add another pair. Use [Delete row] to delete one or more rows.

Lag sequential analysis treats each behavior/modifier combination as a distinct event. For example, if A is a behavior specified to be modified by 1 or 2, then the behavior/modifier combinations A1 and A2 (or A*, if A is not followed by any modifier) are considered to be distinct events.

Event pairs may include global behaviors when codes are allowed to repeat. For example, if A and B are behaviors specified as modified, then A | B may be requested, where A | B refers to "any A" following "any B." However, some combinations such as A1 | A, or A | A1 are not permitted.

Event pairs may not include global behaviors when codes are not allowed to repeat.

*JWatcher's* "Lag Sequential" routines calculate the following statistics:

Observed frequency B | A
Observed frequency A
Probability B
Expected frequency B | A
Standard deviation
Confidence interval 95%
*z*-score
*p*-value

---

**Note:** *Transition Probability B|A, although not reported here by* JWatcher, *may be calculated very easily in the result file by creating a single new column and dividing "observed frequency B|A" by "observed frequency A." See below.*

Each of these statistics is calculated for a specified event pair, such that B | A refers to B given A. We use B | A generically in the statistics selection menu to refer to any combination of behaviors in which A is the "given" or "lag 0" behavior and B is the "target" behavior. Thus "observed frequency A" tabulates the observed frequency of your given behavior, and "probability B" calculates the probability of your target behavior.

The target behavior (B) may either precede or follow the given behavior (A), depending upon the range of lags specified. Statistics will be calculated for every lag within the specified range. A negative lag means that the target behavior will precede the given behavior, whereas a positive lag means that the target behavior will follow the given behavior.

See section 13.8 on how to use sequence analysis for a description of the way break codes and ignored codes affect tabulation.

### *Definitions of Statistics*

See also section 13.12 under "Lag Sequential Analysis" for an example calculation for lag sequential analysis.

#### OBSERVED FREQUENCY B|A

The frequency (count) that the target behavior occurs relative to the given behavior at each specified lag.

#### OBSERVED FREQUENCY A

The frequency (count) that the given behavior occurs in the sequence at each lag. For example, in the sequence {A B C A D}, if A is the given behavior, then A is available as the given code two times at lag 1 (AB, AD), but only one time at lag 2 (AC). The "observed frequency A" is equivalent to the row total for the given behavior if the results were reported in matrix form (see sequence analysis), and can be used to calculate transition probabilities (see below).

#### PROBABILITY B

The probability that the target will occur relative to the given code at each lag. When codes are allowed to repeat, it is the frequency (count) of the target in the overall sequence, divided by the total number of entries in the sequence. When codes are not allowed to repeat, the procedure employs matrix multiplication as described in the example calculations section 13.12 (under "Lag Sequential Analysis").

#### EXPECTED FREQUENCY B|A

The expected frequency that the target occurs relative to the given code. It is calculated based upon the expected mean of the binomial distribution, and is the observed frequency of the given code multiplied by the probability of the target (observed frequency A * probability B).

#### STANDARD DEVIATION

The standard deviation of the expected frequency. It is calculated based upon the binomial distribution, and is the square root of [observed frequency A * probability B *

(1 – probability B)]. Note that this standard deviation is calculated as described in Douglass and Tweed (1979) and Sackett (1979), but not as described in Allison and Liker (1982). To derive the Allison and Liker (1982) standard deviation, multiply the above by the square root of (1 – probability A), where "probability A" refers to the probability of the given behavior in your sequence.

### CONFIDENCE INTERVAL 95%

The upper and lower bounds of the 95% confidence intervals around the expected frequency. It is calculated based upon the normal approximation to the binomial distribution, and is the expected mean ±1.96*(standard deviation).

### Z-SCORE

These are calculated as the [(observed frequency B|A ± $^1/_2$) – expected frequency B|A)]/standard deviation. This calculation is based upon the normal approximation to the binomial distribution, and employs a continuity correction of ± $^1/_2$. Sackett (1979) and Allison and Liker (1982) do not include a continuity correction, nor does the z-score (adjusted residual) advocated by Bakeman and Gottman (1997). To remove the continuity correction, generate a new z-score by subtracting "expected frequency B|A" from "observed frequency B|A" and dividing this result by "standard deviation."

### P-VALUE

The p-value is based upon the z-score, as calculated by *JWatcher*. That is, for a one-tailed test it is based upon the normal approximation to the binomial distribution using a continuity correction. It represents the probability of getting an equal or greater value for the "observed frequency B|A" (if the observed value is larger than the expected), or an equal or lesser value for the "observed frequency B|A" (if the observed value is smaller than the expected), given that the sequence is random.

See example calculations (see section 13.12 "Lag Sequential Analysis") for more details about statistics.

The following table illustrates how to calculate transition probabilities. First, add a column to your result file and label it "transition probability B|A." Then divide "observed frequency B|A" (number of times B occurs in relation to A) by "observed frequency A" (equivalent to row total for A, if this were in matrix form).

```
#LAG SEQUENTIAL STATISTICS
Lags B|A     Observed frequency B|A  Observed frequency  A  Transition probability B|A
        -5                       13                      23  13/23 = 0.5652
        -4                        1                      24  1/24 = 0.0417
        -3                       11                      24  11/24 = 0.4583
        -2                        0                      24  0/24 = 0.0000
        -1                        9                      24  9/24 = 0.3750
         1                        9                      25  9/25 = 0.3600
         2                        0                      24  0/24 = 0.0000
         3                       12                      24  12/24 = 0.5000
         4                        0                      24  0/24 = 0.0000
         5                        8                      24  8/24 = 0.3333
```

As mentioned in the statistics definitions, the standard deviation calculated by *JWatcher* is consistent with Sackett (1979) and Douglass and Tweed (1979), but not with Allison and Liker (1982). To derive the Allison and Liker (1982) standard deviation, multiply *JWatcher's* standard deviation by the square root of (1 – probability A). The "probability A" is the probability of your given behavior, and is found in your results file's general statistics table.

| #GENERAL STATISTICS Behavior/Modifier | Count | Probability |
|---|---|---|
| A | 25 | **0.18** |
| B | 33 | 0.23 |
| C | 48 | 0.34 |
| D | 36 | 0.25 |

| #LAG SEQUENTIAL STATISTICS Lags B\|A | Standard deviation B\|A | Allison and Liker s.d. |
|---|---|---|
| -5 | 2.03 | 2.03 * sqrt(1 – 0.18) = 1.84 |
| -4 | 2.07 | 2.07 * sqrt(1 – 0.18) = 1.87 |
| -3 | 2.07 | 2.07 * sqrt(1 – 0.18) = 1.87 |
| -2 | 2.07 | 2.07 * sqrt(1 – 0.18) = 1.87 |
| -1 | 2.07 | 2.07 * sqrt(1 – 0.18) = 1.87 |
| 1 | 2.11 | 2.11 * sqrt(1 – 0.18) = 1.91 |
| 2 | 2.07 | 2.07 * sqrt(1 – 0.18) = 1.87 |
| 3 | 2.07 | 2.07 * sqrt(1 – 0.18) = 1.87 |
| 4 | 2.07 | 2.07 * sqrt(1 – 0.18) = 1.87 |
| 5 | 2.07 | 2.07 * sqrt(1 – 0.18) = 1.87 |

To remove the continuity correction for *z*-scores, you will need to recalculate *z*-scores as (observed frequency B | A – expected frequency B | A)/standard deviation. You may use the standard deviation provided by *JWatcher* or the recalculated version as per Allison and Liker above.

| #LAG SEQUENTIAL STATISTICS Lags B\|A | Observed frequency B\|A | Expected frequency B\|A | Standard deviation B\|A | z-score with continuity correction removed |
|---|---|---|---|---|
| -5 | 13 | 5.35 | 2.03 | (13 – 5.35)/2.03 = 3.77 |
| -4 | 1 | 5.58 | 2.07 | (1 – 5.58)/2.07 = -2.21 |
| -3 | 11 | 5.58 | 2.07 | (11 – 5.58)/2.07 = 2.62 |
| -2 | 0 | 5.58 | 2.07 | (0 – 5.58)/2.07 = -2.70 |
| -1 | 9 | 5.58 | 2.07 | (9 – 5.58)/2.07 = 1.65 |
| 1 | 9 | 5.81 | 2.11 | (9 – 5.81)/2.11 = 1.51 |
| 2 | 0 | 5.58 | 2.07 | (0 – 5.58)/2.07 = -2.70 |
| 3 | 12 | 5.58 | 2.07 | (12 – 5.58)/2.07 = 3.10 |
| 4 | 0 | 5.58 | 2.07 | (0 – 5.58)/2.07 = -2.70 |
| 5 | 8 | 5.58 | 2.07 | (8 – 5.58)/2.07 = 1.17 |

If you do not wish to remove the continuity correction from *z*-scores, but wish to recalculate them using Allison and Liker standard deviations, then divide the *z*-score by square root(1 – probability A), where "A" refers to your given behavior.

| #GENERAL STATISTICS Behavior/Modifier | Count | Probability |
|---|---|---|
| A | 25 | **0.18** |
| B | 33 | 0.23 |
| C | 48 | 0.34 |
| D | 36 | 0.25 |

```
#LAG SEQUENTIAL STATISTICS
                             z-score with continuity correction, using
Lags B|A      z-score  B|A  Allison and Liker standard deviation
          -5     3.53  3.53/ sqrt(1 - 0.18) = 3.90
          -4    -1.97 -1.97/ sqrt(1 - 0.18) = -2.18
          -3     2.38  2.38/ sqrt(1 - 0.18) = 2.63
          -2    -2.45 -2.45/ sqrt(1 - 0.18) = -2.71
          -1     1.41  1.41/ sqrt(1 - 0.18) = 1.56
           1     1.27  1.27/ sqrt(1 - 0.18) = 1.40
           2    -2.45 -2.45/ sqrt(1 - 0.18) = -2.71
           3     2.86  2.86/ sqrt(1 - 0.18) = 3.16
           4    -2.45 -2.45/ sqrt(1 - 0.18) = -2.71
           5     0.93  0.93/ sqrt(1 - 0.18) = 1.03
```

## 13.11 Complex Sequences

The purpose of this tab is twofold: (1) it enables you to create your own sampling regimens, which may differ from those provided in the other tabs, and (2) it enables you to export tabulated data for analysis in other statistical packages. Results files are comma-delimited text (with the suffix *.com.res). Word-processing or spreadsheet programs may be used to easily reformat the results files for use in a variety of statistics programs.

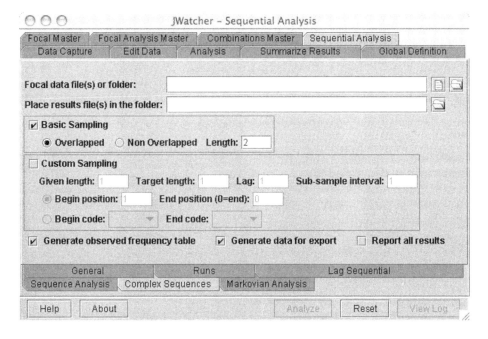

**Note:** *Before committing yourself to using this routine, we strongly advise creating a test file and importing it into your program of interest (after reorganizing the file appropriately) to verify that this routine will work for you.*

To use this tab, you must first specify a focal master file (*.fmf) and other settings in the general tab. However, the calculations for the observed table and export data are based upon the key codes occurring within each data file itself, and not the focal master file. In other words, a behavior may be listed in the focal master file, but if it never occurs, it will not be included in the table or export data. The same applies for modifiers.

To generate data for export using sampling regimes identical to those found in the sequence analysis, Markovian, or lag sequential tabs, see the end of this section, "How to Replicate Sampling from Other Tabs."

For each analysis, you may generate an observed frequency table and/or a list of tabulated data for export. If the "Report all results" box is selected, the observed frequency table will list results for all possible behavioral combinations, including those with counts of zero. The "Report all results" box does not affect the list of export data.

You may use either the "Basic Sampling" or "Custom Sampling" routines of this tab.

## Basic Sampling

Basic sampling requires that you specify the number of consecutive codes to sample at one time (the length of the sample unit) and whether the sampling will be overlapped or non-overlapped.

With overlapped sampling you slide your sampling "window" from the first code, to the second code, to the third code, etc. You are moving from one position in the sequence to the next.

With non-overlapped sampling, your sampling "window" skips one or more positions in the sequence, such that no position is sampled more than once. Sampling occurs at an interval equal to the length of the sample unit.

For example, for the sequence {A B C D E F G}, you may wish to sample units of length 3. In this case, you would generate the following series with overlapped sampling: ABC, BCD, CDE, DEF, EFG. For non-overlapped sampling with length 3, the following series would be produced: ABC, DEF. In other words, sampling occurs at position 1 (A) and then again at position 4 (D) in our example.

## Custom Sampling

Custom sampling enables you to vary the length of both the given and the target units, and to vary the relative position of one with respect to the other (i.e., the lag). You may also vary the sampling interval to create overlapped sampling, non-overlapped sampling, or some other sampling interval. In addition, you may sample portions of the sequence by varying the start and end positions.

### GIVEN LENGTH

We use "given" to mean the criterion event, or "lag 0" event. It is the event for which you want to know what precedes or follows. The length refers to how many codes make up this event. For example, if the sequence is {X Y Z A B C} and the given length is 2, the first given event would be XY, if we assume we are starting from the beginning of the sequence. If the given length were 4, then the first given event would be XYZA.

### TARGET LENGTH

We use "target" to mean the event that precedes or follows the "given" event. The length refers to how many codes make up this event. The "target" event could occur at any specified lag, either positive or negative (see below).

### LAG

Lag refers to the position of the "target" event relative to the "given" event. Lag 1 means that the target is one position ahead of the given event in the sequence. Lag –1 means that the target is one position behind the given event. If the given event comprises more than one code, then positive lags are counted from the last code of the given event. However, negative lags, in this case, are counted from the first code of the given event, not the last code.

For example, consider the sequence {A B C D E F G H I J K}. If the given length is 3, the target length is 2, and the lag is +3, then the first sequence would be {ABCFG}. The given is {ABC}. The lag is counted as three positions ahead of the last code in the given sequence, so three positions ahead of the C brings us to F. The target is FG.

Consider the same sequence. If the given length is 3, the target length is 2, and the lag is –3, then the first sequence would be {DEFAB}. The first code in the sequence from which we can count back three positions (lag –3) is D. Given length = 3, so the given is DEF. Counting back three positions brings us to A. Target length = 2, so the target is AB.

**SUB-SAMPLE INTERVAL**

The sub-sample interval refers to how you move along the sequence when sampling. Standard overlapped sampling would have a sub-sample interval of 1. This means that you slide your "window" from the first code, to the second code, to the third code, etc. You are moving from one position in the sequence to the next (defined to be an interval of 1). A sub-sample interval of 2 would mean that you start at the first code, then move your sampling "window" to the third code, then to the fifth code, etc.

For example, for the sequence {A A B C A}, if we use a given length = 1, target length = 1, and lag = 1, then a sub-sample interval = 1 would produce the following series: AA, AB, BC, CA. The sampling window slides along the sequence one position at a time. A sub-sample interval = 2 would produce the series AA, BC. The sampling window slides along by moving from first to third to fifth position (interval is 2). For this sequence there is nothing to tally beyond the third position.

Note that if the given event consists of more than one code, the interval is counted from the first code of the given event. For example, consider the sequence {A B C D E F G H I J K}. If the given length is 3, the target length is 2, and the lag is 3, then the first sequence would be {A B C F G}, as described above. If our sub-sample interval were 3, then the next sequence would be {D E F I J}. We move three positions ahead from the first position in the given event (A), which brings us to D. We then consider our given event to be DEF (length = 3). Because lag = 3, we count three positions ahead from the last position in the given (F), which brings us to I. The target length = 2, so the target is {I J}. Continuing, the subsequent sequence should begin with {G H I}, but there are no codes available at lag 3, so no other sequence is produced.

## *How to Sample Portions of the Sequence*

**BEGIN POSITION**

This is the position in the overall sequence where tallying begins. For example, for the sequence {A B C X D E F}, "begin position 1" means start at A. "Begin position 3" means start at C. Note that break codes are included when specifying positions in the sequence. For example, if X is specified as the break code, X is considered to be at position 4 and D is considered to be at position 5.

**END POSITION**

This is the position in the overall sequence where tallying ends. For example, for the sequence {A B C D E F G H I J K}, end position 0 means end at K. End position 6 means end at F.

**BEGIN CODE**

Tallying begins at the first occurrence of the specified code. For example, for the sequence {A B C D A B C D A B C D}, if the begin code is D, then tallying starts at the first D, located at position 4 in the sequence.

### END CODE

Tallying ends at the first occurrence of the specified code, after tallying has begun. For example, for the sequence {A B C D A B C D A B C D}, if the begin code is D and the end code is B, then tallying will start at D (position 4) and end at B (position 6).

---

**Note:** *There is a known issue associated with the sampling of a portion of the sequence. The observed frequency table and the data for export will correctly report results based upon the portion of the sequence requested. However, calculations for the general settings section and general statistics section are based upon the entire sequence.*

---

## How to Replicate Sampling from Other Tabs

To replicate sampling for sequence analysis, select custom sampling and specify given length = 1, target length = 1, sub-sample interval = 1. Vary the lag from 1 to 5, depending upon the lag desired. Ensure "Generate data for export" box is selected.

To replicate sampling for Markovian analysis, select basic sampling and specify "overlapped." For first-order models, use length = 2. For second-order models, use length = 3. Ensure "Generate data for export" box is selected.

To replicate sampling for lag sequential analysis, select custom sampling and specify given length = 1, target length = 1, sub-sample interval = 1. Vary lag depending upon lag desired. Ensure "Generate data for export" box is selected.

## How General Tab Settings Affect Tabulation

### MODIFIED BEHAVIORS

When behaviors are modified, each behavior/modifier combination is treated as a distinct event. For example, for the sequence {A1 A2 B A1 C}, where A, B, and C are behaviors and A is modified by 1 or 2, the following series would be produced for basic, overlapped sampling with length = 2: A1A2, A2B, BA1, A1C. When a behavior is modified, observed frequencies will not be provided for the behavior globally (e.g., for A in the above example, where A refers to "any A"). If such statistics are desired, you should rerun the analysis with the behavior unmodified. That is, deselect it in the modifier table of the general tab.

### IGNORED BEHAVIORS

When codes are ignored, sampling occurs as if these codes never occurred in the sequence. For example, for the sequence {A B C D E F}, if B were ignored, the following series would be produced for basic, overlapped sampling with length = 2: AC, CD, DE, EF.

### REPEATED KEY CODES

When repeated codes are ignored, sampling occurs as if the repeated code never occurred in the sequence. For example, for the sequence {A A B B C C}, the following series would be produced for basic, overlapped sampling with length = 2: AB, BC.

### BREAK CODES

When break codes are used, sampling stops at each break code and resumes at the first code immediately thereafter. For example, for the sequence {A B C D E X F G H I} where X is the break code, the following series would be produced for basic, overlapped sampling with length = 3: ABC, BCD, CDE, FGH, GHI. For custom sampling where given = 1, target = 1, lag = 3, sub-sample interval =1, the following series would be produced: AD, BE, FI. For custom sampling where given = 1, target = 1, lag = –3, sub-sample interval = 1, the following series would be produced: DA, EB, IF.

---

**Note:** *The following example illustrates the special case of custom sampling with negative lags and sub-sample intervals greater than 1. Consider the sequence {A A B A C B X B C A B C} where A, B, and C are behaviors and X is the break code. The following series will be generated for given = 1, target = 1, lag = –1, and sub-sample interval = 2: BA, CA, AC, CB. Sampling will begin at the first position in the sequence or after a break code, and if that position cannot be used to sample, then sampling will skip to the next position based upon the sub-sample interval specified (which, in this example, is two positions ahead).*

---

**RESULT FILE FORMAT**

The following example illustrates the format of exported data. Assume the sequence {A A B A C A}. Basic, overlapped sampling with length = 3 will produce the series: AAB, ABA, BAC, ACA. This series will be reported in the result file as follows:

```
#EXPORT DATA
Sample number  Sequence    Code 1      Code 2      Code 3
          1 AAB        A           A           B
          2 ABA        A           B           A
          3 BAC        B           A           C
          4 ACA        A           C           A
```

The series of sampled sequences are listed in the order in which they are sampled, accompanied by the corresponding sample number. Each sampled sequence is additionally broken down into separate columns containing no more than one code per column, to facilitate importation into some statistical packages. The output associated with custom sampling is identical as above, but it will also contain two extra columns listing the given and target sequences, respectively, for each line.

## 13.12 An Example to Illustrate *JWatcher*'s Calculations

### Sequence Analysis

*JWatcher*'s "Sequence Analysis" routines calculate the following statistics:

> Observed matrix
>
> Simple probability matrix
>
> Transitional probability matrix
>
> Expected values, $z$-scores, and $p$-values
>
> Odds Ratio
>
> Yule's Q

The following example is intended to illustrate how each of the above statistics is calculated. See Bakeman and Gottman (1997) for more details.

Assume the sequence {A A B A C A B B C B A A B C A B C C B C A B B C A}.

**General Statistics**

| Behavior/Modifier | Description | Count | Probability |
|---|---|---|---|
| A | Behavior A | 9 | 9/25 |
| B | Behavior B | 9 | 9/25 |
| C | Behavior C | 7 | 7/25 |

The observed matrix reports the frequency with which a behavior follows another behavior as a count. Frequencies are reported in matrix form for all possible event pairs in the data file sequence.

**Observed Matrix**

| | | Lag 1 | | | |
| | | A | B | C | Total |
|---|---|---|---|---|---|
| | A | 2 | 5 | 1 | 8 |
| Lag 0 | B | 2 | 2 | 5 | 9 |
| | C | 4 | 2 | 1 | 7 |
| | Total | 8 | 9 | 7 | 24 |

**Observed Matrix**

| | | Lag 2 | | | |
| | | A | B | C | Total |
|---|---|---|---|---|---|
| | A | 2 | 4 | 2 | 8 |
| Lag 0 | B | 4 | 1 | 4 | 9 |
| | C | 1 | 4 | 1 | 6 |
| | Total | 7 | 9 | 7 | 23 |

**Observed Matrix**

| | | Lag 3 | | | |
| | | A | B | C | Total |
|---|---|---|---|---|---|
| | A | 2 | 1 | 5 | 8 |
| Lag 0 | B | 3 | 5 | 0 | 8 |
| | C | 2 | 2 | 2 | 6 |
| | Total | 7 | 8 | 7 | 22 |

**Observed Matrix**

|  |  | Lag 4 | | | |
|---|---|---|---|---|---|
|  |  | A | B | C | Total |
|  | A | 3 | 4 | 1 | 8 |
| Lag 0 | B | 2 | 2 | 3 | 7 |
|  | C | 1 | 2 | 3 | 6 |
|  | Total | 6 | 8 | 7 | 21 |

**Observed Matrix**

|  |  | Lag 5 | | | |
|---|---|---|---|---|---|
|  |  | A | B | C | Total |
|  | A | 2 | 2 | 3 | 7 |
| Lag 0 | B | 3 | 2 | 2 | 7 |
|  | C | 1 | 4 | 1 | 6 |
|  | Total | 6 | 8 | 6 | 20 |

The simple probability matrix reports the probability that an event pair occurs in the sequence. It is calculated by dividing the observed count for each event pair by the total number of event pairs in the sequence. Probabilities are reported in matrix form for all possible event pairs in the data file sequence. The sum of simple probabilities for all possible event pairs in the matrix is 1.

**Simple Probability Matrix**

|  |  | Lag 1 | | | |
|---|---|---|---|---|---|
|  |  | A | B | C | Total |
|  | A | 2/24 | 5/24 | 1/24 |  |
| Lag 0 | B | 2/24 | 2/24 | 5/24 |  |
|  | C | 4/24 | 2/24 | 1/24 |  |
|  | Total |  |  |  | 24/24 |

This and all subsequent calculations are based upon the observed matrix, so calculations will be shown for lag 1 only, with the same principles applying to lags 2 through 5.

The transitional probability matrix reports the probability, given that one behavior occurs, that another behavior occurs. It is calculated by dividing the observed count for each event pair by the total occurrences of the given event (row total for the given event). Probabilities are reported in matrix form for all possible event pairs in the data file sequence. Each row total sums to 1.

**Transitional Probability Matrix**

| | | A | B | C | Total |
|---|---|---|---|---|---|
| | | | Lag 1 | | |
| | | A | B | C | Total |
| Lag 0 | A | 2/8 | 5/8 | 1/8 | 8/8 |
| | B | 2/9 | 2/9 | 5/9 | 9/9 |
| | C | 4/7 | 2/7 | 1/7 | 7/7 |

Expected values, z-scores, and p-values are reported in matrix form for all possible event pairs in the data file sequence.

---

**Warning:** JWatcher's *algorithms calculate expected values and z-scores (and hence p-values) that apply only when behaviors are allowed to repeat (i.e., each behavior is allowed to follow itself). If behaviors are not allowed to repeat, we advise exporting your tabulated data with JWatcher's Complex Sequences routine, and then analyzing with a general-purpose log-linear program such as SPSS (SPSS Inc., www.spss.com). See Bakeman and Gottman (1997) for further discussion on this topic.*

---

Expected values for a cell are calculated from the observed matrix by multiplying the observed row total for that cell by the observed column total for that cell and then dividing by the observed matrix total. Note that this formula generates expected values assuming independence, that is, no association between the rows and columns of the table. It also assumes that codes are not equiprobable, but rather occurred as often as they in fact did.

**Expected Matrix**

| | | Lag 1 | | |
|---|---|---|---|---|
| | | A | B | C |
| Lag 0 | A | = 8*8/24 | = 8*9/24 | = 8*7/24 |
| | B | = 9*8/24 | = 9*9/24 | = 9*7/24 |
| | C | = 7*8/24 | = 7*9/24 | = 7*7/24 |

## Z-SCORES

Z-scores (adjusted residuals) are calculated using the following formula: z-score for a cell = (observed cell value – expected cell value)/square root [expected cell value *(1 – (observed row total/observed matrix total))*(1 – (observed column total/observed matrix total))]. Assuming that z-scores are normally distributed, and an alpha = 0.05, then values equal or greater than absolute value of 1.96 are considered to differ from random.

**Z-score Matrix**

| | | Lag 1 | | |
|---|---|---|---|---|
| | | A | B | C |
| Lag 0 | A | –0.6124 | 1.7889 | –1.2702 |
| | B | –0.8944 | –1.1975 | 2.2031 |
| | C | 1.5878 | –0.5798 | –1.0292 |

Odds ratio and Yule's Q require that you specify specific event pairs for analysis using the key codes pair table. For each specified event pair, a collapsed 2 × 2 matrix is created. For example, if you specify B | A (B given A), then the collapsed matrix will be composed of A, not A, B, not B, where x, y, z, q are observed counts for each corresponding cell (odds ratio = xq/yz. Yule's Q = (odds ratio – 1)/(odds ratio + 1) or (xq – yz)/(xq + yz).

|  |  | Lag 1 | |
| --- | --- | --- | --- |
|  |  | B | Not B |
| Lag 0 | A | x | y |
|  | Not A | z | q |

Note that Odds ratio varies from zero to positive infinity, with 1 meaning no effect. Yule's Q is a transformation of the odds ratio that varies from –1 to +1, with zero indicating no effect.

**Collapsed 2 x 2 Matrix for B|A**

|  |  | Lag 1 | | |
| --- | --- | --- | --- | --- |
|  |  | B | Not B | Total |
| Lag 0 | A | 5 | 3 | 8 |
|  | Not A | 4 | 12 | 16 |
|  | Total | 9 | 15 | 24 |

Odds ratio = 5*12/3*4 = 5

Yule's Q = (5 – 1)/(5 + 1) = 4/6 = 0.6667, or

Yule's Q = (5*12 – 3*4)/(5*12 + 3*4) = 48/72 = 0.6667

Because the odds ratio and Yule's Q are not typically or often used in studies of animal behavior, we provide some additional explanation here, with the added goal of highlighting what *JWatcher's* calculations will and will not do for you.

The odds ratio is a way of comparing whether the probability of a certain dichotomous event is the same for two groups. For example, say you want to know whether there is a difference in food preferences for wild versus captive rabbits.

|  | Organic | Nonorganic |
| --- | --- | --- |
| Wild | 199 | 1 |
| Captive | 101 | 99 |

The odds that wild rabbits choose organic over nonorganic carrots are 199:1. The odds that captive rabbits choose organic over nonorganic carrots are 101:99.

The odds ratio is the ratio of odds of an event's occurring in one group to the odds of its occurring in another group. The two groups in this case are wild versus captive, and the event of interest may be defined as choosing organic carrots.

The odds ratio is then (199/1)/(101/99) = 195. Wild rabbits are 195 times more likely than captive rabbits to choose organic carrots over nonorganic carrots.

In general, when the odds ratio is 1, the event is equally likely in both groups. When the odds ratio is greater than 1, the event is more likely in the first group. When the odds ratio is less than 1, the event is more likely in the second group.

The value of the odds ratio ranges from zero to positive infinity. When the odds of the first group approach zero, the odds ratio approaches zero. When the odds of the second group approach zero, the odds ratio approaches infinity.

Note that calculations for the odds ratio assume dichotomous variables, organized into a 2 x 2 table.

Although the above example about rabbit and carrots illustrates how to calculate the odds ratio, it does not specifically examine sequences of behavior. In the context of sequences of behavior, you might be interested in knowing whether one particular event is especially likely to follow another particular event. Revisiting our previous example, you might be interested in knowing if chimpanzees are particularly likely to pant hoot after climbing a tree. You may have scored a sequence of behaviors that includes such things as forage, look, walk, run, climb tree, alarm call, groom, etc. You may then use the odds ratio to determine whether chimpanzees are more or less likely to pant hoot after climbing a tree than after other behaviors.

Remember that *JWatcher* will collapse larger tables of observed counts into 2 x 2 tables, and that these 2 x 2 tables are organized as follows, where x, y, z, and q represent observed counts:

|         | Event B | Not B |
|---------|---------|-------|
| Event A | x       | y     |
| Not A   | z       | q     |

Remember that "Not A" includes all behaviors other than Event A, and that "Not B" includes all behaviors other than Event B.

If you are interested in the likelihood that a subject will pant hoot after climbing a tree, *JWatcher* will tabulate the following collapsed table of hypothetical counts from your scored sequence of behaviors:

|                | Pant hoot | Not pant hoot |
|----------------|-----------|---------------|
| Climb tree     | 50        | 100           |
| Not climb tree | 2         | 500           |

The above means that the subject pant hooted 50 times after climbing a tree. It engaged in other behaviors 100 times after climbing a tree. It pant hooted two times after behaviors other than climbing a tree. There were 500 cases in the sequence in which a behavior other than pant hooting followed a behavior other than tree climbing.

The odds that subjects will pant hoot after climbing a tree are 50:100. Thus subjects are 50/100 = 0.5 times more likely to pant hoot after climbing a tree than after any other behavior.

The odds that subjects will pant hoot after any other behavior other than tree climb-ing are 2:500. Thus subjects are $2/500 = 0.004$ times more likely to pant hoot after any behavior other than climbing a tree.

The odds ratio is $0.5/0.004 = 125$. Thus subjects are 125 times more likely to pant hoot after tree climbing than after engaging in any other behavior other than tree climbing.

Note that *JWatcher's* odds ratio will not let you compare two specific events found with-in your sequence. Rather, you must compare a specific event to the occurrence of all other events (Event A versus Not A, Event B versus Not B). For example, you cannot calculate whether subjects are more likely to pant hoot after climbing a tree than they are to look after climbing a tree:

|  | Pant hoot | Look |
| --- | --- | --- |
| Climb tree | 50 | 10 |
| Not climb tree | 2 | 49 |

Nor can you calculate whether subjects are more likely to pant hoot after climbing a tree compared to the likelihood of pant hooting after grooming:

|  | Pant hoot | Not pant hoot |
| --- | --- | --- |
| Climb tree | 50 | 100 |
| Groom | 2 | 12 |

As shown earlier, you may only calculate whether subjects are more likely to pant hoot after climbing a tree compared to all other behaviors:

|  | Pant hoot | Not pant hoot |
| --- | --- | --- |
| Climb tree | 50 | 100 |
| Not climb tree | 2 | 500 |

## Markovian Analysis

*JWatcher's* Markovian analysis will produce the following statistics for every analysis, regardless of statistics selected in the menu:

$U_m$ (maximum uncertainty)
$U_0$ (zero-order uncertainty)
$U_1$ (first-order uncertainty)
$U_2$ (second-order uncertainty)

*JWatcher* will also produce the following statistics (when selected) for first- and second-order models:

Observed matrix
Simple probability matrix
Transitional probability matrix

The following example illustrates how *JWatcher* calculates these statistics. See Hailman and Hailman (1993) for more details.

Assume the sequence {A A B A C A B B C B A A B C A B C C B C A B B C A}. Note that this is the same example as shown in the sequence analysis section.

$U_m$ (maximum uncertainty) = $\log_2 k$, where k = number of different kinds of events. In our example, the sequence is composed of three different types of behaviors (A, B, and C); thus, k = 3 and $U_m = \log_2 3 = 1.585$.

$U_0$ (zero-order uncertainty) = $-\Sigma\, p_i \log_2 p_i$ for i = 1 to k, where $p_i$ is the relative probability of each event, which is calculated as Fi/N. Fi is the frequency of occurrence for each event (count), and N is the total number of events in the sequence.

$N = 25$
$F_A = 9, F_B = 9, F_C = 7$
$p_A = 9/25 = 0.36, p_B = 9/25 = 0.36, p_C = 7/25 = 0.28$
$U_0 = -(0.36 \log_2 0.36 + 0.36 \log_2 0.36 + 0.28 \log_2 0.28) = 1.575$

$U_1$ (first-order uncertainty) = $-\Sigma\, p_{ij} \log_2 p_{i|j}$ for i = 1 to k and j = 1 to k, where P(i|j) is the transitional probability of each event, and P(ij) is the simple probability of each event (a.k.a., "joint probability").

The first-order observed matrix reports the frequency (count) with which a behavior immediately follows another behavior (i.e., lag 1 given lag 0). Counts are reported in matrix form for all possible event pairs in the data file sequence.

The first-order observed matrix is:

|       |       | Lag 1 |   |   |       |
|-------|-------|-------|---|---|-------|
|       |       | A     | B | C | Total |
|       | A     | 2     | 5 | 1 | 8     |
| Lag 0 | B     | 2     | 2 | 5 | 9     |
|       | C     | 4     | 2 | 1 | 7     |
|       | Total |       |   |   | 24    |

The first-order simple probability matrix reports the probability that an event pair occurs in the sequence. It is calculated by dividing the observed count for each event pair by the total number of event pairs in the sequence. Probabilities are reported in matrix form for all possible event pairs in the data file sequence. The sum of simple probabilities for all possible event pairs in the matrix is 1.

The first-order simple probability matrix is:

|  |  | Lag 1 | | | |
| --- | --- | --- | --- | --- | --- |
|  |  | A | B | C | Total |
|  | A | 2/24 | 5/24 | 1/24 | 8/24 |
| Lag 0 | B | 2/24 | 2/24 | 5/24 | 9/24 |
|  | C | 4/24 | 2/24 | 1/24 | 7/24 |
|  | Total |  |  |  | 24/24 |

The second-order transitional probability matrix reports the probability, given that one behavior occurs, that another behavior occurs. It is calculated by dividing the observed count for each event pair by the total occurrences of the given event (row total for the given event). Probabilities are reported in matrix form for all possible event pairs in the data file sequence. Each row total sums to one.

The first-order transitional probability matrix is:

|  |  | Lag 1 | | | |
| --- | --- | --- | --- | --- | --- |
|  |  | A | B | C | Total |
|  | A | 2/8 | 5/8 | 1/8 | 1 |
| Lag 0 | B | 2/9 | 2/9 | 5/9 | 1 |
|  | C | 4/7 | 2/7 | 1/7 | 1 |

Using the formula and numbers above for first-order uncertainty, $U_1 = 1.3734$.

$U_2$ (second-order uncertainty) $= -\Sigma\ p_{ij} \log_2 p_{i|j}$ for $i = 1$ to $k$ and $j = 1$ to all possible ordered pair of preceding events.

The second-order observed matrix is:

|  |  | Lag 1 | | | |
| --- | --- | --- | --- | --- | --- |
|  |  | A | B | C | Total |
|  | AA | 0 | 2 | 0 | 2 |
|  | AB | 1 | 2 | 2 | 5 |
|  | AC | 1 | 0 | 0 | 1 |
|  | BA | 1 | 0 | 1 | 2 |
| Lag 0 | BB | 0 | 0 | 2 | 2 |
|  | BC | 3 | 1 | 1 | 5 |
|  | CA | 0 | 3 | 0 | 3 |
|  | CB | 1 | 0 | 1 | 2 |
|  | CC | 0 | 1 | 0 | 1 |
|  | Total |  |  |  | 23 |

The second-order simple probability matrix is:

|  |  | Lag 1 | | | |
| --- | --- | --- | --- | --- | --- |
|  |  | A | B | C | Total |
|  | AA | 0/23 | 2/23 | 0/23 | 2/23 |
|  | AB | 1/23 | 2/23 | 2/23 | 5/23 |
|  | AC | 1/23 | 0/23 | 0/23 | 1/23 |
|  | BA | 1/23 | 0/23 | 1/23 | 2/23 |
| Lag 0 | BB | 0/23 | 0/23 | 2/23 | 2/23 |
|  | BC | 3/23 | 1/23 | 1/23 | 5/23 |
|  | CA | 0/23 | 3/23 | 0/23 | 3/23 |
|  | CB | 1/23 | 0/23 | 1/23 | 2/23 |
|  | CC | 0/23 | 1/23 | 0/23 | 1/23 |
|  | Total |  |  |  | 23/23 |

The second-order transitional probability matrix is:
Using the above formula and values, $U_2 = 0.8028$.

|  |  | Lag 1 | | | |
| --- | --- | --- | --- | --- | --- |
|  |  | A | B | C | Total |
|  | AA | 0/2 | 2/2 | 0/2 | 2/2 |
|  | AB | 1/5 | 2/5 | 2/5 | 5/5 |
|  | AC | 1/1 | 0/1 | 0/1 | 1/1 |
|  | BA | 1/2 | 0/2 | 1/2 | 2/2 |
| Lag 0 | BB | 0/2 | 0/2 | 2/2 | 2/2 |
|  | BC | 3/5 | 1/5 | 1/5 | 5/5 |
|  | CA | 0/3 | 3/3 | 0/3 | 3/3 |
|  | CB | 1/2 | 0/2 | 1/2 | 2/2 |
|  | CC | 0/1 | 1/1 | 0/1 | 1/1 |

## Lag Sequential Analysis

*JWatcher's* "Lag Sequential" routines calculate the following statistics:

    Observed frequency B | A
    Observed frequency A
    Probability B
    Expected frequency B | A
    Standard deviation
    Confidence interval 95%
    *z*-score
    *p*-value

Each of these statistics is calculated for a specified event pair, such that B | A refers to B given A. We use B | A generically to refer to any combination of behaviors where A is the "given" or "lag 0" behavior and B is the "target" behavior. Thus "Observed frequency A" tabulates the observed frequency of your given behavior and "Probability B" calculates the probability of your target behavior.

The following example is intended to illustrate how each of the above statistics is calculated. See Douglass and Tweed (1979) for a description of the rationale behind the calculations.

Assume the sequence {A A B A C A B B C B A A B C A B C C B C A B B C A}. Also assume that we have specified the event pair B | A for analysis.

Note that this example sequence contains repeating codes.

### General Statistics

| Behavior/Modifier | Description | Count | Probability |
|---|---|---|---|
| A | Behavior A | 9 | 9/25 |
| B | Behavior B | 9 | 9/25 |
| C | Behavior C | 7 | 7/25 |

#### OBSERVED FREQUENCY (TARGET|GIVEN)

The "Observed frequency B | A" calculates the number of times (count) that the target behavior precedes or follows the given behavior at each lag. For example, if we are interested in B | A for the range of lags –5 to +5, then the following table would be produced:

| Lag | Observed frequency B|A |
|---|---|
| –5 | 3 |
| –4 | 2 |
| –3 | 3 |
| –2 | 4 |
| –1 | 2 |
| 1 | 5 |
| 2 | 4 |
| 3 | 1 |
| 4 | 4 |
| 5 | 2 |

Thus, for lag –5, B preceded A three times in the sequence. At lag –4, B preceded A two times. At lag +2, B followed A four times, etc. The lag at which B | A occurred with the greatest frequency is lag +1 with a count of five.

#### OBSERVED FREQUENCY (GIVEN)

The "Observed frequency A" calculates the number of times (count) that the given code occurs at each lag. Note that this statistic is used primarily to generate further statistics such as the expected frequency, standard deviation, confidence intervals, and $z$-scores, and therefore it may not be that useful on its own. You may also use it to calculate transition probabilities in your result file. Finally, be aware that Douglass and Tweed (1979) estimate this value as the number of times the given code occurs in the overall sequence, whereas we calculate it exactly as the number of times the given code is available at each lag. In our example, the following table will be produced:

| Lag | Observed frequency A |
|-----|----------------------|
| –5  | 6                    |
| –4  | 6                    |
| –3  | 7                    |
| –2  | 7                    |
| –1  | 8                    |
| 1   | 8                    |
| 2   | 8                    |
| 3   | 8                    |
| 4   | 8                    |
| 5   | 7                    |

Thus, for lag –5, there are six As for which lag –5 tabulations are possible. For lag +1, there are eight As for which lag +1 tabulations are possible. When the overall sequence is long relative to the lag length, these counts should approach the total count of A in the sequence.

### PROBABILITY (TARGET)

The "Probability B" is the probability that the target code will occur relative to the given code at each lag. It is calculated differently depending upon whether behaviors are allowed to repeat or not.

When codes are allowed to repeat, "Probability B" is simply the frequency of occurrence of the target code in the overall sequence. In this case, "Probability B" = 9/25 = 0.36, regardless of lag.

When codes are not allowed to repeat, "Probability B" is calculated as follows:

For lags ± 1, "Probability B" is P(B)/(1 – P(A)), where P(B) is the frequency of occurrence of target behavior B in the overall sequence and P(A) is the frequency of occurrence of given behavior A in the overall sequence. Using values from our above example, "Probability B" = 0.36/(1 – 0.36) = 0.5625.

> **Note:** *We include values from the above example for the purpose of illustrating calculations only. Technically, they should not be used here because they are derived from a sequence with repeating codes.*

For lag ± 2, the transition probabilities for each pair are given by the matrix M2 where M2 = M1 * M1 (using matrix multiplication).

M1 is constructed for each possible pair of behaviors where P(target) = P(target)/(1 – P(given)) when target does not equal given, and P(target) = 0 when target = given.

To find M1:

|  | | Lag 1 | |
|---|---|---|---|
|  | A | B | C |
| Lag 0   A | = 0 | = 0.36/(1 − 0.36) | = 0.28/(1 − 0.36) |
| B | = 0.36/(1 − 0.36) | = 0 | = 0.28/(1 − 0.36) |
| C | = 0.36/(1 − 0.28) | = 0.36/(1 − 0.28) | = 0 |

Multiplying gives values of:

|  | | Lag 1 | |
|---|---|---|---|
|  | A | B | C |
| Lag 0   A | 0 | 0.5625 | 0.4375 |
| B | 0.5625 | 0 | 0.4375 |
| C | 0.5000 | 0.5000 | 0 |

Therefore, M1 =

$$\begin{vmatrix} 0 & 0.5625 & 0.4375 \\ 0.5625 & 0 & 0.4375 \\ 0.5000 & 0.5000 & 0 \end{vmatrix}$$

From this matrix, we can find that P(B | A) = 0.5625 by looking in the first row, second column.

M2 = M1 * M1 =

|  | A | B | C |
|---|---|---|---|
| A | 0.5352 | 0.2188 | 0.2461 |
| B | 0.2188 | 0.5352 | 0.2461 |
| C | 0.2813 | 0.2813 | 0.4375 |

Thus, P(B | A) at lag ± 2 is 0.2188.

Lag ± 3 probabilities are given by the matrix M3, where M3 = M2 * M1.

Therefore, M3 =

|  | A | B | C |
|---|---|---|---|
| A | 0.2461 | 0.4241 | 0.3298 |
| B | 0.4241 | 0.2461 | 0.3298 |
| C | 0.3770 | 0.3770 | 0.2461 |

Thus, P(B | A) at lag ± 3 is 0.4241.

In general, lag ± k probabilities are given by the matrix Mk, where Mk = M(k – 1) * M1.

### EXPECTED FREQUENCY (TARGET|GIVEN)

The "Expected frequency B|A" is based upon the binomial expected mean, and is calculated as "Observed frequency A" * "Probability B."

Thus for lag +1, the "Expected frequency B|A" is 8 * 0.36 = 2.9, when codes are allowed to repeat. When codes are not allowed to repeat, the "Expected frequency B|A" is 8 * 0.5625 = 4.5.

### STANDARD DEVIATION

The standard deviation is calculated based upon the binomial distribution and is calculated as the square root of ["Observed frequency A" * "Probability B" * (1 – "Probability B")].

> **Note:** *This standard deviation is calculated as described in Douglass and Tweed (1979) and Sackett (1979), but not as described in Allison and Liker (1982).*

For lag + 1, the standard deviation is the square root of [8 * 0.36 * (1 – 0.36)] = 1.4, when codes are allowed to repeat. When codes are not allowed to repeat, the standard deviation is the square root of [8 * 0.5625 * (1 – 0.5625)] = 1.97.

### CONFIDENCE INTERVAL

A 95% confidence interval around the expected mean ("Expected frequency B|A") is calculated based upon the normal approximation to the binomial distribution, using the following formulas:

Lower limit for 95% CI = expected mean – 1.96*(standard deviation)

Upper limit for 95% CI = expected mean + 1.96*(standard deviation)

These formulas are only valid when N*P = 5 and N*(1 – P) = 5, where N is "Observed frequency A" and P is "Probability B." A warning will be produced in the log file when the above criteria are not met.

### BINOMIAL *P*-VALUE (ONE-TAILED) AND *Z*-SCORES

For a one-tailed test, a binomial *p*-value is calculated based upon the normal approximation to the binomial distribution using a continuity correction. Thus the *p*-value is the probability of getting either an equal or greater number of successes (if the number of successes is larger than the expected), or an equal or fewer number of successes (if the number of successes is smaller than the expected), given that the sequence is random. In this case, the number of successes is the "Observed frequency B|A" at each lag.

These *p*-values are derived from z-scores, calculated using the following formula:

Case 1: When observed frequency B | A > expected mean, then *z* = [(observed frequency B | A – 1/2) – expected mean]/standard deviation.

Case 2: When observed frequency B | A < expected mean, then *z* = [(observed frequency B | A + 1/2) – expected mean]/standard deviation.

Case 3: When observed frequency B | A = expected mean, then *p* = 0.5000.

These formulas are only valid when: N*P = 5 and N*(1 – P) = 5, where N is "Observed frequency A" and P is "Probability B." A warning will be produced in the log file when the above criteria are not met.

Note that Sackett (1979), Douglass and Tweed (1979), Allison and Liker (1982) and Bakeman and Gottman (1997) do not employ the continuity correction when calculating *z*-scores.

# Strategies for Using *JWatcher*

Let's review some of the preceeding material. To use *JWatcher*, you must first create an overall ethogram for your species in the *.gdf. Then create an *.fmf from a subset of those behaviors. Once you have an *.fmf, you are ready to score behavior. However, observing behavior ultimately requires you to have an explicit idea of what you are aiming to quantify.

For basic analysis, we suggest that you create an *.faf before scoring behavior, as the process will force you to decide whether or not behaviors are mutually exclusive, whether or not you will ultimately want to subtract or ignore behaviors, which behaviors may or may not have modifiers, whether or not you are interested in understanding something about events or states, and whether or not you will be using conditional analyses. The types of analyses that you wish to undertake will ultimately influence the best way to score behavior. Considering these issues before scoring behavior does not prevent you from changing the *.faf at a later time. In fact, we find the ability to "time window" data one of the most useful functions of *JWatcher* and we routinely analyze data with several *.fafs.

For state analyses, it behooves you to think very clearly about the difference in meaning between "natural" and "all" analyses. This decision applies to both duration and interval statistics. Remember that "natural" analyses will report results only for those durations and intervals that begin and end completely within a time bin (that is, they are not truncated). Both durations and intervals will be truncated by the end of the focal, end of a time bin, beginning of a time bin other than the very beginning of the focal (T = 0), and the onset and termination of a key code specified to be out-of-sight. Additionally, intervals will be truncated by the beginning of the focal (T = 0). Because durations are not truncated by the beginning of the focal, if you are interested in natural durations, you should begin scoring at the true onset of the first behavior. Also note that out-of-sight will have an additional consequence for "all" interval statistics (see section 8.5), in that the onset of out-of-sight will terminate (but not truncate) an interval, and will continue to do so for the entire time that out-of-sight remains on.

There are two ways one could conceivably use *JWatcher* to calculate the proportion of time in sight. One way is to "subtract" the behavior that represents out-of-sight by using the subtract function in "Focal Analysis Master > Exclusions" and then examine the proportion of time statistic. The other way is to specify an out-of-sight key in "Focal Analysis Master > State Analysis" and examine the "proportion of time in sight" statistic. However, designating a key as out-of-sight in the "State Analysis" window will have additional consequences beyond simple subtraction if you are interested in natural durations or natural intervals. Specifically, it truncates natural durations and natural intervals, as described above. If a focal subject is truly out of sight, this is a desirable characteristic.

You should also consider whether to score repeated keystrokes for a given behavior. Repeated keystrokes will affect state analysis statistics such as the number of bouts, average bout duration, and standard deviation of bout duration (see section 8.3).

This issue of repeated keystrokes is particularly relevant when you are planning to score simultaneous streams of behaviors for conditional state analysis. For example, if you have two sets of mutually exclusive behaviors, such that rear (r) and stand (s) are mutually exclusive, and look (l) and forage (f) are mutually exclusive, but each set is nonmutually exclusive with the other, then you have several options for scoring:

Option 1:

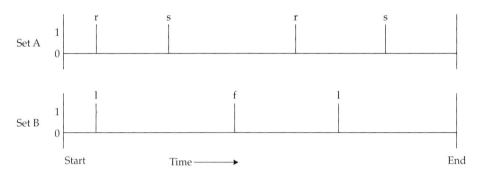

The above represents the sequence of keystrokes as they occur over time. Set A shows the sequence for rear (r) and stand (s), which are mutually exclusive postural changes. Set B shows the sequence for look (l) and forage (f), which are mutually exclusive actions. Behaviors from one set do not turn off behaviors from the other set. With this option, a keystroke is hit when a change occurs within one set of mutually exclusive behaviors, independent of changes that occur in the other set.

Option 2:

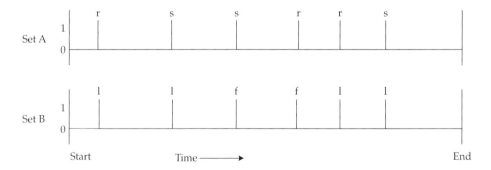

Option 2 represents exactly the same sequence of behaviors as option 1 above. The sequence of keystrokes is shown as they occur over time. With option 2, however, a keystroke is hit for both sets of mutually exclusive behaviors every time a change occurs in either set.

Although option 1 may be more elegant, it may be easier to score option 2 for some people, under some circumstances, or to score a combination of the above. Both options will generate identical values for total time, proportion of time, proportion of time in sight, and conditional proportion of time for all behaviors and also for conditional state combinations (simultaneous occurrence of nonmutually exclusive behaviors). However, count, and hence average bout duration and bout standard deviation, will differ because of the way the program quantifies repeated keystrokes (see section 8.3 for more on repeated keystrokes).

The issue of repeated key codes is also relevant when you are planning to use the "Combinations" routine. For example, if you had scored r (rear look), s (stand look), c (crouch look) to reflect changes in posture while looking, and you now want to convert r, s, and c into one code l (look) with the combinations routine, you will end up with three ls in a row. In other words, the one bout of looking will be described by three repeated keystrokes. Again, this is only an issue for count, average bout duration, and standard deviation of bouts.

When using conditional analyses, you need to pay particular attention to the relationships between behaviors. For example, as explained previously in this manual, for conditional event analysis it is imperative that events and states within an event/state(s) combination be made nonmutually exclusive (see section 8.9). Otherwise, each occurrence of the event will turn off the state(s) of interest, and thus produce potentially unintended results.

It is now possible to score more than one individual per focal using conditional analysis. You would simply define the set of individuals as a mutually exclusive set distinct from your other behaviors of interest. When focusing on individual 1, you would hit 1 (or whatever key code is assigned to this individual), and then score its behavior. When focusing on individual 2, you would hit 2, and then score that individual's behavior. Conditional states analysis could then be used to quantify the behavior for each individual separately. For example, you might quantify time spent foraging, given that individual 1 is included in the focal, or you could quantify time spent foraging and rearing, given that individual 2 is included in the focal. Note that this assumes that you are focusing on one individual at a time.

Multiple users may wish to use different codes to score the same behavior for basic analysis, and then summarize result files reporting full names instead of key codes. However, be aware that conditional states and events are always reported as key codes and that the reliability routine compares key codes only (and not behavior names).

Although not specifically designed to do so, *JWatcher* may also be used for scan-sampling multiple individuals in studies which focus on certain questions. The strategy here would be to specify the set of individuals as behaviors (as opposed to modifiers) in the global definition or focal master file, and to specify their actions as modifiers. For example, you might have individuals 1, 2, and 3, who could engage in foraging (F), looking (L), or walking (W). At each sample time, you would log the individual (behavior) followed by its action (modifier) for every individual in the set. For example, you might log the following:

| Start | Time 1 | Time 2 | Time 3 | EOF |
|-------|--------|--------|--------|-----|
|       | 1F     | 1L     | 1F     |     |
|       | 2F     | 2F     | 2F     |     |
|       | 3L     | 3W     | 3F     |     |

The sequence of key codes in a data file thus would look like this:
Start    1F    2F    3L    1L    2F    3W    1F    2F    3F    EOF

*JWatcher* would then quantify the count (using either state or event analysis) for each of the following:

1—total of all 1

1F

1L

1W

2—total of all 2

2F

2L

2W

3—total of all 3

3F

3L

3W

You would then need to post-process the summarized results file (or single *cd.res file) to create the proportion of observations for each (e.g., count for 1F/count for 1 total).

Sequential analysis assumes that all codes represent a simple sequence (i.e., there are no simultaneously occurring behaviors). Thus, if you intend to conduct both conditional and sequential analyses with one dataset, we advise that you plan your scoring strategy carefully. Depending upon which set of analyses are required, preprocessing (or rescoring) may be necessary to combine simultaneously occurring behaviors into a single behavior code (e.g., standing and looking must be recoded as a single code) for sequential analysis. Note that the combinations routine in its current incarnation will not solve this problem.

Currently, for sequential analysis, there is no way to summarize multiple results files, or to combine multiple data files into one "large" data file for analysis. In principle, it should be possible to combine data files on your own by copying and pasting in a word-processing or spreadsheet program and then adding a break code between files. However, we do not guarantee that this will always work or that you will not encounter unforeseen glitches. See Appendix A for tips on modifying data files using a spreadsheet program.

There are several file management issues relevant to both basic and sequential analyses. When *.dat, *.faf, and *.cmf files are created, the location (i.e., pathway) to the associated *.fmf at the time of creation is recorded. Editing *.dat files, or using *.faf, or *.cmf files for later analysis, requires the *.fmf either to be in the original location (where it was when the above files were created), or in the same folder as the *.dat, *.faf, or *.cmf files. We suggest that you create a directory for each project and not move around the *.fmf, *.faf, or *.cmf files. Data and results files can usually be reorganized as long as the *.fmf stays in its original location.

With respect to files, *JWatcher* will only recognize suffixes of files that are lowercase (e.g., *.dat, *.fmf, *.faf). Sometimes when you copy files from one computer to another, the suffixes become corrupted and are changed to uppercase (e.g., *.DAT, *.FMF, *.FAF). If this happens, you must change the suffixes back to lowercase before using the files with *JWatcher*.

Finally, a tip on scoring behavior: Sometimes transitions between behaviors occur too quickly to be scored accurately. If you are scoring from a videotape and do not wish to use *JWatcher's* video version, you could score behavior viewed at half or quarter speed, and then post-process statistics accordingly. This strategy will always work for sequential analysis because the times associated with key codes are essentially irrelevant. For basic analysis, this strategy will work for some statistics but not others (see Chapter 8 for descriptions of statistics). For example, for state analysis, the count, proportion of time, proportion of time in sight, and conditional proportion of time statistics will not be affected by scoring videos played at different speeds. However, total time and average bout duration will require adjustment. For example, if you score behavior viewed at half speed, you will need to multiply the reported total time by 2 to derive the actual time. The same applies to the average bout duration. Standard deviation of bouts will not easily scale.

# CHAPTER 15

# Learning with *JWatcher*

By now we hope you have a good overview of *JWatcher* and insights into why and how you might use particular routines. We have developed a series of labs that use *JWatcher* to teach students the basics of quantifying behavior and that also provide some experience applying the scientific method. While we use these as group exercises in our classes at UCLA, it is certainly possible to run through them alone.

We maintain a Web site at UCLA (www.jwatcher.ucla.edu) that has the QuickTime videos and other assorted files that accompany each lab. For all labs, you must have QuickTime installed on your computer. Open one or more of the videos in QuickTime while simultaneously running *JWatcher* in another window, or use *JWatcher Video* to simultaneously run both of them within *JWatcher*.

We also provide a pilot analysis of guppy courtship behavior to illustrate the "score once, analyze many times" way that *JWatcher* can be used. Of course, these labs illustrate only a small subset of *JWatcher's* options, but by working through these exercises, you can gain experience using *JWatcher's* routines. We hope that this will help you develop your own focused hypotheses to quantify the behavior that you study.

## 15.1 Observing and Quantifying Behavior

To conduct this lab, first download and use the appropriate *.gdf, *.fmf, and *.faf files and the appropriate QuickTime files. You may also make the *.gdf, *.fmf, and *.faf files on your own. Tips on how to do so are provided at the end of this lab.

Objectives:

1. To understand some of the decisions one must make when constructing an ethogram.
2. To become familiar with the process of quantifying behavioral observations.

Today you will begin to learn about ways to quantify animal behavior. Determining how to quantify behavior is at the essence of testing behavioral hypotheses. An accessible entry into the literature is contained in Paul Martin and Patrick Bateson's excellent book (Martin and Bateson 1993).

Foraging animals must trade-off time allocated to foraging with antipredator (and social) vigilance (Bednekoff and Lima 1998). We have provided a series of two 2-minute video clips of foraging mammals filmed at Rocky Mountain Biological Laboratory (www.rmbl.org), a subalpine field station near Crested Butte, Colorado.

The animals include the following:

1. Squirrel1.mov and squirrel2.mov are golden-mantled ground squirrels (*Spermophilus lateralis*), which are small, asocial, resident ground squirrels. Active during the summer, golden-mantled ground squirrels hibernate throughout the winter. The clips are of two young of the year.
2. Marmot1.mov and marmot2.mov are yellow-bellied marmots (*Marmota flaviventris*), which are mid-sized, social resident ground-dwelling squirrels. Active during the summer, marmots must gain sufficient mass to survive hibernation. The clips are of two young marmots that have been fur-dyed as part of a long term behavioral study. The marmots were recorded in early August, a time when they are actively trying to store fat. Clip one is "blot neck," and clip two is "plus back" (the marmot on the left at the start of the video).
3. Hare1.mov and hare2.mov are snowshoe hares (*Lepus americanus*), which are large, asocial, lagomorphs. Hares are active throughout the year. In the summer their fur blends in with the summer vegetation, while in the winter their pelage turns white—which perfectly matches their snow-covered meadows. Clip one is of an adult hare, while clip two is of a young hare foraging next to a willow thicket.
4. Deer1.mov and deer2.mov are mule deer (*Odocoileus hemionus*). Mule deer are year-round residents of RMBL. We have clips of two females, one with a young (deer1.mov) and one without a young (deer2.mov).
5. Cow1.mov and cow2.mov are domestic cattle (*Bos taurus*) which are grazed, seasonally, in and around the National Forest lands surrounding RMBL. Clips are of a mother (cow1.mov) and her young of the year (cow2.mov).
6. Horse1.mov and horse2.mov are domestic horses (*Equus caballus*), which are also grazed seasonally. Cattlemen use the horses to heard cattle. Clips are of two males foraging in a temporary paddock.

## Developing an Ethogram

An ethogram is a catalog of behaviors. The first thing you must do when quantifying behavior is to come up with a list of behaviors. We are going to develop a "partial ethogram" focusing on foraging and antipredator vigilance. Have a look at one of each of the clips. Focus on the foraging and vigilance behavior. Note that some species can forage while simultaneously looking and some species can look while chewing.

Divide into several groups so that several people are looking at one species. Each group should describe, for a species, the motor patterns used for foraging and for vigilance. An example is:

### HORSE, FORAGING

Subject stands quadrupedally, head down in the vegetation, clipping and ingesting vegetation with its mouth.

Be sure to include the various postures used while acquiring food and looking (i.e., if you see animals looking while chewing, be sure to define a behavior "looking and chewing").

Share your resulting ethogram with the other groups and discuss the specificity of your categories and your definitions.

## Developing a Testable Hypothesis

In order to test behavioral hypotheses, you must have focused questions. Let's consider antipredator vigilance. A number of obvious questions arise when looking at these different video clips. The one we are going to ask today is: *Are there differences among the species in terms of the time allocated to foraging and vigilance?* We are going to test this hypothesis by estimating the time allocated to foraging and vigilance for each of these species. Because we have only two video clips of each species, we will not conduct formal statistical analyses; rather, we will eyeball the differences in mean time allocation and base our conclusion on this comparison.

Assuming there will be differences, discuss what might explain these differences. For instance, species vary in their domestication, body size, and exposure to predators. While RMBL has a variety of predators for small body-sized prey (e.g., coyotes, foxes, weasles, martens, black bears, hawks, and eagles all prey on wild animals at RMBL), larger body-sized animals may be relatively safe from these predators. Wolves are extinct around RMBL, and black bears do not attack deer-sized animals). The video clips include animals of different ages and sexes. How might these influence vigilance? How about group size?

## Quantifying Behavior

For the purpose of this exercise, let's use a simple ethogram that allows us to make comparisons among species.

   f  = head down foraging

   r  = rearing up on two legs while foraging

   l  = standing quadrupedally and looking

   c  = standing quadrupedally and looking while chewing

   u  = standing bipedally and looking while chewing

   w = walking or other locomotion

   x  = other behavior

   o  = out of sight

There are several ways one could estimate the time allocated to foraging and vigilance. We are going to employ a technique called focal animal sampling, whereby we focus on a single subject and note what it is doing. When focusing on a single subject, one can time sample or continuously record behavior. Time sampling involves recording what the subject is doing at predetermined time intervals—say, every 1 second, every 5 seconds, etc. Continuous recording is doing just that, noting every behavioral transition (i.e., from foraging to looking).

There are advantages and disadvantages to each of these recording methods: time sampling necessarily involves missing behavior, but it may be less labor intensive than continuous recording. For animals that engage in behaviors that have relatively long durations, time sampling may be appropriate. In contrast, time sampling animals that quickly change behaviors and engage in a number of different activities over a short period of time may lead to inadequate estimates of time allocation. Of course, the shorter the time interval between samples, the more "continuously" you are recording behavior.

We are going to employ continuous recording to estimate the time allocated to foraging and vigilance in these mammals, and we are going to use an event recorder to help us. Event recorders are computer programs (or dedicated pieces of hardware) that record keystrokes as they occur over time. In our case, keystrokes will represent behavioral transitions. For instance, when the animal is foraging, you will type an "f"; when the animal is looking, you will type "l," etc. Using analysis algorithms included in *JWatcher*, the event recorder, we will then calculate the time allocated to foraging and vigilance.

### Using JWatcher *to Score Behavioral Transitions*

1. Click on the *JWatcher* icon to launch *JWatcher*.
2. In the "Data Capture" tabbed window, name the data file you will be scoring by clicking on the file navigator icon (it looks like a sheet of paper) to the right of the "Focal Data" window. Choose the location where you wish to save your new file. Type in the name of your new file in the "filename" box and click [Open]. Keep the names simple. For instance, name the data file for the first ground-squirrel video clip "squirrel1.dat."
3. Specify a "Focal Master File" (the ethogram, along with additional specifications for recording the focal observation) by clicking on the file navigator icon. In this case, the focal master file is called "lab.fmf."
4. Click the [Next] button at the bottom right to tab into the next page.
5. Answer the two questions by typing the species and the video clip into the boxes below the questions and click the [Next] button to advance.
6. Cue up the video clip. There is a 4-second countdown sequence. When ready, click on the "Start" button. Immediately type the key code representing the behavior the subject is currently engaged in. Whenever the behavior changes, type the key code for the new behavior. Continue for the full 2 minutes (*JWatcher* will automatically time out).

**Note 1:** JWatcher *is case sensitive:* "f" *will* not *be recorded the same way as* "F." *For this exercise, you should* use lowercase letters.

**Note 2:** *If you wish to see a list of the behavioral codes on your computer screen, click the "Behaviors" tab in the upper right corner of the* JWatcher *screen.*

**Note 3:** *If you made a data entry mistake, discard the resulting data file and start again.*

If you are not a good touch typist, you may combine the different types of looking and just type "l," and the different types of foraging and just type "f." If you do this, be sure to also type "x" and "o" (for other behaviors and out-of-sight, respectively).

### Using JWatcher *to Analyze Focal Animal Samples*

1. Once you have scored the video clip or clips, analyze the data by tabbing to the "Analysis" tab.
2. Use the file navigator icon to select the lab.faf—a focal analysis file that specifies the types of analyses we are going to calculate.
3. Use the file navigator tab to select the data file (e.g., squirrel1.dat) to select the data file to analyze.
4. Specify the "Results" folder in the "Observing Behavior" folder as the destination for the results. (Note: this is automatically created—simply verify that you know where it will be placed.)
5. Select "Print results for all behaviors."
6. Click the [Analyze] button at the bottom of the file window to analyze your data.

#### VIEWING THE RESULTS FILES

You will need to use Excel (or another spread-sheet program) to view the results files. There are two results files, *.cd.res, and *.tr.res. The *.cd.res file has the quantitative results, while the *.tr.res has a file that you can open and use to graph the behavioral traces. For today's exercise, let's just open the *.cd.res files.

1. View the *.cd.res file by opening it through Excel. Excel will not automatically recognize *JWatcher* files; you will need to "tell" Excel to "list all file types" or "show all documents." The *.cd.res file is a comma-delimited text file.
2. Once opened, you should see a list of the behavioral codes and several summary statistics for each behavioral code.

   N: Occurrence

   TT: Total time (in milliseconds)

   X: Average time (in milliseconds)

   SD: Standard deviation of the average time (in milliseconds)

   PROP IS: Proportion of time in sight
3. Create a summary results spreadsheet.

### CONSIDER THE FOLLOWING ISSUES

1. Are the species different? How? Why might this be?
2. How would you more formally test the hypothesis that there are differences among the species?
3. What other hypotheses could you test using these data?
4. We did not talk about errors, or the reliability of observers, but these issues are essential for those scoring behavior. There are two types of reliability that are very important here. Inter-observer reliability measures how different observers code the same behavior. Intra-observer reliability measures how the same observer codes the same behavior on multiple occasions. Consider these types of reliability and suggest ways to quantify them. Recall that *JWatcher* has built-in routines to help you do this.

### HOW TO MAKE YOUR OWN GLOBAL DEFINITION FILE, "LAB.GDF"

Open the global definition tab, and click [Add row].

Define the following key codes:

**Enter your ethogram and the key codes below.**

**Define behaviors with a single character:**

| Key Code | Behavior | Description |
|---|---|---|
| c | look chew | standing quadrupe... |
| f | forage | head down; foraging |
| l | stand look | standing quadrupe... |
| o | out of sight | subject is out of sight |
| r | rear up and forage | rearing up bipedall... |
| u | rear up and chew | standing bipedally ... |
| w | locomotion | walking or other lo... |
| x | other | any other behaviors |

Full entries for descriptions are:

| Description |
|---|
| standing quadrupedally and looking while chewing |
| head down; foraging |
| standing quadrupedally and looking |
| subject is out of sight |
| rearing up bipedally while foraging |
| standing bipedally and looking while chewing |
| walking or other locomotion |
| any other behaviors |

Save your file as "lab.gdf."

**HOW TO MAKE YOUR OWN FOCAL MASTER FILE, "LAB.FMF"**

Open the focal master file tab, and click [New].

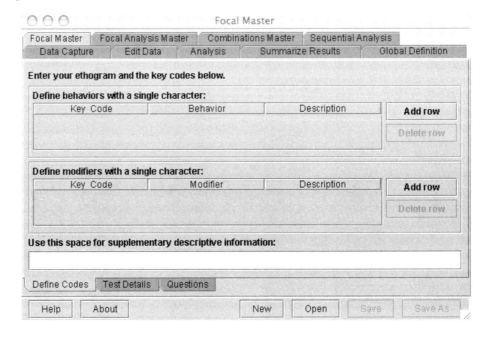

Select "lab.gdf" to load your behaviors:

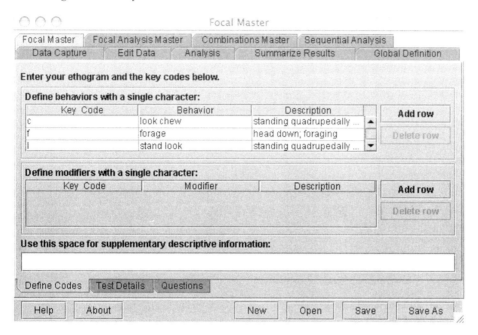

In the "Test Details" window, specify the duration of the focal to be 2 minutes, and have the clock count down:

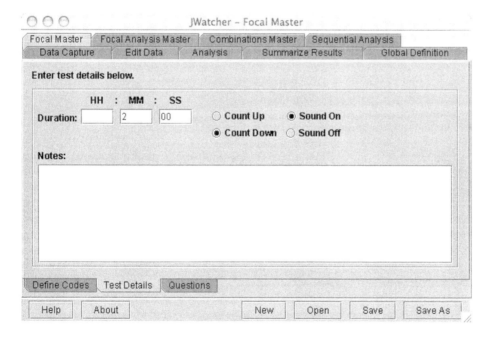

In the "Questions" window, enter "Species" for question 1 and "Video clip" for question 2:

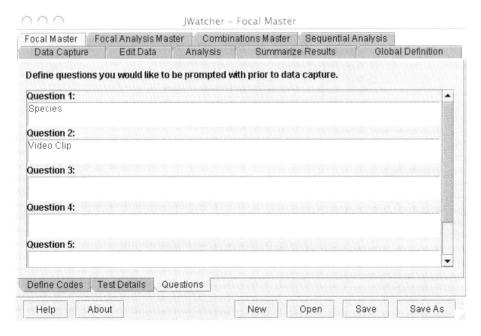

Save the file as "lab.fmf."

### HOW TO MAKE YOUR OWN FOCAL ANALYSIS MASTER FILE, "LAB.FAF"

Open the "Focal Analysis Master" tab, click [New], and select "lab.fmf":

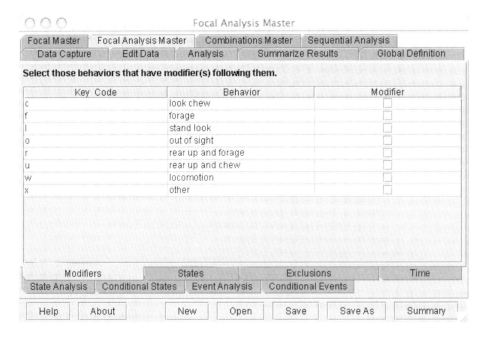

Click on the "State Analysis" window, specify "o" to be the key code representing out-of-sight from the pull-down menu, and select the following statistics in the "All Duration" column:

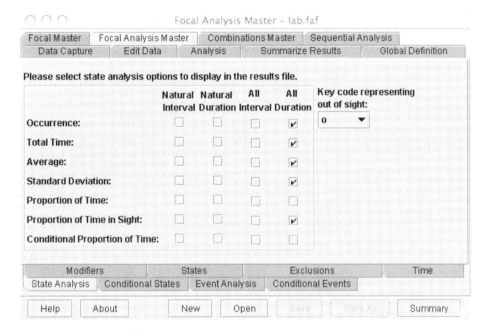

Save your file as "lab.faf."

## 15.2 Comparing Two Recording Techniques

To conduct this exercise, be sure that you have QuickTime loaded. Download the videos from the *JWatcher* Web site (www.jwatcher.ucla.edu) and either open them in a separate window or open them within *JWatcher Video*. You will also need to download flamingo.fmf and flamingo.faf from the Web site or create them on your own. Tips to create these *.fmf and *.faf files are provided at the end of this lab.

The objective of this exercise is to contrast two recording methods. Specifically, we will compare time sampling and continuous recording of focal subjects. You will also learn a few methods to test your inter-observer reliability.

We will use several clips of flamingos videotaped at the Los Angeles Zoo as an example of how to calculate time budgets for animals. Time budgets describe how animals allocate their time to different behaviors. This calculation can be used to show how an animal's behavior varies with changing circumstances, such as predation risk, group size, etc.

Because flamingos generally live in groups, we could potentially estimate their time budgets using either scan sampling (rapidly scanning a group of subjects) or focal sampling (focusing on one subject at a time).

Spend a few minutes looking at one of the flamingo clips. For example, open the file called "Flamingo_group.mov." What are the advantages and disadvantages of using scan sampling compared to focal sampling for calculating time budgets of these flamingos? For calculating time budgets in general?

For the purpose of this exercise, we will use focal samples. You will score behavior from three different individuals, each tracked separately. Each focal sample is approximately 2 minutes in duration.

### Time Sampling

First, we will begin by time sampling (sampling periodically). We will sample the behavior of an individual every 10 seconds. After scoring all three clips, you will calculate your intra-observer reliability or, if you are doing this with a partner, your inter-observer reliability (consistency or repeatability).

In general, time sampling is an efficient and often easy way of collecting data in the field that does not necessarily require any "high-tech" equipment. Pencil, paper, and a simple timing device are all you need, although more fancy event recorders (see below) may also be used.

### VIEWING THE ETHOGRAM

1. Open the video called "Ethogram_NoComp.mov."
2. Click the [Play] button to see a partial ethogram of flamingo behavior.

An ethogram is a catalog of behaviors. The specific ethogram used in a study will depend upon the question asked and on how accurately, and with what specificity, a particular behavior can be scored. Familiarize yourself with the behaviors shown in this ethogram by watching the video a few times.

Note that this ethogram has been chosen arbitrarily. What potential problems do you foresee?

### COLLECTING DATA

Now look at the data sheet ("Time Sampling Check Sheet") on page 168. You will see the same behaviors listed across the top of the page. You will also see a series of rows. Each row will correspond to a tone that you will hear every 10 seconds when viewing the subsequent three focal clips. You should make one check mark per row, in the column corresponding to the behavior that you observe at the tone. Score each video clip only once.

1. Open the QuickTime Player file called "FlamingoA_NoComp.mov" or open it through *JWatcher Video*. Cue up the video clip. There is a 5-second delay before the video begins. Click the [Play] button to view the focal clip. The individual to follow is labeled with an arrow. Record the behavior that you observe at each tone in your data sheet.
2. Repeat with QuickTime Player files called "FlamingoB_NoComp.mov" and "FlamingoC_NoComp.mov."

### CALCULATING OBSERVER RELIABILITY

Once you have completed scoring all three clips, add up the number of times you observed each behavior and enter the totals in the second-to-last row of your data sheet. To study intra-observer reliability, score them again and compare your results. To score inter-observer reliability, compare the results to those that someone else has scored.

Which behaviors were consistently scored? Which were not? Can you explain the inconsistencies? How might you improve your reliability in the future?

Although eyeballing totals is one way to get a feel for your consistency, there are more formal ways of calculating reliability. We will use a simple worksheet to calculate two measures: "r" and "O."

"r" is the correlation coefficient calculated between your observed totals for each behavior and your partner's corresponding totals. A value close to 1.0 means that you were reliable.

"O" is the index of concordance, which is simply the proportion of observations on which you both agreed (scored the same behavior at the same tone). It is calculated by counting the total number of agreements and then dividing by the total number of observations.

Another measure is "K," the kappa coefficient (K), which is basically an index of concordance that has been modified to take into account the number of agreements that you would get due to chance alone. We will not calculate it for time sampling but will revisit kappa later for continuous recording.

1. Use the time sampling reliability worksheet. A filled-in example has been given to you at the back of this exercise (page 170). Enter one set of observations into the "Observer 1's behaviors" column, and the other set of observations into the "Observer 2's behaviors" column. Notice that you should enter the number that corresponds to each behavior (see top row of your check sheet) rather than letters. Whenever both agree for a given line (have the same entry), enter "1" into the "agree" column. Sum your agreements and divide by the total number of entries to calculate "O."
2. In the second part of the time sampling reliability worksheet, enter the total number of times you observed each behavior (see your time sampling check sheet) in each of the two observation files. To calculate "r," you must enter these values into Excel and use the correlation function. The formula is shown in the filled-in example on page 170.

### HOW RELIABLE WAS YOUR SCORING?

"r" and "O" tell you slightly different things. When might it be important to check "O" rather than just "r"?

### CALCULATING THE TIME BUDGET

Finally, in your check sheet, calculate the proportion of time engaged in each behavior by dividing each column total by the total number of observations. This is your time budget.

Do you think that a 10-second time interval enabled us to adequately describe the time budget of these flamingos? Why or why not? In general, what criteria should you use to choose an appropriate time interval?

## Continuous Recording

Now we will go back and score the same three video clips using continuous recording.

Continuous recording (all-occurrence recording to provide a complete record of all behaviors) is more labor intensive, but it will give you a more complete description than time sampling of what occurred during any given time interval.

### CONTINUOUS RECORDING WITH *JWATCHER*

We will use the same ethogram that we just used for time sampling in the previous section. The following key codes will represent behaviors:

| Behavior | Key code |
| --- | --- |
| Aggression | a |
| Forage | f |
| Groom | g |
| Head swing | h |
| Stand look | l |
| Sleep | s |
| Walk | w |
| Wing spread | d |
| Other | x |
| Out-of-sight | o |

1. Click the *JWatcher* icon to launch *JWatcher*.
2. When *JWatcher* first opens, you will be in the "Data Capture" tabbed window.
3. In this window, name the data file you will be scoring by clicking on the file navigator icon (it looks like a sheet of paper) to the right of the "Focal Data" box. Choose the location where you wish to save your new file. Type in the name of your new file in the "File Name" box and click [Open]. Keep the names simple. For instance, name the data files "clipA-1," "clipA-2," "clipB," and "clipC." Note that you will score the first video clip A twice to check your intra-observer reliability.
4. Specify your "Focal Master File" (flamingo.fmf) by clicking on the file navigator icon. This file contains the ethogram along with additional specifications such as the duration for recording the focal observation.
5. Click the [Next] button at the bottom right to tab into the next page.
6. Answer the top question by typing the letter of the video clip into the box below the question and click the [Next] button to advance.
7. Open and cue up the first video clip. Start by scoring A twice, and then score B, followed by C. There is a 5-second delay before each video clip begins. When ready, click on the [Start] button in the "Capture Data" page of *JWatcher*. Immediately type the key code representing the behavior the subject is currently engaged in. Whenever the behavior changes, type the key code for the new behavior. Continue for the 2 full minutes (*JWatcher* will automatically time out).

**Note 1:** *If you wish to see a list of the behavioral codes on your computer screen, click the "Behaviors" tab in the upper right corner of the* JWatcher *screen.*

**Note 2:** *If you made a data entry mistake, stop scoring behavior, discard the resulting data file, and start again.*

### CALCULATING INTRA-OBSERVER RELIABILITY

You will now compare your two files for video clip A using *JWatcher's* reliability routine.

1. Click the "Analysis" tab in the upper menu.
2. In the lower left corner, click on the "Reliability" tab.
3. For the "First Data File," specify clip A-1. For the "Second Data File," specify clip A-2.
4. Name your reliability result file in the "Reliability File Name" box.
5. The result file will automatically be saved to the location shown in the "Reliability File Folder." Make sure you note where it will be saved.
6. Click on the [Calculate Reliability] button to generate the result file.
7. You will need to use Excel (or another spreadsheet program) to view the result file. Open your file through Excel. Excel will not automatically recognize *JWatcher* files; you will need to "tell" Excel to "list all file types" or "show all documents." This result file is a comma-delimited text file.

*JWatcher* reports the overall percent agreement ("O"), overall kappa coefficient ("K"), and the percent agreement for each behavior separately. See the example reliability result file at the end of the exercise.

## USING *JWATCHER* TO ANALYZE FOCAL ANIMAL SAMPLES

Once you have scored all three video clips, you are now ready to use *JWatcher*'s analysis algorithms to calculate time budgets.

1. Click the "Data" tab on the lower left of the "Analysis" window.
2. Use the file navigator icon to select the focal analysis master file (flamingo.faf). The focal analysis file specifies the types of analyses we are going to calculate.
3. Use the file navigator tab to select the data file (e.g., clipB.dat) to select the data file to analyze.
4. Specify the "Results" folder in the appropriate location as the destination for the results. (Note: this is automatically created—simply verify that you know where it will be placed.)
5. Select "Print results for all behaviors."
6. Click the [Analyze] button at the bottom of the file window to analyze your data.

## VIEWING THE RESULTS FILES

You will need to use Excel (or another spread-sheet program) to view the results files. There are two results files, *.cd.res and *.tr.res. The *.cd.res file has the quantitative results, while the *.tr.res has a file that you can open and use to graph the "behavioral traces." For today's exercise, let's just open the *.cd.res files.

1. View the *.cd.res file by opening it through Excel. Excel will not automatically recognize *JWatcher* files; you will need to "tell" Excel to "list all file types" or "show all documents." The *.cd.res file is a comma-delimited text file.
2. Once the file is opened, you should see a list of the behavioral codes and several summary statistics for each behavioral code.

| N | Occurrence |
|---|---|
| PROP IS | Proportion of time in sight |

If your animal never went out-of-sight, then "proportion of time" and "proportion of time in sight" should be the same. The "proportion of time in sight" for your behaviors is your time budget.

Fill out the data sheet for your continuous recording results (on page 172).

## COMPARING CONTINUOUS RECORDING VERSUS TIME SAMPLING

Compare your results for time sampling versus continuous sampling. Did continuous recording give you a better estimate of flamingo time budgets than time sampling? If you were to collect more data, which recording rule would you use in the future? Why?

**Time Sampling Check Sheet**

| Tone | 1 Aggress | 2 Forage | 3 Groom | 4 Head swing | 5 Stand look | 6 Sleep | 7 Walk | 8 Wing spread | 9 Other | 10 Out sight |
|---|---|---|---|---|---|---|---|---|---|---|
| A.1 | | | | | | | | | | |
| A.2 | | | | | | | | | | |
| A.3 | | | | | | | | | | |
| A.4 | | | | | | | | | | |
| A.5 | | | | | | | | | | |
| A.6 | | | | | | | | | | |
| A.7 | | | | | | | | | | |
| A.8 | | | | | | | | | | |
| A.9 | | | | | | | | | | |
| A.10 | | | | | | | | | | |
| A.11 | | | | | | | | | | |
| A.12 | | | | | | | | | | |
| A.13 | | | | | | | | | | |
| B.1 | | | | | | | | | | |
| B.2 | | | | | | | | | | |
| B.3 | | | | | | | | | | |
| B.4 | | | | | | | | | | |
| B.5 | | | | | | | | | | |
| B.6 | | | | | | | | | | |
| B.7 | | | | | | | | | | |
| B.8 | | | | | | | | | | |
| B.9 | | | | | | | | | | |
| B.10 | | | | | | | | | | |
| B.11 | | | | | | | | | | |
| B.12 | | | | | | | | | | |
| B.13 | | | | | | | | | | |
| C.1 | | | | | | | | | | |
| C.2 | | | | | | | | | | |
| C.3 | | | | | | | | | | |
| C.4 | | | | | | | | | | |
| C.5 | | | | | | | | | | |
| C.6 | | | | | | | | | | |
| C.7 | | | | | | | | | | |
| C.8 | | | | | | | | | | |
| C.9 | | | | | | | | | | |
| C.10 | | | | | | | | | | |
| C.11 | | | | | | | | | | |
| C.12 | | | | | | | | | | |
| C.13 | | | | | | | | | | |
| Total | | | | | | | | | | |
| Percent | | | | | | | | | | |

**Time Sampling Reliability Worksheet**

| Tone | Observer 1's behavior | Observer 2's behavior | Agree |
|---|---|---|---|
| A.1 | | | |
| A.2 | | | |
| A.3 | | | |
| A.4 | | | |
| A.5 | | | |
| A.6 | | | |
| A.7 | | | |
| A.8 | | | |
| A.9 | | | |
| A.10 | | | |
| A.11 | | | |
| A.12 | | | |
| A.13 | | | |
| B.1 | | | |
| B.2 | | | |
| B.3 | | | |
| B.4 | | | |
| B.5 | | | |
| B.6 | | | |
| B.7 | | | |
| B.8 | | | |
| B.9 | | | |
| B.10 | | | |
| B.11 | | | |
| B.12 | | | |
| B.13 | | | |
| C.1 | | | |
| C.2 | | | |
| C.3 | | | |
| C.4 | | | |
| C.5 | | | |
| C.6 | | | |
| C.7 | | | |
| C.8 | | | |
| C.9 | | | |
| C.10 | | | |
| C.11 | | | |
| C.12 | | | |
| C.13 | | | |

| Behaviors | Observer 1's total | Observer 2's total |
|---|---|---|
| Aggression | | |
| Forage | | |
| Groom | | |
| Head swing | | |
| Stand look | | |
| Sleep | | |
| Walk | | |
| Wing spread | | |
| Other | | |
| Out of sight | | |

| | |
|---|---|
| Total agree | |
| Total entries | |
| "O" | |
| "r" | |

## Time Sampling Reliability Worksheet—WORKED EXAMPLE

| Tone | Observer 1's behavior | Observer 2's behavior | Agree |
|------|------|------|------|
| A.1 | 6 | 9 | 0 |
| A.2 | 6 | 6 | 1 |
| A.3 | 6 | 6 | 1 |
| A.4 | 5 | 5 | 1 |
| A.5 | 5 | 5 | 1 |
| A.6 | 5 | 5 | 1 |
| A.7 | 3 | 3 | 1 |
| A.8 | 3 | 3 | 1 |
| A.9 | 3 | 3 | 1 |
| A.10 | 5 | 5 | 1 |
| A.11 | 5 | 5 | 1 |
| A.12 | 5 | 5 | 1 |
| A.13 | 3 | 3 | 1 |
| B.1 | 2 | 2 | 1 |
| B.2 | 3 | 3 | 1 |
| B.3 | 3 | 3 | 1 |
| B.4 | 5 | 5 | 1 |
| B.5 | 3 | 3 | 1 |
| B.6 | 3 | 3 | 1 |
| B.7 | 7 | 7 | 1 |
| B.8 | 5 | 5 | 1 |
| B.9 | 5 | 5 | 1 |
| B.10 | 4 | 5 | 0 |
| B.11 | 4 | 5 | 0 |
| B.12 | 4 | 5 | 0 |
| B.13 | 4 | 5 | 0 |
| C.1 | 7 | 7 | 1 |
| C.2 | 2 | 2 | 1 |
| C.3 | 9 | 9 | 1 |
| C.4 | 5 | 5 | 1 |
| C.5 | 5 | 5 | 1 |
| C.6 | 8 | 8 | 1 |
| C.7 | 7 | 7 | 1 |
| C.8 | 5 | 5 | 1 |
| C.9 | 4 | 4 | 1 |
| C.10 | 8 | 8 | 1 |
| C.11 | 4 | 4 | 1 |
| C.12 | 4 | 4 | 1 |
| C.13 | 4 | 4 | 1 |

| Behaviors | Observer 1's total | Observer 2's total |
|------|------|------|
| Aggression | 0 | 0 |
| Forage | 2 | 2 |
| Groom | 8 | 8 |
| Head swing | 8 | 4 |
| Stand look | 12 | 16 |
| Sleep | 3 | 2 |
| Walk | 3 | 3 |
| Wing spread | 2 | 2 |
| Other | 1 | 2 |
| Out of sight | 0 | 0 |

To calculate "r," you need to correlate observer 1's totals with observer 2's totals. In Excel, use the CORREL (array 1, array 2) function, such that array 1 is the list of Observer 1's totals (0, 2, 8, 8, 12, 3, 3, 2, 1, 0), and array 2 is the list of Observer 2's totals (0, 2, 8, 4, 16, 2, 3, 2, 2, 0). In the formula below, B2:B11 refers to array 1, and C2:C11 refers to array 2.

| | |
|------|------|
| Total agree | 34 |
| Total entries | 39 |
| "O" | = 34/39 = 0.872 |
| "r" | = CORREL(B2:B11, C2:C11) = 0.918 |

**EXAMPLE RELIABILITY RESULT FILE**

Total key code entries:

| | |
|---|---|
| obs1.dat | 39 |
| obs2.dat | 39 |

This reliability file compares two data files, obs1.dat and obs2.dat. There are 39 entries in each file.

#CONFUSION MATRIX

| Key codes | d | f | g | h | l | s | w | x | Total obs1.dat |
|---|---|---|---|---|---|---|---|---|---|
| d | 2 | 0 | 0 | 0 | 0 | 0 | 0 | 0 | 2 |
| f | 0 | 2 | 0 | 0 | 0 | 0 | 0 | 0 | 2 |
| g | 0 | 0 | 8 | 0 | 0 | 0 | 0 | 0 | 8 |
| h | 0 | 0 | 0 | 4 | **4** | 0 | 0 | 0 | 8 |
| l | 0 | 0 | 0 | 0 | 12 | 0 | 0 | 0 | 12 |
| s | 0 | 0 | 0 | 0 | 0 | 2 | 0 | **1** | 3 |
| w | 0 | 0 | 0 | 0 | 0 | 0 | 3 | 0 | 3 |
| x | 0 | 0 | 0 | 0 | 0 | 0 | 0 | 1 | 1 |
| Total obs2.dat | 2 | 2 | 8 | 4 | 16 | 2 | 3 | 2 | 39 |

The confusion matrix shows which key codes co-occurred in the sequence. The number of agreements are shown along the diagonal. Disagreements are highlighted in bold. There were four times when the code "h" occurred in obs1.dat but the code "l" occurred in obs2.dat, and there was one time that "s" occurred in obs1.dat but "x" occurred in the other file.

#STATISTICS

| Key codes | obs1.dat | obs2.dat | Both agree | YN | NY | Disagree | % agreement | Kappa |
|---|---|---|---|---|---|---|---|---|
| d | 2 | 2 | 2 | 0 | 0 | 0 | 100 | |
| f | 2 | 2 | 2 | 0 | 0 | 0 | 100 | |
| g | 8 | 8 | 8 | 0 | 0 | 0 | 100 | |
| h | 8 | 4 | 4 | 4 | 0 | 4 | 50 | |
| l | 12 | 16 | 12 | 0 | 4 | 4 | 75 | |
| s | 3 | 2 | 2 | 1 | 0 | 1 | 66.67 | |
| w | 3 | 3 | 3 | 0 | 0 | 0 | 100 | |
| x | 1 | 2 | 1 | 0 | 1 | 1 | 50 | |
| Total | 39 | 39 | 34 | 5 | 5 | 10 | **87.18** | 0.8386 |

The statistics section gives the overall percent agreement as a percent (in bold, 87.18%), and the overall kappa coefficient as a proportion (0.8386). The percent agreement for each behavior is also given separately. The codes "h," "l," "s," and "x" did not have perfect agreement between the two files.

## Continuous Recording Data Sheet

| | Key code | a | f | g | h | l | s | w | d | x | o |
|---|---|---|---|---|---|---|---|---|---|---|---|
| | | Aggress | Forage | Groom | Head swing | Stand look | Sleep | Walk | Wing spread | Other | Out sight |
| N | A | | | | | | | | | | |
| | B | | | | | | | | | | |
| | C | | | | | | | | | | |
| | Total | | | | | | | | | | |

| | | | | | | | | | | | |
|---|---|---|---|---|---|---|---|---|---|---|---|
| PropIS | A | | | | | | | | | | |
| | B | | | | | | | | | | |
| | C | | | | | | | | | | |
| | Average | | | | | | | | | | |

### HOW TO MAKE YOUR OWN FOCAL MASTER FILE, "FLAMINGO.FMF"

Open the focal master file tab, and click [Add row].

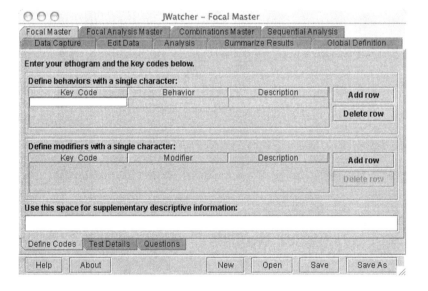

Define the following key codes:

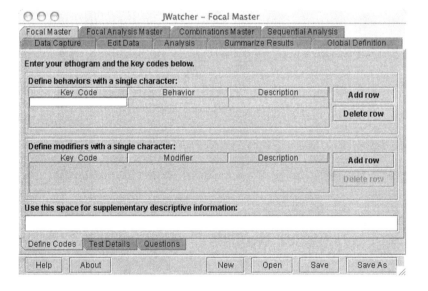

In the "Test Details" window, specify the duration of the focal to be 2 minutes, and have the clock count down:

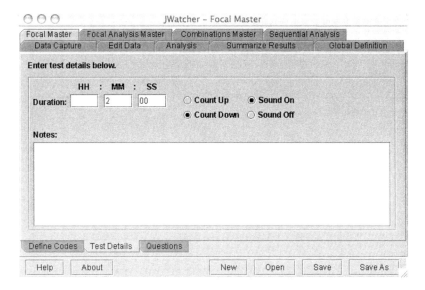

In the "Questions" window, enter "Video clip" for question 1:

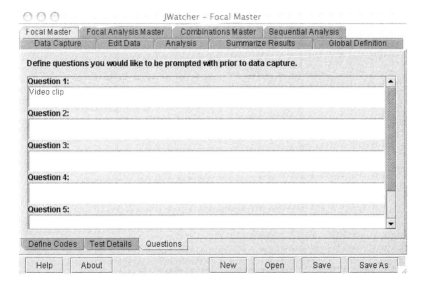

Save the file as "flamingo.fmf."

**HOW TO MAKE YOUR OWN FOCAL ANALYSIS MASTER FILE, "FLAMINGO.FAF"**

Open the "Focal Analysis Master" tab, click [New], and select "flamingo.fmf":

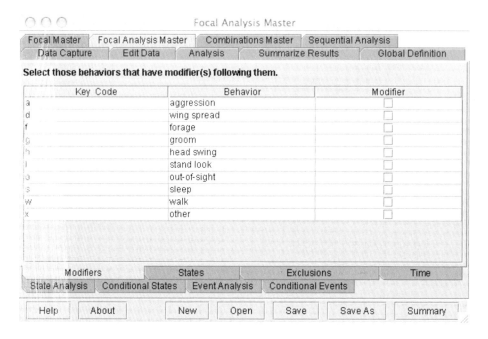

Click on the "State Analysis" window, specify "o" to be the out-of-sight key from the pull-down menu, and select "Occurrence" and "Proportion of Time in Sight" in the "All Duration" column:

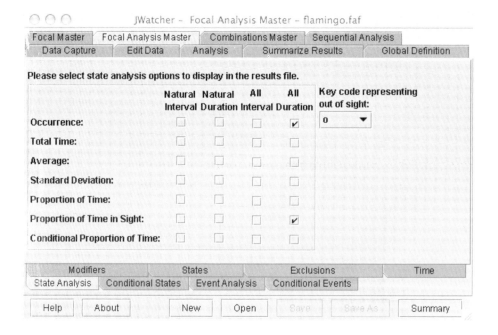

Save your file as "flamingo.faf."

## 15.3 Observing and Quantifying Behavioral Sequences

This exercise was developed in collaboration with Barbara Clucas, and we thank her for the excellent videos.

To conduct this exercise, be sure that you have QuickTime loaded. Download the videos from the *JWatcher* Web site (www.jwatcher.ucla.edu) and open them with QuickTime. This exercise is not designed for *JWatcher Video*. You will also need to download SSA.fmf from the Web site or create it on your own.

When watching an animal, you might observe some actions that appear to occur in a "stereotyped" sequence. Your dog may always circle three to four times before settling down, or your cat may frequently groom itself in the same way, first licking its front legs and then moving to its tail. Animal behavior researchers have historically been very interested in these stereotyped actions because they often represent a "species-specific behavior" (that is, the same sequence of behavioral actions are reliably found in most individuals of a species and are slightly to completely different from those of other species). Konrad Lorenz (one of the founders of Ethology) believed these stereo-typed behavioral patterns were similar to morphological traits and could be used to help understand the evolution of behavior. In his famous 1941 paper, "Comparative studies of the motor patterns of Anatinae," Lorenz described stereotyped display patterns of 20 birds using 48 characters (e.g., "body-shaking") and used the similarities and differences of these behavioral actions to construct a "phylogeny" (a hypothesis about evolutionary relationships) of these species. Methods used to describe behavioral patterns have greatly advanced since Lorenz's time and we now have techniques that allow for a more sophisticated analysis of behavior, such as "sequential analyses."

In this lab exercise, you will learn about techniques of observing, scoring, and quantifying behavioral patterns. You will watch videos of a behavioral sequence exhibited by two species of ground squirrels (genus: *Spermophilus*) and determine the transition probabilities of the behaviors involved in the sequence (a transition probability is the probability that one behavior will follow another behavior). The transition probabilities will help you decide whether these species exhibit stereotyped behavior patterns, and they will allow you to compare the pattern between species.

### An Introduction to "Snake Scent Application" in Ground Squirrels

Rattlesnakes have been a major predator of ground squirrels for millions of years and this coexistence has led to the evolution of several unique antipredator strategies in ground squirrels. For instance, in some species of ground squirrels adults are resistant to rattlesnake venom and will actively harass and attack these predators. Here you will observe another rattlesnake-related behavior. Some species of ground squirrels exhibit a very peculiar behavior when they encounter anything that is saturated in snake scent. For example, California ground squirrels and rock squirrels will chew on shed snakeskin and apply it to their fur by licking their bodies. This behavior, called "snake scent application" (SSA), is also found in other rodents (e.g., chipmunks and mice). Rodents are a major prey source for snakes. Why do you think rodents apply their predator's scent?

Researchers have proposed several hypotheses for the function of SSA in ground squirrels: an antipredator function, an antiparasite function, and/or a social alarm cue function. These researchers are currently testing the alternative hypotheses experimentally. However, before testing the function of a behavior, they needed to have a good description of the behavior.

In order to describe the behavior systematically, the researchers quantified SSA across a certain number of individuals in both California ground squirrels and rock squirrel species. By quantifying the application behavior, they could determine if ground squirrels apply snake scent following a stereotyped pattern. In the future, this information can be used to make comparisons across multiple ground squirrel species, similar to Lorenz's work with the display pattern in birds.

You will watch videos of SSA behavior from two species of ground squirrel: California ground squirrels (*S. beecheyi*) and rock squirrels (*S. variegatus*). To obtain the videos, a researcher staked out a shed skin of a sympatric rattlesnake species (*Crotalus atrox* for rock squirrels, and *C. viridis oreganus* for California ground squirrels) and surrounded it with a minimal bait trail (sunflower seeds) to attract the squirrels to the skin. The squirrels were marked with numbers (fur dye) to identify individuals. Each video represents a different individual. The study sites were in Winters, California (California ground squirrels), and Caballo, New Mexico (rock squirrels), in county or state parks where squirrels are used to cars. The squirrels were videotaped from a car, approximately 20–30 m away.

1. Open up the QuickTime Player file called "SSA_Sp1." This video shows a California ground squirrel engaged in SSA.
2. Click on the [Play] button to see SSA behavior. Note that after chewing the shed snakeskin, the ground squirrel applies the snake scent to several sections of its body.

You may wish to play videos at half speed to more easily view behaviors. To play videos at half speed in QuickTime, select "Window" from the main menu, then "Show A/V Controls."

**Note:** *As designed, this exercise cannot be conducted using* JWatcher Video.

### PART 1—COLLECTING DATA

**Observing the behavior**  You will be scoring SSA behavior using *JWatcher*. The ethogram for this exercise will be composed of the body sections to which ground squirrels apply snake scent after chewing shed snakeskins.

1. Familiarize yourself with the names of the different parts of the ground squirrel body by looking at the figure below.

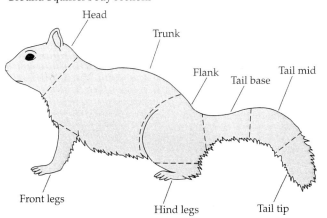

Ground Squirrel body sections

2. Watch the video "SSA_Sp1" again. In the table on the left below, under "Body Sections," write down the body sections to which the squirrel applies the snake scent.

| Behavior | | | Sequence of application |
|---|---|---|---|
| | Chew | | 1. Chew |
| | Body sections | | 2. |
| Apply to | e.g., flank | | 3. |
| | | | 4. |
| | | | 5. |
| | | | 6. |
| | | | 7. |
| | | | 8. |
| | | | 9. |
| | | | 10. |

3. Next you will write down the sequence of the application behavior in the table above on the right (next to the numbers); starting with "chew" (written for you), write down the body sections to which the ground squirrel applies the scent. In other words, score a behavior every time the ground squirrel switches from applying scent to one body section to applying it to the next. For example, "chew – flank – hind leg – flank – tail base," etc.

To which section of its body did the ground squirrel apply the snake scent first? Second? Third?

**Checking your reliability**   Checking your reliability is a crucial part of any study. You need to ensure that you can consistently score the behaviors defined in the ethogram from one time to the next (intra-observer reliability) and that multiple people scoring behavior in a study are all scoring the same behavior (inter-observer reliability).

For this exercise, you will be using a predefined ethogram that links each behavior with a single key code. The key codes and behaviors that they represent are shown in the table below.

| | Behavior | Key code |
|---|---|---|
| Start with | Chew | c |
| Apply to | Head | d |
| | Front legs | f |
| | Hind legs | h |
| | Flank | k |
| | Tail base | b |
| | Tail mid | m |
| | Tail tip | t |
| | Trunk | u |
| End with | Break (also use when uncertain) | x |

Note that one of the behaviors represents a "break code." You will be scoring multiple videos consecutively. You will score "break" between different video clips. You should also score "break" when you cannot tell what behavior is taking place.

Since we are interested in the sequence of anointment behaviors, we will not score other behaviors such as "look," "run away," "groom," "tail flip," etc. However, do score "chew" whenever you see a squirrel chewing a piece of snakeskin to acquire more scent.

1. Open up the QuickTime Player file called "SSA_Sp2." This file contains video of a rock squirrel engaged in SSA. Watch the video once without scoring anything.
2. Play the video again and score the application sequence using your key codes under "Application Sequence (Your 1st try)."

Then, replay the video and score it again under "Application Sequence (Your 2nd try)." Compare your results with those of your partner.

Note that you may wish to play the video at half speed, to pause, or to use the scroll bar to examine behaviors more closely.

| Your 1st try | Your 2nd try | Partner's 1st try | Partner's 2nd try |
|---|---|---|---|
| Application sequence | Application sequence | Application sequence | Application sequence |
| | | | |
| | | | |
| | | | |
| | | | |
| | | | |
| | | | |
| | | | |
| | | | |
| | | | |
| | | | |
| | | | |
| | | | |
| | | | |

Was your own scoring consistent (repeatable)? Were there any differences between yours and your partner's? Which body segments were most difficult to score reliably?

Think about the ethogram. What problems did you encounter? How will you handle these problems?

**Thought exercise** If two people are scoring these videos, should one individual score species A and the other individual score species B? Why or why not?

**Scoring behavior** First you will need to score behavioral sequences using the ethogram defined above by hitting the appropriate key code every time you observe a behavior. Later you will use *JWatcher's* analysis routines to describe the pattern of transitions from one behavior to the next.

1. Click on the *JWatcher* icon to launch *JWatcher*.
2. When *JWatcher* first opens, you will be in the "Data Capture" window. In this window, name the data file you will be scoring by clicking on the file navigator icon (it looks like a sheet of paper) to the right of the "Focal Data" box. Type in the name of your new file in the "File Name" box. Keep the names simple. For instance, name the data file for the California ground squirrel video clips as "Species1." Choose the location where you wish to save your new file and click [Open].
3. Specify your "Focal Master File" by clicking on the file navigator icon. Select "SSA.fmf." This loads the predesignated ethogram that links key codes with behaviors. Remember that this file contains the ethogram along with additional specifications such as the duration for recording the focal observation.
4. Click [Next] twice at the bottom right to tab into the next "Capture Data" page.
5. Answer the top question by typing the species common name into the box below the question and click [Next] to advance.
6. Open and cue up the video clips in the folder "Species1" (California ground squirrels). Start with clip 1 and then score clips 2 through 6. When ready, click [Start] in the "Capture Data" page of *JWatcher*. Then start the first video. Immediately type the key code representing the "chew" behavior when the video starts. Note that you will need to reactivate the *JWatcher* window by clicking on it first; otherwise the key codes will not register.

   Whenever the squirrel begins applying the snake scent, type the key code for that specific body section, and then for the body section to which the squirrel switches, and so forth. Score the SSA behavior until the video ends and type your key code for "break code." *Do not click* [Stop] *between videos.* Continue scoring the rest of the videos for Species2 the same way. When you have finished all videos, click [Stop].
7. Click [New] and rename the data file (e.g., "Species2") and then repeat Steps 3 through 5 above, this time scoring the video clips in the folder "Species2" (rock squirrels). Note that there are a total of 12 rock squirrel clips.

At the end, you should have two data files, one for each species.

---

**Note:** *If you wish to see a list of the behavioral codes on your computer screen, click [Behaviors] in the upper right corner of the* JWatcher *screen.*

---

For this analysis, the exact time during which the behaviors occur is not important. We are interested in the sequence only. Thus you may play the videos at half speed or use the scroll bar to view the behaviors more slowly, if either of these makes scoring easier. Do not worry if there is a lag between the time when you see the behavior occurring and the time when you hit the key code.

If you made a data entry mistake, you have several options. You may stop scoring behavior, discard, and delete the resulting data file, and start again. Or, once you have finished scoring an entire data file, you may open it in the "Edit Data" window and fix your mistakes. Note that you will have to remember exactly where the mistake occurred to do this. Alternatively, if you have trouble touch-typing the key codes, you may write down the list of behaviors on a piece of paper and then type them into *JWatcher* when you have finished watching the video.

If you cannot tell which body segment is being anointed, then score "break" but do your best to figure it out first.

### PART 2—ANALYZING YOUR DATA

**Sequential analysis**   Once you have scored all video clips for both species, you are now ready to use *JWatcher's* analysis algorithms to analyze SSA sequences. Analyzing data files is a three-part process. First you must specify the general parameters for your sequential analyses. Then you must choose which analysis type to use (we will be using "Sequence Analysis"). Finally, you must run your data files through an analysis routine to generate results files.

1. To begin to analyze your data, click on the "Sequential Analysis" tab in the upper menu to open the window. Click on the file navigator icon to the right of the "Focal Master File" field to load your project's ethogram (SSA.fmf). If you do not see this file currently displayed, specify the location where it was saved in the upper part of the window.
2. Once the ethogram has been loaded, indicate what key code was used as your "Break Code" by clicking on the down arrow and selecting "x." Then select to have repeated key codes "ignored" (you should not have any repeated key codes). For this exercise, we did not have any repeated codes because we are interested in the transitions from one body section to another.
3. Click on the "Sequence Analysis" tab in the lower left menu. Then select the same focal master file that you selected in step 1. A results file name will automatically appear in the space below. Select your first data file (e.g., Species1.dat) by clicking on the file icon to the right of the focal data file box. Your results file will be saved in the folder shown in the box below. Make sure you note where your results will be saved so that you can access them later.
4. Check the "Lag 1" box. "Lag 1" means that we are interested in the behavior that immediately follows another.
5. Check the "Observed Matrix" and the "Transitional Probability Matrix" boxes.
6. Click [Analyze] at the bottom of the file window to analyze your data. *JWatcher* will then inform you if there are any errors or warnings in your analysis. Click [OK] to view the log. You may get a warning if you hit a key that is not defined in your ethogram. If this is the case, go to the "Edit Data" tab and open your file, correct the error in the "Key Pressed" column by clicking on the relevant cell, deleting the mistake, and retyping the correct behavior. Finally, save the corrected file.
7. Repeat steps 1 through 6 for your second data file (e.g., Species2.dat).

**Viewing the results files**   You will need to use a text-editor, a word-processor, or spreadsheet program to view the results files. Find your results folder and there should be one two result files (e.g., Species1.seq.res and Species2.seq.res) along with the log file. Results files are comma-delimited texts.

**Explanation of "sequence analysis"**   Sequence analysis algorithms quantify the frequency with which one behavioral event follows another behavioral event. For example, we are interested in knowing the frequency that "apply to tail base" follows "apply to flank" in the SSA sequence.

The observed matrix shows the number of times that each behavior followed another in the sequence, reported as a count. The behaviors listed in the "Lag 1" row follow behaviors listed in the "Lag 0" column. For example, in an arbitrarily created observed matrix shown below, "Flank" follows "Chew" 21 times, "Tail Base" follows "Chew" 22 times, and "Tail mid" follows "Chew" 29 times. The total number of times that "Chew" occurred in the sequence with a behavior following it is 100. The total number of times that "Flank" occurred in the sequence following a behavior is 106.

### Observed Matrix

|  |  | Lag 1 |  |  |  |  |  |
|---|---|---|---|---|---|---|---|
|  |  | Chew | Flank | Tail base | Tail mid | Tail tip | Total |
|  | Chew | 0 | 21 | 22 | 29 | 28 | 100 |
|  | Flank | 0 | 0 | 19 | 18 | 20 | 57 |
|  | Tail base | 0 | 5 | 0 | 22 | 23 | 50 |
| Lag 0 | Tail mid | 0 | 12 | 12 | 0 | 37 | 61 |
|  | Tail tip | 0 | 68 | 8 | 9 | 0 | 85 |
|  | Total | 0 | 106 | 61 | 78 | 108 | 353 |

A transition probability is the probability that one behavior will follow another. Looking at the example matrix below, we see that the probability that "Flank" follows "Chew" is 0.21, the probability that "Tail base" follows "Chew" is 0.22, and the probability that "Tail mid" follows "Chew" is 0.29. These transition probabilities are calculated directly from the observed matrix shown above. For example, to calculate the probability that "Flank" follows "Chew," you would divide the number of times that "Flank" followed "Chew" (21) by the total number of times that "Chew" occurred in the sequence with any behavior following it (row total for "Chew" = 100). Thus, the transitional probability would be 21/100 = 0.21.

### Transitional Probability Matrix

|  |  | Lag 1 |  |  |  |  |  |
|---|---|---|---|---|---|---|---|
|  |  | Chew | Flank | Tail base | Tail mid | Tail tip | Total |
|  | Chew | 0 | 0.21 | 0.22 | 0.29 | 0.28 | 1.0 |
|  | Flank | 0 | 0 | 0.33 | 0.32 | 0.35 | 1.0 |
| Lag 0 | Tail base | 0 | 0.10 | 0 | 0.44 | 0.46 | 1.0 |
|  | Tail mid | 0 | 0.20 | 0.20 | 0 | 0.60 | 1.0 |
|  | Tail tip | 0 | 0.80 | 0.09 | 0.11 | 0 | 1.0 |

Notice that a behavior cannot follow itself; therefore, the diagonal of this matrix is composed of zeros. Look at the row for "Chew." We see that no behavior is more likely to follow "Chew" than any other (all between 21% and 29%). Now look at the row for "Tail tip." In this case, "Flank" is far more likely to follow "Tail tip" (80% of the time) than "Tail base" or "Tail mid" (~10% of the time). Notice that the probabilities for each row sum to 1.0. In a completely stereotyped behavior, one behavior may always follow another (100% of the time) to the exclusion of all other behaviors.

PART **3**—INTERPRETING YOUR RESULTS

**Constructing transition diagrams** A transition diagram is a visual depiction of the transition probabilities. Arrows are drawn between behaviors, with the thickness of the arrow reflecting the frequency of the transition. The thicker the arrow, the higher the probability that this particular transition will occur. The direction of the arrow shows which behavior follows which.

1. Under "General Statistics," check all behaviors (body sections) that had counts higher than 10. These will be the "Lag 0" behaviors that you will examine in your transitional probability matrix. Since those below 10 were rare, we will exclude them for this lab exercise.
2. Under "Transitional Probability Matrix," circle all transition probabilities in your matrix that are higher than 0.1000. These will be the transitions you draw in Figure 2 (see step 3). For example, in the example matrix shown above, the transition from flank (f) to tail base (b) is 0.33.
3. Using the figure on the next page, fill in transition arrows of SSA for both species, also label them with the exact number. Use the arrow width legend and corresponding probability to draw in transitions from one box to another starting with "Tail base" to "Chew."

**Transition diagrams**

(A) Rock squirrel (*Spermophilus variegatus*)

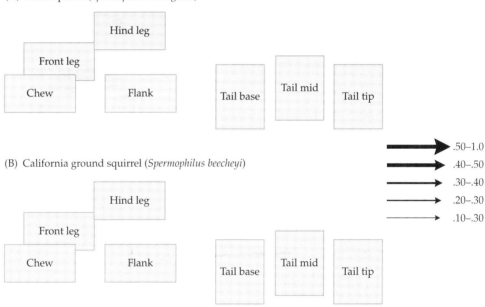

(B) California ground squirrel (*Spermophilus beecheyi*)

Consider the following questions: What transition was most likely to happen (e.g., had the highest transition probability)? Do you see a pattern to the application of snake scent? Does the application of snake scent follow a stereotyped pattern? Do you see any species differences? Do you think that these results are reliable? Why or why not? What might explain any species differences? How would you test hypotheses about species differences? Could SSA behavior be used to create a phylogeny?

**HOW TO MAKE YOUR OWN FOCAL MASTER FILE, "SSA.FMF"**

Open the focal master file tab and click [Add row].

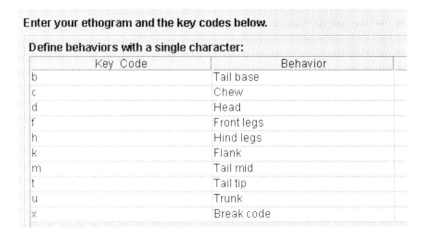

Define the following key codes:

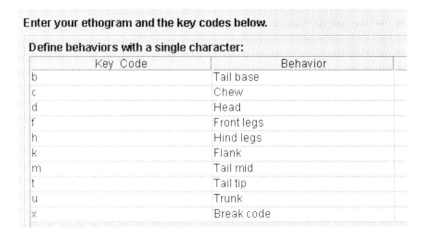

You do not need to specify anything in the "Test Details" window or the "Questions" window.

Save the file as "SSA.fmf.

## 15.4 Guppy Courtship: Using Both Sequential Analysis and Basic Analysis to Conduct a Pilot Study

By working through this exercise, you will employ a series of *JWatcher's* routines to examine a specific behavioral question: Does courtship behavior differ between dull and bright male guppies? Please note that this exercise is illustrative only; sample sizes are too small to draw convincing conclusions.

Guppies (*Poecilia reticulata*) are small, sexually dimorphic fish that are often used in studies of sexual selection and mate choice (e.g., Endler 1980; Grether 2000). Females are typically larger than males and are silvery grey in color, whereas males are brightly colored, often with dramatic orange patches and black spots (Houde 1997). Males engage in conspicuous courtship displays in which they position themselves in front of, or to the side of, a female, arch their bodies into an S-shaped curve, and shudder. This display is called a "sigmoid" display (Baerends et al. 1955). Guppies are native to freshwater streams of Trinidad, Tobago, and northeastern South America, where they live in mixed sex nonterritorial groups with no specific breeding season.

Many previous studies have focused on female choice of males based on their coloration and behavior (Houde 1997), but relatively fewer studies have looked specifically at male behavior (Kolluru and Grether 2005). In this exercise, we will first explore whether the sequential pattern of courtship might differ between dull and bright males. We will define brightness as the amount of orange coloration. We will then examine whether the duration and rate of sigmoid displays differs between the two groups of males.

In the photographs below (taken from a video), we provide some examples of relatively bright males and relatively dull males. The bright males have a greater proportion of their body colored with orange spots.

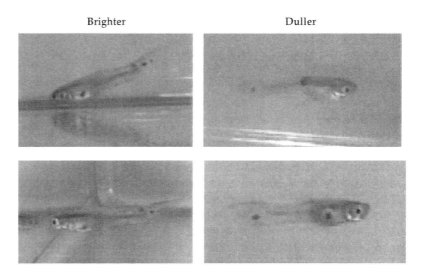

Brighter                    Duller

To begin examining these questions, we conducted 2-minute continuous focal observations on ten male-female pairs. Five of these pairs had bright males, and five had dull males. Before conducting the focal samples, we isolated each pair into a small holding tank. Different females were used for each pair.

You may download QuickTime versions of these focal samples at our Web site (www.jwatcher.ucla.edu).

We used the following ethogram to score male behavior:

| | |
|---|---|
| **Swim towards** | Actively following side or behind, pursuing or chasing female |
| **Swim away** | Retreat from female, head facing away, or rapidly displaced by attacking female with head in either direction |
| **Float** | Immobile, head not oriented toward female |
| **Sigmoid** | S-shaped shudder, ranging from low intensity, slight body flicks while engaging female, to high intensity, extended sigmoid displays |
| **Posture** | Floating or hovering near female with head oriented towards female, but not with sigmoid, may move backwards while still facing female, or move slowly backwards and forwards while facing female throughout. Male's head within 2–3 body lengths of female. |
| **Non-directed swimming** | Eating, pacing along glass while not specifically following female, includes gulping air from surface |
| **Attack** | Bite or charge female resulting in rapid displacement |
| **Not visible** | Break between files, or behavior not able to be discerned |

Our ethogram was based upon the types of behaviors that we observed in our holding tank and those that we believed could be scored reliably. As it turned out, these behaviors could not be scored very reliably because the onset and offset of the various categories were often hard to discern. Thus, any results that we report based upon our initial scoring of the data files with the above ethogram are intended only to illustrate the process of analyzing behavioral data. A classic, comprehensive ethogram is contained in Baerends et al. (1955).

We initially scored each male as its own data file and created a total of ten files. For sequence analysis, we then combined all the dull males into one data file and the bright males into another data file, using the spreadsheet program Excel. Thus we ended up with two combined data files. When combining files, we placed a break code (not visible) between each original file.

It became immediately apparent that we would need to score considerably more transitions to adequately describe the sequential pattern of courtship in either group. However, before forging ahead and committing ourselves to a large-scale time-consuming effort to collect more data, we decided to run some pilot tests. It is these pilot tests that we use to illustrate our approach.

We began our exploration by using the combined files to compare the sequences of dull versus bright males. First we calculated the overall frequencies for each behavior; then we calculated transition probabilities (for lag 1) and drew kinematic graphs.

Using *JWatcher*'s sequence analysis routine, we found that:

For bright males:

```
#GENERAL STATISTICS
Behavior/modifier  Description             Count      Probability
a                  Swim away                 31         0.1713
f                  Float                      9         0.0497
n                  Non-directed swimming     12         0.0663
p                  Posture                   32         0.1768
s                  Sigmoid                   52         0.2873
t                  Swim toward               45         0.2486
Total                                       181
```

For dull males:

```
#GENERAL STATISTICS
Behavior/modifier  Description             Count      Probability
a                  Swim away                 40         0.2116
f                  Float                      5         0.0265
n                  Non-directed swimming     13         0.0688
p                  Posture                   32         0.1693
s                  Sigmoid                   41         0.2169
t                  Swim toward               58         0.3069
Total                                       189
```

Because "Float" and "Nondirected swimming" have relatively few observations, we combined these categories into a single new category, "Other," for subsequent analyses.

For bright males:

```
#GENERAL STATISTICS
Behavior/modifier  Description                      Count      Probability
a                  Swim away                          31         0.1722
p                  Posture                            32         0.1778
s                  Sigmoid                            52         0.2889
t                  Swim toward                        45         0.25
x                  Other (float +non-directed swim)   20         0.1111
Total                                                180
```

For dull males:

```
#GENERAL STATISTICS
Behavior/modifier  Description                      Count      Probability
a                  Swim away                          40         0.2128
p                  Posture                            32         0.1702
s                  Sigmoid                            41         0.2181
t                  Swim toward                        58         0.3085
x                  Other (float +non-directed swim)   17         0.0904
Total                                                188
```

Just eyeballing the numbers quickly, we see that there probably is no difference in the overall distribution of frequencies between bright and dull males. To test this formally, we ran a chi-square test using SPSS. We found that:

**Chi-square tests**

|  | Value | df | p-value (2-sided) |
|---|---|---|---|
| Pearson Chi-Square | 4.154 | 4 | 0.386 |
| Likelihood ratio | 4.163 | 4 | 0.384 |
| Number of valid cases | 368 | | |

Thus there is no difference in the distribution of frequencies between bright and dull males for the particular behaviors that we scored. If these data were more representative, we might be justified in concluding that males court similarly despite variable coloration.

We returned to *JWatcher's* sequence analysis routine and calculated an observed frequency matrix for our list of behaviors.

For bright males:

**Observed Matrix**

| | | Lag 1 | | | | | |
|---|---|---|---|---|---|---|---|
| | | Swim away | Posture | Sigmoid | Swim toward | Other | Total |
| | Swim away | **0** | 3 | 8 | 12 | 6 | 29 |
| | Posture | 8 | **0** | 16 | 2 | 5 | 31 |
| Lag 0 | Sigmoid | 13 | 14 | **0** | 17 | 5 | 49 |
| | Swim toward | 8 | 11 | 22 | **0** | 3 | 44 |
| | Other | 2 | 3 | 6 | 8 | **0** | 19 |
| | Total | 31 | 31 | 52 | 39 | 19 | 172 |

For dull males:

**Observed Matrix**

| | | Lag 1 | | | | | |
|---|---|---|---|---|---|---|---|
| | | Swim away | Posture | Sigmoid | Swim toward | Other | Total |
| | Swim away | **0** | 1 | 7 | 22 | 7 | 37 |
| | Posture | 8 | **0** | 11 | 9 | 3 | 31 |
| Lag 0 | Sigmoid | 13 | 10 | **0** | 16 | 1 | 40 |
| | Swim toward | 15 | 19 | 19 | **0** | 5 | 58 |
| | Other | 4 | 1 | 4 | 7 | **0** | 16 |
| | Total | 40 | 31 | 41 | 54 | 16 | 182 |

In this example, behaviors cannot logically repeat. The main diagonal will therefore be composed of structural zeros (as opposed to sampling zeros); these are highlighted in bold. Notice that there are several cells with very low sample sizes.

We then calculated transition probabilities.

For bright males:

**Transitional Probability Matrix**

| | | Lag 1 | | | | | |
|---|---|---|---|---|---|---|---|
| | | Swim away | Posture | Sigmoid | Swim toward | Other | Total |
| | Swim away | 0 | 0.10 | 0.28 | 0.41 | 0.21 | 1 |
| | Posture | 0.26 | 0 | 0.52 | 0.06 | 0.16 | 1 |
| **Lag 0** | Sigmoid | 0.26 | 0.29 | 0 | 0.35 | 0.10 | 1 |
| | Swim toward | 0.18 | 0.25 | 0.50 | 0 | 0.07 | 1 |
| | Other | 0.10 | 0.16 | 0.32 | 0.42 | 0 | 1 |

For dull males:

**Transitional Probability Matrix**

| | | Lag 1 | | | | | |
|---|---|---|---|---|---|---|---|
| | | Swim away | Posture | Sigmoid | Swim toward | Other | Total |
| | Swim away | 0 | 0.03 | 0.19 | 0.59 | 0.19 | 1 |
| | Posture | 0.26 | 0 | 0.35 | 0.29 | 0.10 | 1 |
| **Lag 0** | Sigmoid | 0.33 | 0.25 | 0 | 0.40 | 0.02 | 1 |
| | Swim toward | 0.26 | 0.33 | 0.33 | 0 | 0.08 | 1 |
| | Other | 0.25 | 0.06 | 0.25 | 0.44 | 0 | 1 |

Using these transition probabilities, we drew kinematic graphs for each transition with a probability greater or equal to 0.10.

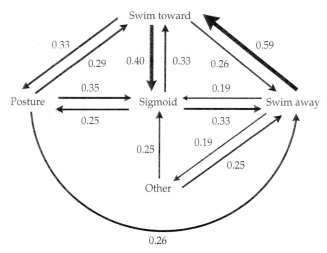

**Bright males**

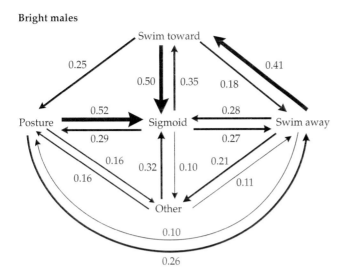

(Not shown: arrow from "Other" to "Swim toward" with transition probability of 0.42 for bright males and 0.44 for dull males.)

From these kinematic graphs, it appears that dull and bright males have similar courtship patterns. One potentially noteworthy difference seems to be that once posturing, bright males are perhaps more likely to sigmoid display than dull males, rather than pursue (swim toward) the female.

Of course, the huge caveat for this pilot analysis is that data are insufficient and small differences in the observed matrix could potentially have large misleading effects on the transition probabilities. The other caveat is that, just by looking at these numbers, we have no idea whether they describe any pattern that differs from random.

To examine which transition differs from random, if any, we might calculate $z$-scores and look for those that are greater (or less) than 1.96. However, *JWatcher's* sequence analysis routine assumes that behaviors are allowed to repeat. Since our behaviors do not repeat, this would not be an appropriate test. For example, *JWatcher* would report the following $z$-scores for our data:

For bright males:

### Z-score

|  |  | Lag 1 |  |  |  |  |
|---|---|---|---|---|---|---|
|  |  | Swim away | Posture | Sigmoid | Swim toward | Other |
|  | Swim away | −2.77 | −1.18 | −0.34 | **2.64** | 1.82 |
|  | Posture | 1.25 | −2.88 | **2.86** | −2.38 | 1.00 |
| **Lag 0** | Sigmoid | 1.83 | **2.27** | −5.45 | **2.38** | −0.22 |
|  | Swim toward | 0.03 | 1.40 | **3.31** | −4.16 | −1.04 |
|  | Other | −0.90 | −0.27 | 0.14 | **2.14** | −1.63 |

For dull males:

**Z-score**

|  | | Lag 1 | | | | |
| --- | --- | --- | --- | --- | --- | --- |
|  | | Swim away | Posture | Sigmoid | Swim toward | Other |
| | Swim away | –3.62 | **–2.60** | –0.5886 | **4.44** | **2.44** |
| | Posture | 0.57 | –2.77 | 1.90 | –0.09 | 0.19 |
| **Lag 0** | Sigmoid | 1.82 | 1.52 | –3.86 | 1.62 | –1.59 |
| | Swim toward | 0.87 | **3.86** | **2.26** | –5.99 | –0.06 |
| | Other | 0.31 | –1.20 | 0.25 | 1.29 | –1.30 |

Notice that the diagonals (representing repeated behaviors) indicate that repeats frequently occurred significantly less often than would be expected by chance. However, repeats are not allowed to occur for this analysis. Strictly, this analysis should be interpreted with caution. Values significant at the 0.05 level (other than at structural zeros) are shown in bold.

A correct calculation of z-scores, given that repeats are not allowed, would involve exporting our data with *JWatcher's* complex sequences routine and then running the analysis in SPSS. To do so, we selected basic, overlapped sampling with length = 2 in the complex sequences tab. This means that we are sampling the same way as above for sequence analysis (lag 1). We then took the exported list of transitions and used this list to run a general log-linear analysis in SPSS, specifying structural zeros for the repeats.

We found that for dull males, the table-wise chi-square was significant at the 0.05 level for both the Pearson and the likelihood ratio chi-square. Three transitions had adjusted residuals greater than 1.96, and one transition had an adjusted residual less than 1.96.

- Adjusted residuals >1.96

    Swim away to swim toward

    Swim away to other (float or nondirected swimming)

    Swim toward to posture

- Adjusted residuals <1.96

    Swim away to posture

This pattern is similar to what we derived using z-scores based upon repeating codes, except that the transition from "swim toward" to "sigmoid" is no longer significant.

For bright males, the table-wise chi-square was significant at the 0.05 level for both the Pearson and the likelihood ratio chi-square. But only one transition had an adjusted residual less than 1.96. There were no transitions with adjusted residuals greater than 1.96.

- Adjusted residuals <1.96

    Posture to swim toward

This pattern is substantially different from what we derived using z-scores based upon repeating codes; in that calculation five transitions had adjusted residuals greater than

1.96, and now there are none. In both cases, the number of transitions from "posture" to "swim toward" was significantly less than expected due to chance alone.

The important point here is that the pattern of significance is very different using a log-linear analysis specifying structural zeros as opposed to the one described by incorrectly using adjusted residuals ($z$-scores) based upon repeating codes, particularly for the bright males.

We wondered earlier whether bright males, once posturing, were more likely to sigmoid display than dull males, rather than swimming toward the female. Only part of this story is upheld by the adjusted residuals calculated with the log-linear method, in that bright males are less likely than chance to swim toward the female following posturing. However, once posturing, neither bright nor dull males are more likely than chance to engage in any particular behavior.

In general, $z$-scores are sensitive to sample size. By increasing our sample size we might be able to identify additional transitions that are more likely to occur than chance. However, because $z$-scores are sensitive to sample size, we also must be concerned about using them to make cross-table comparisons, such as comparing dull versus bright males, when sample sizes between the tables differ.

When the number of individuals observed is small, spurious results can occur by chance. For instance, we combined five dull males into one file and five bright males into another file. Although the focal length for each male was consistently 2 minutes, the data file for different males may have contained drastically different numbers of transitions. If this were true, one male with a disproportionately high number of transitions might dominate the category and create spurious results.

Another possible way to ask whether the courtship sequence differs for dull males versus bright males is to perform $t$-tests on the transition probabilities, using individual data files. For example, we might be interested in knowing what precedes the sigmoid display and whether there is a difference between bright and dull males. Of course, posing this question assumes that we have an adequate sample size of transitions for each individual to properly estimate the transition probabilities.

To illustrate this, we first extracted the transition probabilities of interest from each individual's result file. We then compared the list for dull males to the list for bright males. For this example, we asked whether the transition probabilities from posture to sigmoid, and posture to swim toward, differ between dull and bright males.

The following table shows the list of transition probabilities extracted from the results files:

| Posture to sigmoid | | Posture to swim toward | |
|---|---|---|---|
| Bright | Dull | Bright | Dull |
| 0.57 | 0.43 | 0.29 | 0.57 |
| 0.33 | 0.17 | 0.00 | 0.17 |
| 0.50 | 0.38 | 0.00 | 0.38 |
| 0.50 | 0.33 | 0.00 | 0.00 |
| 0.67 | 0.50 | 0.00 | 0.25 |

We ran independent sample $t$-tests using SPSS, and found that there were no significant differences for either case (posture to sigmoid: $t = 1.964$, df = 8, $p = 0.085$; posture to swim toward: $t = -1.923$, df = 8, $p = 0.091$). Using the arcsine square root transformation typically applied to proportions yielded similar results (posture to sigmoid: $t = 1.940$, df = 8, $p = 0.088$; posture to swim toward: $t = -2.082$, df = 8, $p = 0.071$).

As mentioned above, we were also interested in whether the rate and the duration of sigmoid displays differ between dull and bright males. To examine this question, we used *JWatcher's* basic analysis, and using "All" statistics, quantified the rate (count per minute in sight), proportion of time in sight, and average duration for the sigmoid display. We analyzed each of the ten individual data files (not the two combined data files). We then ran independent sample $t$-tests in SPSS to compare the two groups.

We found no significant differences (rate of sigmoid display: $t = 2.151$, df = 8, $p = 0.064$; average duration of sigmoid: $t = -0.807$, df = 8, $p = 0.443$; proportion of time engaged in sigmoid: $t = 1.194$, df = 8, $p = 0.267$).

|  | Coloration | N | Mean | Standard deviation |
|---|---|---|---|---|
| Rate of sigmoid (N/min) | Bright | 5 | 4.53 | 1.510 |
|  | Dull | 5 | 2.70 | 1.151 |
| Average duration of sigmoid (ms) | Bright | 5 | 3815.5 | 1163.47 |
|  | Dull | 5 | 5446.4 | 4364.04 |
| Proportion of time in sigmoid | Bright | 5 | 0.288 | 0.0671 |
|  | Dull | 5 | 0.217 | 0.1149 |

Watching the guppies in our holding tank, we noticed that some individuals seemed less active. These guppies spent more time floating or swimming slowly, whereas other individuals spent more time rapidly pacing along the glass or rapidly swimming from one side of the tank to the other. This was true for both males and females. Thus we wondered whether dull and bright males differ in activity level. We also wondered whether the rate or duration of sigmoid displays by males is correlated with female activity level. Does female activity level differ when females are paired with dull compared to bright males?

To answer these questions, we needed some measure of "activity level." Because the fish were enclosed in a small tank, the more a fish swam around, the more it necessarily turned, changing directions as it swam. We thus decided to quantify the rate of turning by hitting a key every time an individual changed direction or started swimming after floating immobile. We quantified the turning rate (number of turns per minute in sight) for both males and females.

Using an independent sample $t$-test in SPSS, we found that there was no difference in turn rate between dull and bright males ($t = 0.678$, df = 8, $p = 0.517$).

**Males**

|  | Group | N | Mean | Standard deviation |
|---|---|---|---|---|
| Turn rate (N/min) | Bright | 5 | 28.133 | 13.0754 |
|  | Dull | 5 | 22.400 | 13.6721 |

Similarly, there was no difference in turn rate between females paired with dull or bright males ($t = 0.173$, df = 8, $p = 0.867$).

### Females

| | Group | N | Mean | Standard deviation |
|---|---|---|---|---|
| Turn rate (N/min) | With bright males | 5 | 27.229 | 26.2926 |
| | With dull males | 5 | 24.800 | 17.2141 |

Using a Pearson correlation in SPSS, we found that the number, average duration, and proportion of time in sight that a male was engaged in a sigmoid display were not correlated with female turn rate.

### Female Turn Rate Correlated With

| | Pearson correlation | p-value |
|---|---|---|
| Sigmoid number | 0.506 | 0.135 |
| Sigmoid average duration | –0.090 | 0.805 |
| Sigmoid proportion of time in sight | 0.262 | 0.465 |

Another possible metric of "activity level" might have been the amount of time spent floating immobile, but we did not score this for females, and therefore do not pursue this analysis here.

This example has illustrated the interactive way in which you can study behavior. By scoring behavior once and then analyzing it many times in different ways, you can test a series of focused hypotheses and thereby develop a detailed understanding of behavior.

# Tips on Modifying Data Files Using A Spreadsheet Program

In general, it is always best to use the EDIT tab to make alterations to your data files. However, there are circumstances when this may not be practical or possible. For example, you may wish to combine two or more data files into one larger file, which cannot be done directly with *JWatcher*.

In principle, data files may be modified and saved as comma-delimited text files (*.csv) and still be used by *JWatcher*. Although we provide suggestions about how to modify your files using a spreadsheet program, we do not guarantee that you will not encounter unforeseen problems. We recommend that you undertake such an endeavor with care, and always double-check and proof your files by reopening them in the EDIT tab. We also recommend that you run a test file through the entire process of analysis before committing to a larger scale effort of modifying many files.

To begin, open your data file in a spreadsheet program (such as Excel) as a comma-delimited text file.

```
FirstLineOfData=25
#----------------------------------------------------------
# Name: test1.dat
# Format: Focal Data File 1.0
# Updated: Tue Oct 17 13:21:18 PDT 2006
#----------------------------------------------------------

FocalMasterFile=/My computer/My Folder/alphabet.fmf

# Observation started: Thu Oct 05 10:06:28 PDT 2006
StartTime=1160067988093
# Observation stopped: Thu Oct 05 10:07:28 PDT 2006
StopTime=1160068048093

Answer.1=1399-1400
Answer.2=Adult
Answer.3=Female
Answer.4=treatment 1
Answer.5=
Answer.6=

#BEGIN DATA
        479  a
      21512  b
      23865  c
      34545  d
      60000  EOF
```

Before making any modifications, save the file as comma-delimited text (CSV) using another name for the saved file. Essentially, you want make sure that you retain an original unmodified copy of your data file in case things go awry.

The focal master file associated with this data file (and its directory at the time that this data file was created) is given in the 8th row, after "FocalMasterFile=." You may modify this, but remember that the correct focal master file must be associated with each data file to ensure that analysis proceeds correctly in many cases.

The total duration of the data file is calculated as the "StopTime" minus the "Start-Time." For the file above, the total duration of the session is 1160068048093 – 1160067988093 = 60000 milliseconds. Note that this corresponds to the time associated with "EOF" (End-of-focal or End-of-file). To modify the total duration of the file using a spreadsheet, you must change the difference between the start and stop times. Changing the time next to EOF in a spreadsheet will have no effect. (In the EDIT tab, you must change the time next to the EOF to modify the total duration of the file; *JWatcher* will then automatically adjust the start/stop time difference.)

> **JWatcher Quirk #1:** *It does not matter what time is entered next to EOF in the spreadsheet. To change the EOF time, you must change the difference between the start and stop times in rows 11 and 13, respectively.*

Answers may be modified, but we recommend that you use the EDIT tab to do so, whenever possible. If you do modify answers here, do not introduce commas.

The key codes and associated times are listed after #BEGIN DATA. Times are listed in milliseconds. Remember that there are 60 minutes in an hour, 60 seconds in a minute, but 1000 milliseconds in a second. To easily convert from the time format '00:00:00:00' (hours:minutes:seconds:first two digits of milliseconds) to cumulative milliseconds, use the EDIT tab to do the conversions in either direction.

> **JWatcher Quirk #2:** *Key codes must be preceded by a space to be recognized as a behavior or modifier.*

If you type new codes into your spreadsheet, make sure they are preceded by a space. If they are not preceded by a space, then *JWatcher* will not recognize them as an entry, and will consider the cell to be blank. These entries will be ignored during analysis. This includes " EOF," which must also be preceded by a space.

> **Warning:** *If you used numbers to represent behaviors or modifiers, then Excel may treat these entries as numbers instead of text, and may remove the space in front. One suggestion is to use the find/replace function, and replace each number with = " 1" or = " 2" and so forth. To be clear, you should type the equals sign, followed by the open quotation mark, followed by a space, followed by a number, and ending with the close quotation mark. If you simply type a space followed by a number into the replace box then Excel may continue to treat the entry as a number, and your problem will not be solved. Another suggestion is to use JWatcher's Combinations routine to substitute a different code for the number in your data files, prior to manipulating them in Excel.*

To verify that all codes are recognized once you are done making modifications, open your new data file in the EDIT tab. Cells with unrecognized codes will be blank. Also check that your EOF time is correct.

**Note:** *The code " EOF" must be present as the final line in your data file, even though the time associated with it is irrelevant.*

## For Sequential Analysis

If you are combining multiple data files into one data file for sequential analysis only, then the times associated with each key code will be irrelevant. In this case, you may simply cut and paste the codes without worrying about adjusting the times. For example, you might have the following three files to combine:

```
#BEGIN DATA
      479  a
    21512  b
    23865  c
    34545  d
    60000  EOF


#BEGIN DATA
      236  d
    56239  b
    58001  a
    60000  EOF


#BEGIN DATA
      107  c
    60000  EOF
```

You could specify another code (e.g., 'x') to be a 'break' code (see the section on Sequential Analysis in Chapter 8) to put between files, and then simply stick them together leaving the time codes as is.

```
#BEGIN DATA
      479  a
    21512  b
    23865  c
    34545  d
    60000  x
      236  d
    56239  b
    58001  a
    60000  x
      107  c
    60000  EOF
```

## Basic Analysis Using the Focal Analysis Master

For basic analysis, you must adjust your times to be chronological. We mainly leave it to you to determine the best way to adjust times based upon your data. However, we do provide a simple example below, in which three files are combined in the order given. We assume for the sake of simplicity that the next file begins where the former leaves off, and that there is no intervening break between files.

The procedure is to leave the first file as is, and then take the difference in times between successive key codes for the second and third files.

```
File #1
        Time Key code
           0  a
       21512  b
       23865  c
       34545  d
       60000  EOF


File #2
        Time Key code                              Difference
           0  c
       56239  b           =56239-0                     56239
       58001  a           =58001-56239                  1762
       60000  EOF         =60000-58001                  1999


File #3
           0  d
       60000  EOF         =60000-0                     60000
```

Then add each difference to the previous time (for the second and third files).

```
New file
                          Previous time +
        Time Key code     difference = new time   Difference
           0  a
       21512  b
       23865  c
       34545  d
       60000  c
      116239  b           =6000+56239=116239        56239
      118001  a           =116239+1762=118001       1762
      120000  d           =118001+1999=120000       1999
      180000  EOF         =120000+60000=180000      60000
```

Remember that *JWatcher* will not recognize 180000 as the EOF time, unless you also change the difference between start and stop times to be 180000 (see above).

When using Mac OS X, data files with suffix *.csv may be opened in the EDIT tab by changing the "Files of Type" setting from "Focal Data File (*.dat)" to "All files." However, to analyze the new data file, you must change the suffix of your new file from *.csv back to *.dat.

**JWatcher Quirk #3:** *When using Mac OS X, your data files must have the suffix* *.dat, *otherwise you will not be able to analyze them.*

When using a PC, you should be able to both edit and analyze data files with suffix *.csv.

# Log File Warnings and Errors

## Log File Warnings

### *Reliability*

1. At least one of the key code entries in [data file] contains a comma. Commas will alter the format of the reliability results file. Analyzing anyway.
2. Specified .dat files were not created with the same fmf. Analyzing anyway.

### *All Tabs*

3. Code [some code] at offset [some time] is not in focal master [fmf file]. Ignoring code.
4. Modifier [some modifier] at offset [some time] does not follow a behavior. Ignoring modifier.
5. Modifier [some modifier] at offset [some time] follows an already modified behavior [some behavior-modifier pair]. Ignoring modifier.
6. There are no code entries in the focal data file. Analyzing anyway.
7. Scoring from first code [some code] but this behavior is ignored.
8. Length of time bin [time bin duration] is greater than length of focal data capture session [data capture duration].

### *Sequential Analysis—Complex Sequences*

9. The range of positions specified is invalid since either BEGIN code or END code does not appear in the data file. Analysis will proceed for all positions available within the data file.
10. The range of positions specified is invalid since BEGIN position is greater than END position. Analysis will proceed for all positions available within the data file.
11. The range of positions specified is invalid since either BEGIN position or END position or both exceed those found in the data file. Analysis will proceed for all positions available within the data file.

### *Sequential Analysis—Lag Sequential*

12. The range of lags specified exceeds that found in the data file. Analysis will proceed for those lags available within the data file.
13. The range of lags specified is invalid since FROM lag is greater than TO lag. Analysis will proceed for those lags available within the data file.
14. For data file [data file], at least one $z$-score, $p$-value and/or confidence interval may not be valid. The $z$-score, $p$-value and confidence interval are calculated with

a normal approximation that is valid only when N*P > 5 and N*(1 – P) > 5, where N is the observed frequency of the given event (lag 0) and P is the probability for the target event (precedes or follows the given event). The following pairs/lags are affected: [pairs].

### Sequential Analysis—Runs

15. The sample size of at least one of the dichotomous variables is less than 20 in the data file [data file]. This test is calculated using a normal approximation that may not be valid when the sample size is small. Analyzing anyway.
16. General tab settings do not apply to the runs test. The runs test requires data files to contain a sequence of dichotomous variables only, such that each variable consists of a single key code. Any selections made in the general tab with respect to focal master file, modifiers, ignored behaviors, break code, or consecutively repeating codes will be disregarded for this test. Analyzing anyway.
17. Code [some code] at offset [some time] is either not defined in the focal master file associated with this data file, or is defined to be a modifier. Undefined codes and modifiers will be ignored for the runs test. Ignoring code.

### Summary Results

18. The summary result file has more than 254 columns. This file may be incompatible for use with some spreadsheet programs such as Microsoft Excel.
19. The summary result file has more than 254 columns. This file may be incompatible for use with some spreadsheet programs such as Microsoft Excel.

### Data Analysis

20. The focal master for focal data is [fmf name]. This does not match the focal master [fmf name] in focal analysis master. Analyzing anyway.

### Combinations—Combine Key Codes

21. There are no code entries in the focal data file. Combining anyway.
22. The focal master for focal data is [fmf file]. This does not match the focal master [fmf file] in combinations master. Combining anyway.
23. Focal master file associated with specified combinations master file [fmf name] does not exist or could not be loaded. Proceeding with analysis anyway.

### Sequential Analysis—All But Runs

24. The focal master file is not specified in the General tab. Analyzing anyway using the focal master file in the data file(s). Analysis will proceed assuming that all behaviors are unmodified.
25. The name and directory of the focal master file [fmf name] associated with the data file [dat file] does not match the name and directory of the focal master file [fmf name] specified in the General tab. A mismatch in contents between focal master files could potentially produce erroneous results.
26. Code [some code] at offset [some time] is specified to have a modifier following it but is unmodified. Analyzing anyway.
27. Modifier [some code] at offset [some time] follows an already modified behavior. Ignoring modifier and analyzing anyway.
28. Code [some code] at offset [some time] is not defined in the focal master file associated with this data file. Ignoring code.

## Log File Errors

### Analysis

1. Offset [some time] matches or exceeds the duration of the data capture session [" +  dataDuration + "].

2. No complete time bins to report on.
3. No complete or truncated time bins to report on.
4. The number of time bins calculated is [number of bins]. Greater than MAX_BINS is too many to attempt to score!
5. Code [some code] at offset [some time] is later than focal data EOF time. Skipping analysis.
6. Code [some code] at offset [some time] is earlier than previous entry. Skipping analysis.
7. Behavior Code [some code] in FMF but missing from focal analysis master [faf file]. Ignoring behavior.
8. Offset [offset to score from] matches or exceeds the duration of the data capture session [data capture duration]. Skipping analysis.
9. Scoring from first occurrence of code [behavior to score from] but this behavior is ignored. Skipping analysis.
10. Behavior to score from [behavior to score from] not found in focal data. Skipping analysis.
11. Length of focal data session [data capture duration] is less than or equal to scoring offset [offset to score from]. Skipping analysis.

### Sequential Analysis—Complex Sequences

12. There are no codes to analyze in the data file [data file]. Skipping this file.

### Sequential Analysis—Lag Sequential

13. There are no codes to analyze in the data file [data file]. Skipping this file.

### Sequential Analysis—Markovian

14. There are no codes to analyze in the data file [data file]. Skipping this file.

### Sequential Analysis—Runs

15. Data file [data file] has zero or more than two variables, where each variable consists of a single key code. Runs test cannot be performed. Skipping this file.
16. Unable to find the focal master file [fmf file] associated with this data file [data file]. Skipping analysis of this data file. Please place the focal master in the same directory with the data file.

### Sequential Analysis—Sequence

17. There are no codes to analyze in the data file [data file]. Skipping this file.

### Data Analysis

18. No results have been selected for reporting in this focal analysis master.
19. Behaviors in the related focal master [fmf file] have changed.
20. Unable to save results to [results file]. [Exception message]

### Combinations

21. Combinations master [cmf name] does not specify any codes to replace. No files were combined.
22. Unable to save combined data to [cmf file]. [Exception message]

### Reliability

23. Encountered problems while loading one of the data files. Processing aborted: [exception message].
24. Specified .dat files do not begin with the same key code since at least one of them has no key code entries. Skipping analysis.
25. Specified .dat files do not begin with the same key code. Skipping analysis.
26. Unable to save results to [reliability file].

### Sequential Analysis—All

27. Encountered problems while loading data file [file]. Skipping this file: [Exception message]
28. Unable to save results to [sequential result file]. [Exception message]

### Summary

29. Encountered problems while loading result file [result file]. File skipped.
30. Result file [result file] will not be summarized with other result files in the directory [user directory], since it has not been analyzed in the same way as the first result file in the directory. File skipped.
31. Nothing to summarize, since there are no result files in the specified directory.
32. Unable to save results to [summary file]. [Exception message]

### Sequential Analysis—All But Runs

33. Unable to find the focal master file [fmf file] associated with this data file [data file]. Skipping analysis of this data file. Please place the focal master in the same directory with the data file.

# Compatibility with *JWatcher* 0.9 Files

Data files scored with Version 0.9 are compatible for use with all applicable Version 1.0 routines; therefore, no rescoring of existing data files is necessary (but see exception below).

Global definition and focal master files created by Version 0.9 should be opened and resaved in Version 1.0, after verifying that no unintended alterations have occurred. Note that a number of key codes previously allowed in Version 0.9 global definition and focal master files are no longer able to be defined in Version 1.0 (see section 4, Global Definition for more details—the six key codes are \ | : = , . ). If your previous global definition and focal master files contain any of these codes, we suggest that you create entirely new files in the new version. Version 0.9 data files containing these codes will be able to be analyzed, but these codes will be ignored, and thus information may be lost. If your Version 0.9 data files intentionally contained any of these key codes then you will need either to edit them or rescore.

Focal analysis master files created by Version 0.9 must be updated within the new version before use to prevent unexpected results. Open, fix any inconsistencies, and resave. All of your original selections should be preserved *except for one case within the Event Analysis window* (see below). Files not updated may still be analyzed, but we have not extensively tested these results.

Event Analysis window: In Version 0.9, two analyses (event count and interval occurrence) were combined into one check box. In the new version, these two analyses are now separated into two independent check boxes. If you had selected the "Event Count and Interval Occurrence" box in Version 0.9, you won't get the "Event Count" box checked in the new version. Therefore, you must update this portion manually.

Combinations master files created by Version 0.9 should not be used with Version 1.0. We suggest creating entirely new combination master files with Version 1.0, and rerunning the combine key codes routine. See section 9, Combinations.

Version 1.0 files are not compatible for use with Version 0.9.

# Literature Cited

Alberto, P. A. & Troutman, A. C. 1995. *Applied Behavior Analysis for Teachers, 4th ed.* Columbus: Merill Publ. Co.

Alcock, J. 2005. *Animal Behavior, 8th ed.* Sunderland, MA: Sinauer Associates, Inc.

Allison, P. D. & Liker, J. K. 1982. Analyzing sequential categorial data on dyadic interaction: a comment on Gottman. *Psych. Bull.,* **91,** 393–403.

Altmann, J. 1974. Observational study of behaviour: sampling methods. *Behaviour,* **49,** 227–267.

Baerends, G. P., Brouwer, R. & Waterbolk, H. T. 1955. Ethological studies on *Lebistes reticulatus* (Peters), I. An analysis of the male courtship pattern. *Behaviour,* **8,** 249–334.

Bakeman, R. 1983. Computing lag sequential statistics: the ELAG program. *Behav. Res. Methods Inst.,* **15,** 530–535.

Bakeman, R. & Gottman, J. M. 1997. *Observing Interaction: An Introduction to Sequential Analysis, 2nd ed.* Cambridge: Cambridge Univ. Press.

Bakeman, R. & Quera, V. 1995. Log-linear approaches to lag-sequential analysis when consecutive codes may and cannot repeat. *Psych. Bull.,* **118,** 272–284.

Bednekoff, P. A. & Lima, S. L. 1998. Randomness, chaos and confusion in the study of antipredator vigilance. *Trends Ecol. Evol.,* **13,** 284–287.

Bekoff, M. 1975. Animal play and behavioral diversity. *Am. Nat.,* **109,** 601–603.

Blumstein, D. T. & Daniel, J. C. 2002. Isolation from mammalian predators differentially affects two congeners. *Behav. Ecol.,* **13,** 657–663.

Blumstein, D. T. & Daniel, J. C. 2005. The loss of anti-predator behaviour following isolation on islands. *Proc. R. Soc. Series B,* **272,** 1663–1668.

Blumstein, D. T., Evans, C. S. & Daniel, J. C. 1999. An experimental study of behavioural group size effects in tammar wallabies (*Macropus eugenii*). *Anim. Behav.,* **58,** 351–360.

Bond, A. B. & Kamil, A. C. 1999. Searching image in Blue jays: facilitation and inter-ference in sequential priming. *Anim. Learn. Behav.,* **27,** 461–471.

Breithaupt, T. & Eger, P. 2002. Urine makes the difference: chemical communication in fighting crayfish made visible. *J. Exp. Biol.,* **205,** 1221–1231.

Brown, G. R. & Dixson, A. F. 1999. Investigating the role of postnatal testosterone in the expression of sex differences in behavior in infant Rhesus macaques (*Macaca mulatta*). *Horm. Behav.,* **35,** 186–194.

Brown, J. S. 1999. Vigilance, patch use, and habitat selection: foraging under predation risk. *Evol. Ecol. Res.,* **1,** 49–71.

Butler, M. A. 2005. Foraging mode of the chameleon, *Bradypodion pumilum*: a challenge to the sit-and-wait versus active forager paradigm? *Biol. J. Linn. Soc.,* **84,** 797–808.

Campbell, D. T. & Stanley, J. C. 1963. *Experimental and Quasi-Experimental Designs for Research.* Chicago: Rand McNally College Publishing Company.

Caro, T. 2005. *Antipredator Defenses in Birds and Mammals.* Chicago: University of Chicago Press.

Catchpole, C. & Slater, P. J. B. 1995. *Bird Song: Biological Themes and Variations.* Cambridge: Cambridge University Press.

Clucas, B. A., Rowe, M. P., Owings, D. H. & Arrowood, P. C. In press. Snake scent application in ground squirrels (*Spermophilus* spp.): A novel form of antipredator behaviour? *Anim. Behav.*

Corke, M. J. & Broom, D. M. 1999. The behaviour of sheep with sheep scab, *Psoroptes ovis*, infestation. *Vet. Parisitol.,* **83,** 291–300.

Coss, R. G. & Goldthwaite, R. O. 1995. The persistence of old designs for perception. *Persp. Ethology,* **11,** 83–148.

Coss, R. G. & Moore, M. 2002. Precocious knowledge of trees as antipredator refuge in preschool children: an examination of aesthetics, attributive judgments, and relic sexual dinichism. *Ecol. Psych.,* **14,** 181–222.

Coulson, G. 1989. Repertoires of social behaviour in the Macropodoidea. In: *Kangaroos, Wallabies and Rat-Kangaroos, Vol. 2* (Ed. by G. Grigg, P. Jarman, and I. Hume), pp. 457–473. Chipping Norton, New South Wales, Australia: Surrey Beatty & Sons.

Dawkins, M. 1971. Shifts of 'attention' in chicks during feeding. *Anim. Behav.,* **19,** 575–582.

Dawson, G., Frey, K., Self, J., Panagiotides, H., Hessl, D., Yamada, E. & Rinaldi, J. 1999. Frontal brain electrical activity in infants of depressed and nondepressed mothers: relation to variations in infant behavior. *Dev. Psychopath.,* **11,** 589–605.

Douglas, J. M. & Tweed, R. L. 1979. Analysing the patterning of a sequence of discrete behavioural events. *Anim. Behav.,* **27,** 1236–1252.

Eckstein, R. A. & Hart, B. L. 2000. The organization and control of grooming in cats. *Appl. Anim. Behav. Sci.,* **68,** 131–140.

Eide, H., Quera, V. & Finset, A. 2003. Exploring rare patient behaviour with sequential analysis: an illustration. *Epidemiologia e Psichiatria Sociale,* **12,** 109–114.

Endler, J. A. 1980. Natural selection on color patterns in *Poecilia reticulata*. *Evolution,* **34,** 76–91.

Evans, C. S., Gaioni, S. J. & McBeath, M. K. 1984. A microcomputer system for the measurement of avian heart rate. *Bird Behaviour,* **6,** 41–45.

Fernández-Juricic, E., Campagna, C. & San Mauro, D. 2003. Variations in the arrangement of South American sea lion (*Otaria flavescens*) male vocalizations during the breeding season: patterns and contexts. *Aquatic Mamm.,* **29,** 2.

Ficken, M. S., Hailman, E. D. & Hailman, J. P. 1994. The chick-a-dee call system of the Mexican chicadee. *Condor,* **96,** 70–82.

Fossi, J. J., Clarke, D. D. & Lawrence, C. 2005. Bedroom rape: sequences of sexual behavior in stranger assaults. *J. Interpers. Viol.,* **20,** 1444–1466.

Ganslosser, U. 1989. Agonistic behaviour in Macropodids: A review. In: *Kangaroos, Wallabies and Rat-Kangaroos, Vol. 2* (Ed. by G. Grigg, P. Jarman, and I. Hume), pp. 475–503. Chipping Norton, New South Wales, Australia: Surrey Beatty & Sons.

Goodall, J. 1986. *The Chimpanzees of Gombe.* Cambridge: Belknap Press of Harvard University Press.

Gosling, S. D. 2001. From mice to men: what can we learn about personality from animal research? *Psych. Bull.,* **127,** 45–86.

Gottman, J., Markman, H. & Notarius, C. 1977. The topography of marital conflict: a sequential analysis of verbal and non-verbal behavior. *J. Marriage Fam.,* **39,** 461–477.

Grether, G. F. 2000. Carotenoid limitation and mate preference evolution: a test of the indicator hypothesis in guppies (*Poecilia reticulata*). *Evolution,* **54,** 1712–1724.

Hailman, E. D. & Hailman, J. P. 1993. *UNCERT User's Guide.* Madison: University of Wisconsin Zoology Department.

Hailman, J. P., Ficken, M. S. & Ficken, R. W. 1987. Constraints on the structure of the combinatorial "chick-a-dee" calls. *Ethology,* **75,** 62–80.

Hill, C. M. 2000. Conflict of interests between people and baboons: crop raiding in Uganda. *Int. J. Primatol.,* **21,** 299–315.

Holm, S. 1979. A simple sequentially rejective multiple test procedure. *Scand. J. Stat.,* **6,** 65–70.

Houde, A. E. 1997. *Sex, Color, and Mate Choice in Guppies.* Princeton: Princeton University Press.

Hurt, C. R., Stears-Ellis, S., Hughes, K. A. & Hedrick, P. W. 2004. Mating behaviour in endangered Sonoran topminnow: speciation in action. *Anim. Behav.,* **67,** 343–351.

Irwin, D. M. & Bushnell, M. M. 1980. *Observational Strategies for Child Study.* New York: Holt, Rinehart, and Winston.

Jander, U. & Jander, R. 1993. Randomness in ontogeny. On antennal grooming in the milkweed bug *Oncopeltus fasciatus. Ethology,* **94,** 89–108.

Keppel, G. 1991. *Design and Analysis: A Researcher's Handbook, 3rd ed.* Upper Saddle River, New Jersey: Prentice Hall.

Ketola, R., Toivonen, R. & Viikari-Juntura, E. 2001. Interobserver repeatability and validity of an observational method to assess physical loads imposed on the upper extremities. *Ergonomics,* **44,** 119–131.

Khanzanie, R. 1996. *Statistics in a World of Applications, 4th ed.* New York: Harper Collins.

Kobayashi, T. & Watanabe, M. 1986. An analysis of snake-scent application behaviour in Siberian chipmunks (*Eutamias sibiricus asiaticus*). *Ethology,* **72,** 40–52.

Kolluru, G. R. & Grether, G. F. 2005. The effects of resource availability on alternative mating tactics in guppies (*Poecilia reticulata*). *Behav. Ecol.,* **16,** 294–300.

Krause, J. & Ruxton, G. D. 2002. *Living in Groups.* Oxford: Oxford University Press.

Langley, C. M., Riley, D. A., Bond, A. B. & Goel, N. 1996. Visual search for natural grains in pigeons (*Columba livia*): search images and selective attention. *J. Exp. Psychol.: Anim. Behav. Proc.,* **22,** 139–151.

Lehner, P. N. 1996. *Handbook of Ethological Methods, 2nd ed.* Cambridge: Cambridge University Press.

Lusseau, D. 2003. Effects of tour boats on the behavior of bottlenose dolphins: using Markov chains to model anthropogenic impacts. *Cons. Biol.,* **17,** 1785–1793.

Martin, P. & Bateson, P. 1993. *Measuring Behaviour: An Introductory Guide, 2nd ed.* Cambridge: Cambridge University Press.

Miller, B. J. & Anderson, S. H. 1989. Courtship patterns in induced oestrous and natural oestrous domestic ferrets (*Mustela putorius furo*). *J. Ethol.,* **7,** 65–73.

Miller, B. J. & Anderson, S. H. 1990. Comparison of black-footed ferret (*Mustela nigripes*) and domestic ferret (*M. putorius furo*) courtship activity. *Zoo Biol.,* **9,** 201–210.

Molles, L. E., Hudson, J. D. & Waas, J. R. 2006. The mechanics of duetting in a New Zealand endemic, the Kokako (*Callaeas cinerea wilsoni*): song at a snail's pace. *Ethology,* **112,** 424–436.

Owings, D. H., Coss, R. G., Mckernon, D., Rowe, M. P. & Arrowood, P. C. 2001. Snake-directed antipredator behavior of rock squirrels (*Spermophilus variegatus*): population differences and snake-species discrimination. *Behaviour,* **138,** 575–595.

Oxley, G. & Fleming, A. S. 2000. The effects of medial preoptic area and amygdala lesions on maternal behavior in the juvenile rat. *Dev. Psychobiol.,* **37,** 253–265.

Peters, R. A. & Evans, C. S. 2003. Design of the Jacky dragon visual display: signal and noise characteristics in a complex moving environment. *J. Comp. Physiol. A* **189,** 447–459.

Peters, R. A. & Ord, T. J. 2003. Display response of the jacky dragon, *Amphilbolurus muricatus* (Lacertilia: Agamidae), to intruders: A semi-Markovian process. *Austral Ecol.,* **28,** 499–506.

Redolat, R., Oteriono, M. C., Carrasco, M. C., Berry, M. S. & Brain, P. F. 2000. Effects of acute administration of nicotine and lobeline on agonistic encounters in male mice. *Aggr. Behav.,* **26,** 376–385.

Rice, W. R. 1989. Analyzing tables of statistical tests. *Evolution,* **43,** 223–225.

Ropeik, D. & Gray, G. 2002. *Risk: A Practical Guide for Deciding What's Really Safe and What's Really Dangerous in the World Around You.* Boston: Houghton Mifflin Co.

Sackett, G. P. 1979. The lag sequential analysis of contingency and cyclicity in behavioral interaction research. In: *Handbook of Infant Development* (Ed. by J. D. Osofsky), pp. 623–649. New York: Wiley.

Sanderson, P. M., McNeese, M. D. & Zaff, B. S. 1994. Handling complex real-world data with two cognitive engineering tools: COGENT and MacSHAPA. *Behav. Res. Methods Inst. Comp.,* **26,** 117–124.

Shannon, C. E. & Weaver, W. 1949. *The Mathematical Theory of Communication.* Urbana: University of Illinois Press.

Siegel, S. & Castellan, N. J., Jr. 1988. *Nonparametric Statistics for the Behavioral Sciences, 2nd ed.* New York: McGraw-Hill.

Sih, A., Bell, A. M., Johnson, J. C. & Ziemba, R. E. 2004. Behavioral syndromes: an integrative overview. *Q. Rev. Biol.,* **79,** 241–277.

Slooten, E. 1994. Behavior of Hector's dolphin: classifying behavior by sequence analysis. *J. Mamm.,* **75,** 956–964.

Sokal, R. R. & Rohlf, F. J. 1995. *Biometry: The Principles and Practice of Statistics in Biological Research, 3rd ed.* New York: W. H. Freeman and Company.

Suggs, D. N. & Simmons, A. M. 2005. Information theory analysis of patterns of modulation in the advertisement call of the male bullfrog, *Rana catesbeiana. J. Acoust. Soc. Am.,* **117,** 2330–2337.

Tinbergen, N. 1951. *The Study of Instinct.* Oxford: Oxford Univ. Press.

Tinbergen, N. 1960. The natural control of insects in pine woods: I. Factors influencing the intensity of predation by songbirds. *Arch. Neerland. Zool.,* **13,** 265–343.

Van Hooff, J. A. R. A. M. 1982. Categories and sequences of behavior: methods of description and analysis. In: *Handbook of Methods in Non-Verbal Behavior Research* (Ed. by K. R. Scherer and P. Ekman), pp. 362–439. Cambridge: Cambridge University Press.

Verbeke, G. & Molenberghs, G. 2000. *Linear Mixed Models for Longitudinal Data.* New York: Springer-Verlag.

Waas, J. R. 1991. The risks and benefits of signalling aggressive motivation: a study of cave-dwelling little blue penguins. *Behav. Ecol. Sociobiol.,* **29,** 139–146.

Whiten, A. & Barton, R. A. 1988. Demise of the checksheet: using off-the-shelf miniature hand-held computers for remote fieldwork applications. *Trends Ecol. Evol.,* **3,** 146–148.

Winer, B. J. 1962. *Statistical Principles in Experimental Design.* New York: McGraw-Hill Book Company.

Wright, N. & McGowan, A. 2001. Vigilance on the civil flight deck: incidence of sleepiness and sleep during long-haul flights and associated changes in physiological parameters. *Ergonomics,* **44,** 82–106.

# Index